AMERICAN Headway

Proven success beyond the classroom

THIRD EDITION

Teacher's Book

Liz and John Soars

Amanda Maris

OXFORD
UNIVERSITY PRESS

Contents

Introduction

American Headway 1

American Headway 1, Third Edition is for students who already have some basic knowledge of the language. They may have recently completed a beginner course or they may be returning to language learning after a break and need to review key language before being able to progress further.

New language is introduced systematically and at a steady pace, allowing students to increase their knowledge of the language and build their confidence. Listening material is provided across three class CDs. New vocabulary is introduced gradually and there are regular controlled-practice activities, allowing students to activate the language in a supported way. There are also free-practice activities where students have the ability to start focusing on their fluency. In the Everyday English sections, useful chunks of language are presented which students can use in several different social contexts.

Student Book Organization

The organization of *American Headway 1, Third Edition* is similar to other levels of *American Headway, Third Edition*. Each unit has the following:

- Starter
- Presentation of new language
- Practice
- Skills – always speaking, combined with listening or reading, with a writing section for each unit at the back of the book
- Vocabulary
- Everyday English

Starter

The Starter section is designed to be a warm-up to the lesson and has a direct link with the unit to come.

Presentation of new language

New language items are presented through texts, often as conversations, which students can read and listen to at the same time. This enables students to relate the spelling to the sounds of English, and helps with pronunciation, as well as form and use.

The main verb forms taught are:

- *to be*
- Simple Present
- *can/can't*
- *was/were/could*
- Simple Past
- *I like* and *I'd like*
- Present Continuous
- *going to*
- Infinitive of purpose
- Present Perfect

There are *Grammar Spots* in the presentation sections. Thes[e] aim to focus students' attention on the language of the unit. There are questions to answer, charts to complete, and shor[t] exercises. The *Grammar Spot* is reinforced in the Grammar Reference section at the back of the book.

Practice

This section contains a variety of controlled and free-practice exercises. The primary skills used are speaking and listening, but there is also some reading and writing.

There are information gap exercises, group discussions, information transfer listening exercises, pronunciation exercises, and a lot of personalized activities. There are exercises where the aim is overt analysis of the grammar, such as *Check it*.

Vocabulary

There is a strong lexical syllabus in *American Headway 1, Third Edition*. Vocabulary is introduced systematically and it is reviewed and recycled throughout. Lexical sets are chosen according to two criteria. They complement the grammatical input, for example, jobs and free-time activities with the Simple Present; or shopping items for count and noncount nouns. However, they are mainly chosen for their usefulness. Level 1 students need to build on their vocabulary set and they primarily need words for everyday life. Students also work on word patterns in the form of collocations. Knowledge of common collocations can really help improve a student's level of fluency. The book covers noun + noun combinations as well as verb + noun combinations, such as *drive a car* or *look after children*. Students also focus on other patterns throughout the book, such as opposite adjectives and adverbs.

Skills

Listening

Regular listening sections, in dialogue or monologue form, provide further practice of the language of the unit and help to develop students' ability to understand the main message of the text.

Reading

At the beginning of the book the reading texts are relatively short and are carefully graded to allow students to build on their previous knowledge and to increase their confidence as they start a new level. As students move through the book, the texts quickly become longer and more challenging, with students being exposed to increasing amounts of new lexis. This encourages them to start deducing meaning from context and enables them to engage with more complex reading texts.

Speaking

In the presentation sections, students have the opportunity to practice the pronunciation and intonation of new language. In the practice sections, less-controlled exercises lead to free-speaking practice.

There are many speaking exercises based around the listening and reading activities, including regular role plays. There are speaking opportunities before a text to launch the topic and create interest; and there are speaking activities after a text, often in the form of discussion.

Writing

Writing is primarily practiced in a separate section at the back of the Student Book. This comprises 12 complete writing lessons related to the unit which can be used at the teacher's discretion. The writing syllabus provides models for students to analyze and imitate.

Everyday English

This is an important part of the syllabus of *American Headway, Third Edition*. Students have the opportunity to practice chunks of language used in formal and informal situations. Students learn phrases for requests and suitable responses, for use while shopping, when asking for directions, and for many other situations. Students also learn about appropriacy, as there is a focus on how to sound polite by choosing suitable phrases and using proper intonation.

Grammar Reference

This is at the back of the Student Book, and it is intended for use at home. It can be used for review or reference.

Review

Regular review of grammar and vocabulary is provided throughout the book. There is a photocopiable activity for each of the 12 units at the back of this Teacher's Book. These photocopiables are also available on iTools, along with 12 additional photocopiable activities.

Workbook with iChecker

All the language input – grammatical, lexical, and functional – is revisited and practiced. iChecker Online Self-Assessment offers additional content for self-study in the form of progress checks and test-preparation lessons. Students can download and play all the Workbook audio files when they access iChecker material.

Teacher's Book

The Teacher's Book offers the teacher full support both for lesson preparation and in the classroom. Each unit starts with a clear overview of the unit content from the Student Book, along with a brief introduction to the main themes of the unit and a summary of additional materials that can

be used. Within each unit, the highlighted sections indicate opportunities for additional activities with *Suggestions* and *Extra activities*. This allows for further work on key language or skills when appropriate.

Testing Program

The *American Headway, Third Edition* Testing Program is available online for easy access. The testing materials include Unit tests, Stop and Check tests, Progress tests, Exit tests, and Skills tests with audio files. See instructions on the inside back cover for how to access the Testing Program.

Assessment tools to evaluate progress

Teachers can track students' progress, analyze their results, and plan more personalized learning. Automatic grading frees teachers' time to concentrate on teaching and helps teachers more easily report on progress.

iTools

In addition to the complete Student Book and Workbook content onscreen, teachers have access to audio and video files with optional scripts, as well as additional resources, such as customizable versions of 24 photocopiable activities, video worksheets, and PowerPoint™ presentations.

Video

Brand new video clips, along with classroom worksheets are available on the new *American Headway 1, Third Edition* iTools as well as online. There are 12 clips, one for each unit. The language and topic in each clip are linked to the relevant Student Book unit. The majority of the clips follow a documentary style and include native speaker interviews.

Finally!

The activities in *American Headway 1, Third Edition* are designed to enable students to build on their knowledge of the language and to allow them to activate what they have learned. There is also an emphasis on increasing confidence so that students feel able to actively participate in short conversations and discussions. We hope that students will enjoy using the book and that it will give them a real sense of progression in their language learning.

1 You and me

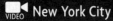

am/is/are • *my/your/his/her* • Verbs – *have/go/live/like* • Possessive *'s* • **Word groups** • **Everyday conversations**

📹 VIDEO ◀ New York City

As you begin *American Headway 1*, you are probably starting a new course with a new group of students. The main goal of this first unit is that students get to know each other and you, and you get to know them. In addition to this focus on personal information, students also practice greetings and expressions from everyday conversations.

LANGUAGE INPUT

GRAMMAR

am/is/are (SB p. 2, p. 7)
my/your/his/her (SB p. 2, p. 3, p. 7)
Verbs – *have/go/live/like* (SB p. 4)
Possessive *'s* (SB p. 4)

- Practicing *be* in all persons (affirmative/negative/questions).
- Reviewing subject pronouns and possessive adjectives.
- Recognizing and using basic verbs to talk about everyday life (*I* form).
- Understanding *'s* for possession and as the short form of *is*.

VOCABULARY

Opposite adjectives (SB p. 7)
The family (SB p. 8)

- Focusing on key adjectives and their opposites in context.
- Practicing vocabulary to ask and answer about your family.

EVERYDAY ENGLISH

Everyday conversations (SB p. 9)

- Using greetings and key expressions in everyday situations.

SKILLS DEVELOPMENT

READING

A student's blog (SB p. 6)

- Reading about a student's experiences in school and with a family in the United States.

LISTENING

Five conversations in a student's day (SB p. 7)

- Listening for key information in five short conversations and completing a chart. **CD1 14** (SB p. 114)

SPEAKING

Talking about you (SB p. 3)
The family (SB p. 8)

- Exchanging personal information.
- Talking about your family.

WRITING

You and your life (SB p. 5)
A blog – Keeping an online journal (SB p. 100)

- Writing key information about yourself.
- Completing blog entries with blanks, then writing an entry to read aloud.

MORE MATERIALS

Photocopiables – Everyday conversations (TB p. 144)   **Tests** (Online)   **Video** (iTools and Online)

STARTER (SB p. 2)

1   **CD1 2** Say your own name – *I'm (Liz)* – and point to yourself to make the meaning clear. Write your name on the board and then spell it out, pointing to each letter in turn. Focus students' attention on the letters in exercise 1 and tell the students that they are going to listen to the alphabet. Play the recording and have students just listen.

Say *A, B, C* and then invite students to continue. Encourage students to help one another if students have problems with individual letters. Write down the letters students get wrong or don't know, paying particular attention to *a, e, g, i, j, q, r, u, w,* and *y,* which often cause problems for students. Drill the letters which students found difficult. Play the recording again as reinforcement if necessary.

2   Invite a few students to say their first name. Check that students understand alphabetical order by writing the letters *a–g* on the board in random order and asking students to reorder them alphabetically. Then ask students to stand up in alphabetical order by their first names and say their name. If appropriate, repeat this, getting progressively faster each time.

Encourage students to memorize as many names as they can. If appropriate, play a memory game by pointing to individual students and yourself, and having the class say the correct names. Encourage students in a multilingual class to pronounce one another's names (and your name!) as accurately as possible. If there are not too many students in the class, write their names on the board so that everyone can begin to learn them.

EXTRA ACTIVITY

Reinforce the alphabet by having students categorize the letters according to their sound:

/eɪ/	a h j k
/i/	b c d e g p t v z
/ɛ/	f l m n s x z
/aɪ/	i y
/oʊ/	o
/u/	q u w
/ɑr/	r

HELLO! (SB p. 2)

am / is / are – my / your

1   Write your own first name and last name on the board. Point to each name as you say "first name" and "last name." Elicit some first names and last names from the class. Teach the question *How do you spell that?* and briefly review the alphabet from the *Starter* section.

CD1 3 Play the recording once and have students read and listen. Then ask them to point to Tim and the interviewer in the photo. Ask *Where are Tim and the interviewer?* (at a business conference).

Play the recording a second time. Students repeat as a class. Play the recording again then practice it in both open pairs (i.e., students ask and answer the questions across the room with the rest of the class listening) and closed pairs (i.e., the whole class working in pairs). Make sure students can accurately produce the contracted forms *name's, what's,* and *I'm,* and the falling intonation on the *wh*-questions.

GRAMMAR SPOT

Focus students' attention on the contractions. Ask students to circle the contracted forms in exercise 1.

2   Focus students' attention on the example. Ask them to complete the conversation. Remind students to use contracted forms. Ask students to point to Carla and Mike in the photo.

CD1 4 Play the recording and let students check their answers.

Answers and audio script
C Hello. My name's Carla. What's **your** name?
M Mike.
C **Where** are you from, Mike?
M **I'm** from Miami. Where **are** you from?
C **I'm from** Miami, too!
M Oh! Nice to meet you!

Ask students to practice the conversation in open and closed pairs. If students sound a little flat, encourage a wide voice range, particularly on the last two lines of the conversation. Also highlight the contrastive stress in: *I'm from Miami. Where are you from?*

3   This is a mingle activity. Demonstrate the conversation first in open pairs, and then have students move around the class and talk to as many people as possible. Monitor and check for accurate pronunciation. Don't let this activity go on too long. If you have a large class, it will be impossible for all the students to talk to everyone.

ADDITIONAL MATERIAL

Workbook Unit 1
Ex. 1   Nice to meet you!
Ex. 2   Countries and nationalities

PERSONAL INFORMATION (SB p. 3)

he/she – his/her

> ⚠ **POSSIBLE PROBLEMS**
>
> - Note that in the negative of *be*, American Headway 1 uses the contracted forms of *not*, not the contracted forms of the verb, i.e., *she isn't, they aren't, you aren't, we aren't*, rather than *she's not, they're not, you're not, we're not*. Try to stick to these forms when you speak to the class. The contraction ~~I amn't~~ isn't possible, and the correct form is shown in the Grammar Spot on p. 3.
> - Where other languages will answer a *Yes/No* question with simply *yes* or *no*, English prefers to add a short answer. Without the short answer, the speaker can sound a little abrupt. Having been introduced to contracted forms, students are tempted to use them in short answers, for example, *Are you married? ~~Yes, I'm~~*, but this is not possible.
> - The names of the characters are pronounced /tɪm freɪzər/ and /soʊfiə məˈlinə/.
> - Lower-level students often have difficulty reading phone numbers and email addresses fluently. In English we give phone numbers using single figures 0–9, and 0 is pronounced *oh*. Be prepared to give a lot of practice during this presentation and also in later lessons. It's a good idea to prepare a list of fictitious email addresses and phone numbers from a range of countries before the lesson to help students with this.

1 Point to the photo of Tim and ask *What's his name?* Then point to the photo of Sofia and say *This is Sofia*. Check comprehension of the key categories in bold in the chart and then give students time to read about Tim and Sofia.

Focus students' attention on the information about reading email addresses. Write a number of fictitious email addresses on the board and have students practice reading them aloud.

2 **CD1 5** Focus students' attention on the incomplete questions and on the example. Play the recording through once. Students listen and complete the questions. Play the recording a second time if necessary. With weaker classes, you can complete the questions orally as a class first and then play the recording for reinforcement.

Ask students to write the answers on the board to make sure they are using the short form *What's* and the full form *is* correctly. Point out that *isn't* is the negative, and that *n't* is the short form of *not*.

Answers and audio script
1 What's his **last** name?
   Frasier
2 **What's** his first name?
   Tim
3 Where's **he** from?
   Chicago
4 How old **is** he?
   30
5 What's **his** phone number?
   312-555-0749

6 **What's his** email address?
   tfrasier@mail.com
7 Is **he** married?
   No, he isn't.

Review the way we read phone numbers (see *Possible problems* in the first column on this page). Before student practice the questions and answers in closed pairs, let them practice in open pairs. Highlight the voice range and intonation of the questions – questions with a question word start high and then fall. With weaker classes, be prepared to drill the forms and spend less time on the intonation.

3 **CD1 6** This exercise highlights the use of *she* and *her* to talk about women and girls. Focus students' attention on the incomplete questions and on the example. Play the recording through once. Students listen and complete the questions. Play the recording a second time if necessary. With weaker classes, you can complete the questions orally as a class first and then play the recording to reinforce the language points.

Answers and audio script
1 What's **her** last name?
2 What's **her** first name?
3 Where's **she** from?
4 How old **is she**?
5 What's **her** phone number?
6 **What's her** email address?
7 **Is she** married?

Highlight the use of *he/his* to talk about Tim and *she/her* to talk about Sofia. Emphasize the difference by asking *What's his/her name?* and *Where's he/she from?* about the students in the class. With weaker classes, drill the questions with the whole class and correct any mistakes in the use of *he/she* and *his/her* carefully.

Have students practice the questions and answers in open pairs before repeating in closed pairs. If necessary, highlight the voice range and intonation again. With weaker classes, be prepared to drill the forms and spend less time on the intonation.

GRAMMAR SPOT

1 Focus students' attention on the affirmative forms in the chart. Make sure students understand that there is a long form and a short form for each verb.

Focus students' attention on the negative forms in the chart. Give some true negative examples to reinforce the meaning, e.g., *I'm not (Hungarian). You aren't (Danish).* Elicit the negative forms for *he* and *she* and drill the pronunciation if necessary.

Answers

Affirmative	Negative
I am = I'm	I'm not
you are = you're	you aren't
he is = he's	he **isn't**
she is = she's	she **isn't**

2 Highlight the use of the subject pronouns by pointing to yourself for *I* and students in the class for *you*, *he*, and *she*. Give students time to write the missing possessive adjectives and then check the answers.

Answers	
Pronouns	**Possessive adjectives**
I	my
you	**your**
he	**his**
she	her

▶▶ Read Grammar Reference 1.1–1.2 on p. 130 together in class and/or ask students to read it at home. Encourage them to ask you questions about it.

Grammar p 98-99 ex. 4A a

Talking about you

⚠ **POSSIBLE PROBLEMS**

This section consolidates the *wh-*questions and also includes a *yes/no* question and short answers. Having focused on the short forms in affirmative sentences, students may be tempted to use a short form in affirmative short answers. The Caution box covers this and highlights that we can't say ~~Yes, I'm.~~ At this early stage, don't give a long explanation of what short answers are and how they operate. It is better to let students see them in context and use them in controlled exercises.

4 This is the students' first opportunity to personalize the language in this section, so try to make sure that they work with a partner that they don't know.

Ask the question *Are you married?* and elicit the answers *Yes, I am./No, I'm not.* Focus students' attention on the note about short answers and point out that we can't say *Yes, I'm.*

With weaker classes, briefly review commonly confused letters of the alphabet *a, e, i, o, u, m* and *n, c* and *k*, etc. and how to read phone numbers. You could also elicit a range of answers to the questions from several students and drill the question forms, before students do the pairwork.

Students ask and answer the questions with a partner. Monitor and check for correct formation of questions and short answers, and for correct pronunciation and intonation.

EXTRA ACTIVITIES

• You can reinforce the use of *he/she* and *his/her* by asking students to work with a new classmate and tell him/her about their partner in exercise 4. Students can also tell the rest of the class about their partner for further practice.

• You can give regular practice of phone numbers (and numbers in general) and email addresses in dictation activities, either with you dictating or with the students working in pairs.

Teacher dictation: Dictate five or six phone numbers/email addresses, writing them down yourself so that you have a way of checking. Students write the numbers/addresses as you say them, and then write them on the board to check.

Pair dictation: Students prepare a list of phone numbers/email addresses to dictate to their partner and then exchange lists to check.

ADDITIONAL MATERIAL

Workbook Unit 1
Ex. 3   Personal information

NICK'S FAMILY (SB p. 4)

Verbs – *have/go/live/like*

NOTE

The purpose of this section is to introduce/review some high-frequency verbs to allow students to give everyday information about themselves. It is not intended to be a full presentation of the Simple Present and so students practice just the *I* form. Don't include any questions in the Simple Present about this section, as a complete review/presentation of the Simple Present is given in Units 2 and 3.

Some basic family words are included in the text and in the Practice section (*brother, sister, parents, mother, father, grandmother*). This vocabulary is reviewed and extended in *Vocabulary and speaking* on SB p. 8.

1 **CD1 7** Pre-teach/check students' understanding of the words *salesman* and *girlfriend*. Focus students' attention on the photo and say *This is Nick Wilson.* Ask *How old is he? Where is he from?* Play the recording once. Students listen and follow along in their books. With weaker students, you can ask students to point to the correct photo as they read and listen. Elicit the answers to the pre-questions (He's 19. He's from Boston.)

2 Give students time to complete the sentences, using *have*, *go, live*, and *like*.

CD1 8 Play the recording and let students check their answers.

Answers and audio script
1 I **go** to Northeastern University.
2 I **have** a brother and a sister.
3 I **live** with my parents in a house in Boston.
4 My family really **likes** Lily!

3 Elicit possible endings to the sentences, providing any necessary vocabulary, e.g., *college, language school, husband, wife*, etc.

Put students in pairs to exchange their information. Monitor and help as necessary.

Possessive 's

> ⚠ **POSSIBLE PROBLEMS**
>
> Students may have problems distinguishing the
> contracted forms *he's/she's/it's* and the marker for
> possessive *'s*. The Grammar Spot for this section clarifies
> the usage, but be prepared to review this point regularly
> to help students in both speaking and writing.

4 Go over the Grammar Spot with the class.

GRAMMAR SPOT

Focus students' attention on the use of *'s* as the
contraction of *is* and as an indicator of possession.
Refer students back to the text about Nick. In pairs,
students underline examples of possessive *'s* and circle
examples of *'s* as the contraction of *is*.

> **Answers**
> **Possession**
> brother's name
> sister's name
> ***is***
> My name's Nick Wilson.
> He's 16 and he's in high school.
> She's 23, and she's married.
> Her name's Lily. She's great!

▶▶ Read Grammar Reference 1.3 on p. 130 together in class, and/or ask
students to read it at home. Encourage them to ask you questions
about it. *Grammar p 99 ex 4aB*

5 Focus students' attention on the example. Get two strong
students to model the example question and answer. Ask
Who's Matt? and elicit the answer (*He's Nick's brother.*)

Students ask and answer the questions in closed pairs.
Monitor and check for correct use of the possessive *'s* and
contracted forms of *be*. If students have problems, drill
the questions and answers and have students repeat in
closed pairs.

> **Answers**
> 2 Who's Rosie? She's Nick's sister.
>   Who's Peter? He's Nick's father.
>   Who's Helen? She's Nick's mother.
>   Who's Lily? She's Nick's girlfriend.
> 3 He's a salesperson.
> 4 She's a teacher.

EXTRA ACTIVITY

Students will need regular review of the possessive *'s*.
You can do this in a later lesson by asking ten or so
students for a photo or other personal item. Put them all
in the middle of the room. Students then have to point to
a photo/an object and say *That's my sister. That's Maria's
cell phone*, etc.

PRACTICE (SB p. 5)

be – am, is, are

1 This exercise reinforces a range of forms of the verb *to be*,
including questions and short answers. Have students
complete the sentences, working individually.

CD1 9 Give students time to check their answers in pairs
then play the recording for a final check.

> **Answers and audio script**
> 1 Where **are** you from?
> 2 "**Are** you from Boston?" "Yes, I **am**."
> 3 "How old **are** you?" "**I'm** 15."
> 4 "**Are** your sisters married?" "No, they **aren't**."
> 5 I like you. You**'re** my friend.
> 6 Marc **isn't** from the US, he's from Canada.
> 7 "**Is** your mother a doctor?" "No, she **isn't**."
> 8 **I'm not** Brazilian. I'm Costa Rican.

2 This exercise gives further practice in distinguishing
the meaning of *'s* – short form of *is* or possession. Focus
students' attention on the examples, then have students
complete the task, working individually. Elicit a range of
answers from the class. If there is disagreement, write the
sentences on the board for analysis with the whole class.

> **Answers**
> 3 is   4 is   5 possession   6 possession

Pronunciation

3 **CD1 10** This exercise tests students' ability to listen
carefully and discriminate between similar words and
phrases.

Play number 1 as an example and elicit the correct
sentence (b). Play the rest of the recording. Students
choose the sentences they hear. You can make this
exercise productive by asking students to read the pairs of
sentences aloud.

> **Answers and audio script**
> 1 **b** She's from Mexico.
> 2 **a** What's his name?
> 3 **a** Your English is good.
> 4 **a** Where's she from?
> 5 **b** He's a teacher from Canada.
> 6 **b** We aren't American.

Spelling

4 Briefly review the alphabet, prioritizing letters that
students have problems with. Point out that numbers 1–3
are names and that 4 and 5 are email addresses. Explain
that students will hear the information in a short context,
but they should listen for just the missing letters and parts
of the email addresses.

CD1 11 Play number 1 as an example and elicit the
missing letters, writing the complete name on the board.

Play the rest of the recording without stopping. If necessary,
play the recording again to allow students to complete
any missing answers. Don't keep repeating the recording,

however, as students need to get used to isolating key information fairly quickly, as they would in real life.

Check the answers by having students write them on the board. Make sure they have recorded the dots correctly in the email addresses.

> **Answers and audio script**
> 1 VANESSA
> 2 JOSEPH BOWEN
> 3 KATIE MATTHEWS
> 4 g.hunt8@wahoo.com
> 5 zac.yates@mail.co.us
>
> **CD1 11**
> 1 My name's Vanessa. That's V - A - N - E - S - S - A. Vanessa.
> 2 My first name's Joseph. That's J - O - S - E - P - H. My last name's Bowen. That's B - O - W - E - N. Joseph Bowen.
> 3 My name's Katie Matthews. That's Katie K - A - T - I - E. Matthews M - A - T - T - H - E - W - S.
> 4 My email address is g.hunt8@wahoo.com. That's G dot H - U - N - T eight at wahoo dot com.
> 5 My email address is zac.yates@mail.co.us. That's Zac Z - A - C, dot Yates, Y - A - T - E - S, at mail dot co dot US.

Talking about you

5 This exercise reinforces the verb *to be* in a range of persons, and allows students to make true sentences about themselves. Pre-teach/check students' understanding of *at home*, *at work*, and *café* by using pictures or simple explanations.

> **Answers**
> There are no set answers for this exercise, but monitor and check students haven't made mistakes in the forms of *to be*.

Have students compare their answers in pairs.

Writing

6 After quite a lot of oral class work, the silent, individual work in this exercise provides variety and balance.

Focus students' attention on the sentence starters and elicit a range of possible endings. The starter *I'm a …* requires a job or the word *student*. In the sentences about family, point out that students can change the key word, e.g., *sister → brother; father → mother.*

Give students time to write about themselves, using the sentence starters. (If you are short of time, students can do this task for homework.)

Students read their description to the class, or to their classmates in small groups. Don't overcorrect students if they make a lot of pronunciation mistakes; the goal is for students to show what they can do, and to say a little about themselves and their families. They can't do everything at once!

ADDITIONAL MATERIAL

Workbook Unit 1
Ex. 4   Possessive *'s*
Ex. 5   Verbs – *have/go/live/like*

A student's blog

> **ABOUT THE TEXT**
>
> This is the first piece of extensive skills work in *American Headway 1*. The goal of this section is to recycle key language and expose students to new language in a relatively natural context. The choice of text type – a blog – will be familiar to the majority of students and reflects communication in the real world. This section also provides a link to the Writing section on SB p. 100.
>
> After an introduction and vocabulary work, students read and listen to the blog at the same time. This might be considered an unnatural activity, but this technique is used only in the early stages of the book to help build confidence. Elementary learners typically find reading easier than listening, because they can recognize cognates without the interference of different pronunciation. However, if they read the blog silently at their own speed, they could become distracted by unknown and unimportant vocabulary. Reading and following the recording allows them to follow the material in a more fluent way.
>
> The places mentioned in the blog are:
>
> Boston – one of the oldest cities in the US, famous for its many historical sights
>
> Boston University – a well-known prestigious, private university in Boston with 33,000 students
>
> Museum of Fine Arts – one of the largest public art museums in the US; it has a diverse collection of European and American art
>
> The following vocabulary items might be new:
>
> – the adjectives in exercise 2 SB p. 6
>
> – *blog* (a type of Internet diary), *speak fast, understand, international, park* (n), *gallery, free, go by subway*
>
> With weaker students, pre-teach/check students' understanding of the vocabulary or assign it as homework prior to the lesson. However, if you feel your students don't need so much support, simply encourage them to use the context to help them understand the new vocabulary.

1 Introduce the topic by writing *Boston* on the board and letting students tell you anything they know. Refer them to the photos and elicit information about what's in the photos – Fanueil Hall Marketplace (a very popular historic marketplace and meeting hall), the Boston Hatch shell, and the Charles River. *fænyəl*

Elicit the names of any other places that students know in Boston.

2 With weaker students, you may want to pre-teach/check students' understanding of the adjectives if you didn't assign them for homework (see *About the text* above). Check the pronunciation of the following adjectives, which can cause problems:

beautiful /ˈbyutəfl/, interesting /ˈɪntrəstɪŋ/, friendly /ˈfrɛndli/.

Make sure that students understand the idea of noun + adjective collocation. Write the following examples on the board and indicate the ones which are and aren't possible: *a friendly person* ✓ / *language* ✗ / *place* ✓ / *book* ✗.

Also check that students understand the use of *a/an* in sentences 1 and 4: *a* + adjective beginning with a consonant; *an* + adjective beginning with a vowel. Elicit two examples, e.g., *a beautiful city/an expensive city*.

Put the students into pairs to complete the sentences. Monitor and help as necessary.

Elicit a range of possible answers from the class. Ask students to justify their answers in simple English as best they can. Try not to let students give their reasons in L1!

> **Possible answers**
> Answers will depend on students' own opinions but these are possible collocations.
> 1 Boston is/isn't a/an big/small/nice/beautiful/expensive/ interesting/friendly/cold/sunny city.
> 2 The people are/aren't nice/interesting/friendly.
> 3 The weather is/isn't cold/sunny.
> 4 English is/isn't a/an beautiful/interesting/difficult/easy language.

3 See the note about vocabulary in *About the text*. Refer students back to the text about Nick on SB p. 4 and ask what they can remember about him. Then focus students' attention on the photo of Amanda. Explain that she is a student in Boston and that the Wilsons are her host family.

CD1 12 Play the first two lines of the blog and have students follow in their books. Focus students' attention on the examples. Play the rest of the recording and then have students complete the true/false task. Give students time to compare their answers in pairs and correct the false sentences. Check the answers with the class.

> **Answers**
> 3 ✓
> 4 ✗ She isn't in a small school. She's in a big school.
> 5 ✓
> 6 ✗ They aren't all from Asia. They're from **Mexico, Japan,** Turkey, Argentina, Korea, and China too.
> 7 ✗ She isn't Amanda's teacher. She's Nick's sister.
> 8 ✗ It isn't expensive. It's free.
> 9 ✗ It isn't difficult. It's easy.
> 10 ✓

4 Students often have problems with the formation of questions, so this task provides further practice. Focus students' attention on the example and remind students to focus on the answers to help them form the questions.

Give students time to complete the questions, working individually. Then put students in pairs to ask and answer. Monitor and check for accurate question formation.

CD1 13 Play the recording and let students check their answers. Students practice the questions and answers again. If necessary, drill the questions for pronunciation practice, encouraging accurate intonation.

> **Answers and audio script**
> 1 Where's Amanda from? Brazil.
> 2 **Where's** her school? In a fun part of Boston.
> 3 What's **her teacher's** name? Charlotte.
> 4 **What's her family's** name? Wilson.
> 5 **Where's their house**? In Boston.
> 6 How **old are** the two brothers? Matt's 16 and Nick's 19.
> 7 **Is the weather** OK? Yes, it is. It's cold and sunny.

5 Give students a few minutes to discuss their answers in small groups. Elicit a range of answers from the class.

> **Answers**
> We can see the Wilson family and their house, her school, some students, and her teacher, and Fanueil Hall Marketplace, Boston Hatch shell, and the Charles River.

Listening

6 This is the first listening task in *American Headway 1* without some written support. Reassure the students that the conversations are very short and they only have to listen for the key information to complete the chart. With weaker students, refer students back to Amanda's blog on p. 7, briefly review the names of the people she knows and write them on the board.

CD1 14 Tell students they are going to listen to Amanda in five different situations. Play the first conversation, pausing the recording to elicit the answers (see *Answers* below).

Play the rest of the recording, pausing after each conversation to allow students to write their answers. Check the answers with the class.

> **Answers and audio script**
>
> | **Where's Amanda?** | **Who is she with?** |
> | --- | --- |
> | 1 at home | Peter Wilson |
> | 2 at school/in class | her teacher, Charlotte |
> | 3 at school | another student |
> | 4 at the Museum of Fine Arts | a museum assistant |
> | 5 in a café | a server |
>
> **CD1 14**
> 1 P Goodbye, Amanda! Have a good day at school!
>   A Thank you, Peter. And you have a good day at work!
> 2 C Good morning, Amanda. Where's your homework?
>   A It's here, Charlotte.
> 3 A Hello, Cristo. Where are you from?
>   CR I'm from Mexico.
> 4 A A ticket, please.
>   B The Museum of Fine Arts is free for college students.
>   A Oh, good! Thank you!
> 5 A A coffee, please.
>   B Certainly. Here you are.

If you have time, refer students to the audioscript on p. 114 and have them practice the conversations in pairs.

Vocabulary work

SUGGESTION

Students can use dictionaries to help them with the vocabulary work on adjectives and their opposites.

7 Focus students' attention on the example to check that students understand the concept of opposites. Have students work in pairs or small groups to pool their knowledge. With weaker students, write the missing opposites (see *Answers* below) on the board in random order for them to match.

Check the answers with the class, drilling the pronunciation of the adjectives as necessary. You can ask students to mark the stress on words with two syllables or more.

SUGGESTION

You can give students further practice with the adjectives in this section by giving the names of countries, cities, famous people, names of cars, etc. and eliciting possible descriptions, e.g., *a Ferrari – a fast car/an expensive car.*

GRAMMAR SPOT

This section reviews and extends the affirmative forms of the verb *to be* and the possessive adjectives that students first learned on SB p. 3.

1 Focus students' attention on the examples. Then have students complete the chart, referring to Amanda's blog if necessary. Make sure students provide the full forms, as in the examples. Check the answers.

Answers
I am
you **are**
he **is**
she **is**
it **is**
we **are**
they **are**

2 Focus students' attention on the examples. Then have students complete the chart, again referring to Amanda's blog if necessary. Check the answers.

Answers

I	my
you	**your**
he	**his**
she	**her**
we	**our**
they	their

▶▶ Review Grammar Reference 1.1–1.2 on p. 130 together in class and/or ask students to read it at home. Encourage them to ask you questions about it.

ADDITIONAL MATERIAL

Workbook Unit 1
Ex. 7 Adjectives
Ex. 8 Reading and listening

WRITING (SB p. 100)

A blog

Keeping an online journal

NOTE

This is the first main writing activity in *American Headway 1*. Students are provided with a clear framework for each section of their writing, building on the format they saw in Amanda's blog on SB p. 7. There is also a speaking stage in which students talk about their blog and read a section aloud to the class.

You may have students do the main writing task for homework, but it's worth spending some class time preparing students for the writing, particularly with weaker classes.

SUGGESTIONS

- If your students have access to a computer and the Internet, you can have them write and upload their blogs for other classes to read. These can be updated as the students progress through the course.

- If you have access to video equipment, it's a good idea to record the students when they read their blog aloud. Students usually overcome any initial shyness and soon get used to being recorded. It can be interesting to repeat the same task at a later stage, using a different topic, and let students compare the two talks. This can provide a concrete indicator of progress and so add to students' overall motivation.

1 Ask the questions to the whole class. If any students write a blog, ask what they write about.

2 Ask students if they can remember the topics in Amanda's blog (a welcome section with personal information, the first day at school, information about Boston).

Focus students' attention on the three sections in the blog on SB p. 100. Give students a few minutes to read through the sections and think about possible information they could include. Elicit a range of possible answers from the class. Provide any necessary vocabulary, checking both spelling and pronunciation. Students complete the blog individually.

3 Ask two confident students to demonstrate the activity. Remind the student who is talking not to read all of the text aloud but to use the notes to help him/her remember key information. The student who is listening should show interest and ask a few simple questions if possible. Divide the students into pairs to talk about their blog. Monitor but try not to interfere or over-correct as this is primarily a fluency activity.

4 Brainstorm possible topics for the blog, e.g., a favorite sport/music/food/city/possession. Remind students that they should choose topics that they can write about in the present tense, using *be* and *I like/love/go/have* … . Provide any necessary vocabulary, checking both spelling and pronunciation.

If you assign the writing task for homework, remind students to check their work when they have finished. If you do the task during class time, monitor students carefully and help as necessary.

Give students a few moments to read their blog to themselves and prepare to read it aloud. Monitor and help, checking for potential pronunciation problems.

Let students who feel confident read their blogs first. Ask that the rest of the class pay attention and avoid interrupting. Encourage them to write down any questions they want to ask. There probably won't be time to hear every student in a single lesson, so set up a timetable of who will read their blog in the subsequent classes. Don't make the less confident students have to wait until the end!

If you collect the writing for checking, do a light mark up, only highlighting major errors so as not to limit students' confidence.

VOCABULARY AND SPEAKING (SB p. 8)

The family

SUGGESTION

If possible, it's a nice idea to base family descriptions on real photos. Bring in photos of your family and ask students to do the same. If you have a small enough class, sit them around you and talk about the photos slowly but naturally and pass them around. Encourage students to ask questions, following the models in exercise 4 on p. 8.

This section reviews and extends the family words students learned on SB p. 4. Introduce the topic by talking about your immediate family in a natural way but using the language students have learned, e.g., *I have a …*, *My mother's name is …*, *She's (age)*, etc.

1 Focus students' attention on the diagram and the example. Elicit another example, e.g. *husband and wife*, to show that the words work in male and female pairs.

Students work in pairs to complete the diagram. Monitor and help as necessary.

Check the answers, drilling the pronunciation of the words as necessary. Students may need help with the word stress, vowel sounds, and silent letters in the following:
*grand*mother, *grand*father
niece /nis/   nephew /ˈnɛfyu/   aunt /ænt; ɑnt/
daughter /ˈdɔtər/

Answers
father and mother
husband and **wife**
son and daughter
brother and sister
grandfather and **grandmother**

uncle and **aunt**
nephew and **niece**
boyfriend and girlfriend

2 This exercise reinforces the vocabulary from exercise 1 and also introduces *cousins*, *children*, and *parents*. Focus students' attention on the example and then give students time to complete the sentences, working in pairs.

Check the answers, drilling the pronunciation of the words as necessary.

Answers
2 grandmother
3 aunt
4 uncle
5 nephew
6 niece
7 parents
8 children
9 cousins

3 This is another short listening task that students do without the support of the written text. Students have learned all the language in the script and so should be able to match the names to the people in the family tree without too much difficulty.

Focus students' attention on the family tree. Ask *Who's Joseph?* and have students point to the correct person in the family tree. Explain that students are going to hear Joseph talking about his family. Check the pronunciation of the names in the box, particularly *Andrea* /ˈændriə/ and *Odile* /oʊˈdil/.

CD1 15 Now focus attention on Joseph and play the recording as far as … *he's 25*. Say *Andrea?* and get students to point to the correct person in the family tree (*Joseph's sister*). Repeat for Richard (*Joseph's brother*).

Play the rest of the recording to the end and give students time to check their answers in pairs. With weaker students, pause the recording after each piece of key information. Play the recording again if necessary to let students check/complete their answers. Then check the answers with the class.

Answers and audio script

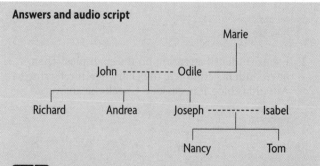

CD1 15

Joseph My family isn't very big. I have a sister, Andrea, she's 18, and a brother Richard, he's 25. They're not married. I'm married, **uh**, my wife's name is Isabel. We have two children, a daughter, Nancy, that's N - A - N - C - Y, she's 4, and a son, Tom, he's only six months old. We live near my parents. My dad's name is John and my mom's is Odile, that's O - D - I - L - E. She's French. My grandmother lives with them, her name's Marie. She's my mom's mom.

1 Demonstrate the activity by writing the names of your extended family on the board and talking about them. Give the information quite slowly but naturally and then ask a few questions to check understanding, e.g., *Who's this?*, *How old is she?*, etc.

Students write down the names of some of their relatives on a piece of paper. Model the example questions and answers in open pairs, encouraging the correct stress pattern. Students then exchange pieces of paper with a partner and ask and answer questions about each other's families.

Monitor and check for correct use of *be*, possessive *'s*, and possessive adjectives. Go over any common errors after the pairwork in a later lesson, but don't overcorrect during the task.

SUGGESTION

With weaker students, or if students are having problems with the possessive *'s*, write the following on the board:

| Who's Joseph? | 's = is |
| He's Andrea's brother. | 's = possessive, not *is* |

Refer students to **CD1 15** on p. 114 as reinforcement. Get them to look at the examples of *'s* and check what they mean.

5 Demonstrate the activity with two strong students. Give students time to exchange information in pairs. Some students may try to ask follow-up questions that require the Simple Present, e.g., *Where do they live?* Just note this if it happens but don't give any correction/explanation if students make mistakes. The Simple Present is covered in Units 2 and 3 of the course.

EXTRA ACTIVITIES

- Have students draw their own family tree as a mini-project (and have their family photos ready if relevant). Divide the class into new pairs and have students ask about each other's family. Then ask a few students to choose someone in a family tree or in a photo and give a brief description of him/her. The person can be from their own or their partner's family.

- Give students further practice on families and possessive *'s* by referring to famous people. Draw the family tree of a famous family, e.g., the British or Spanish royal family and get students to ask and answer questions with *Who?* Alternatively, you can prepare true/false statements about the family relationships. You could also try a quiz based on famous people. Prepare questions based on relationships that your students will know, e.g., *Who's Kate Middleton?* (*She's Prince William's wife.*) Be prepared to modify the questions to suit the age and experience of individual groups.

ADDITIONAL MATERIAL

Workbook Unit 1
Ex. 6 The family

EVERYDAY ENGLISH (SB p. 9)

Everyday conversations

This section introduces and practices expressions for short conversations in everyday situations.

1 This exercise reviews the language used in greetings, both in informal and slightly more formal situations. Write on the board *Hi, Pete!* and *Good morning, Mr. Simpson.* Ask *Which conversation is with a friend?* and elicit *Hi, Pete!* Explain that some of the expressions are for talking to friends (informal) and some are for talking to people you don't know very well (more formal).

Choose a confident student and elicit the following model:

T Hi, (*name of student*). How are you?
S Fine, thanks. And you?
T Pretty good, thanks.

Elicit a more formal model, using two confident students.

Students continue building conversations, using the lines in the boxes. Monitor and check for appropriate use of the greetings and for pronunciation, particularly voice range. If students sound flat, use **CD1 16** as a model to help with intonation.

2 **CD1 16** Tell students that there are four short conversations on the recording, each in a different situation. Play the recording, pausing after each conversation to ask *Friends or not?* (conversations 1 and 2 are friends; 3 and 4 aren't friends and are slightly more formal).

If students had problems with intonation, play the recording again as a model and have them repeat chorally and individually.

Audio script
1 A Hello, Sally. How are you?
  B OK, thank you. And you?
  A Fine, thanks.
2 A Hi, Pete. How are you?
  B All right, thanks. And you?
  A Not bad, thank you.
3 A Good morning, Mr. Simpson. How are you?
  B Pretty good, thank you. And you?
  A Fine, thank you.
4 A Hello, Mrs. Brown. How are you?
  B Fine, thank you. And you?
  A Not bad.

Students then practice making more conversations, using the expressions in exercise 1.

3 Focus students' attention on the photos. Ask *Who are the people? Where are they?* about each one. Focus students' attention on the example in conversation 1 and elicit the other missing words (see *Answers* below).

Students work in pairs and complete the conversations with the expressions given. Monitor and help as necessary.

CD1 17 Play the recording and have students check their answers. If students ask about any of the grammar in the expressions, e.g., *Can I ...?*, refer the students back to the context and explain the use in relation to the situation. There's no need to go into a grammatical explanation of *can* at this stage.

1 **A** Bye, Mom! It's time for school.
   B Goodbye, honey. Have **a good day**!
   A Thanks. See you **later**.
2 **C** Good morning!
   D Good morning! **Can** I have a coffee, an espresso, please?
   C Yes, **of course**. Anything else?
   D No, thank you.
3 **E** **Good afternoon**! Can I **help** you?
   F No, thank you. We're **just** looking.
   E That's OK.
4 **G** Frank. **This is** Gina. She's from our New York office.
   H Hello, Gina. Nice **to meet** you.
   I Hello, Frank. **Pleased** to meet you, too.
5 **J** Thank goodness it's Friday! **Bye**, Ian.
   K Bye, Derek. Have **a good weekend**.
   J Thanks. Same **to you**.
   K See you on Monday.
6 **L** Good night! Sleep **well**.
   M Good night! **See you** in the morning.

4 Students practice the conversations with a partner. Then ask them to memorize two or three of the conversations and act them out for the rest of the class. Acting out conversations can improve students' pronunciation considerably. Remind them of the importance of voice range. If students have problems, play relevant conversations from **CD1 17** again and have students repeat chorally and individually.

SUGGESTIONS

- Encourage students to use these expressions in class whenever appropriate, e.g., saying hello and goodbye at the start and end of class, introducing someone, asking for something with *Could I have …?* You could put key phrases on a classroom poster.
- Students can think of other situations when these expressions would be useful and write or act out parallel conversations.

ADDITIONAL MATERIAL

Workbook Unit 1
Ex. 9   Everyday conversations

Photocopiable Activity

UNIT 1   Everyday conversations TB p. 144

Note: This activity is best used in a later lesson as reinforcement and not straight after finishing SB p. 9.

Materials: one copy of the worksheet cut up per pair of students; push pins or tape

Procedure: This is a running dictation race, in which students have to memorize and dictate key lines from four short conversations. The first pair of students to complete the conversations accurately wins. Alternatively, the activity can be done as a conventional dictation, with the students working face to face.

- Explain that students are going to do a dictation activity in the form of a race. Display all the Student A worksheets on one side of the room and all the Student B worksheets on the opposite wall.

- Pre-teach/check understanding of *How do you spell …? Can you repeat that, please?*, and basic punctuation: period, question mark, and comma.
- Divide the class into A/B pairs. Students write the headings *Conversation 1, 2, 3,* and *4* on a piece of paper on their desk. They then take turns being a runner and a writer. Student A starts by running to their worksheet, memorizing the first line of Conversation 1, running back, and dictating the line to Student B, including the punctuation. Student B then runs to their worksheet, memorizes the next line, runs back and dictates the line to Student A.
- Students continue until they have written out all four conversations on their piece of paper. Check each pair's work for accuracy as they finish. The first pair to finish all four conversations correctly wins.

Don't forget!

Workbook Unit 1
Ex. 10 The alphabet
Ex. 11 Possessive adjectives
Ex. 12 Plural nouns
Grammar Reference (SB p. 130)
Word List Unit 1 (SB p. 139)
Students can translate the words, learn them at home, or transfer some of them to their vocabulary notebook.

Tests (Online)
Unit 1 Test

Video (iTools and Online) ´

Additional photocopiables and PPT™presentations (iTools)

2 A good job!

Simple Present (1) – *he/she/it* • Questions and negatives • Jobs • What time is it?
VIDEO ◀ A day in the life

The themes of this unit are jobs and people's work routines. These themes lend themselves to the practice of the grammatical goal – the third person singular of the Simple Present. The skills work includes a reading text about an Indian teenager who is also a teacher, and listening and speaking activities to reinforce question and answer forms and the vocabulary of jobs.

LANGUAGE INPUT

GRAMMAR
Simple Present (1) – *he/she/it* (SB p. 10)
Questions and negatives (SB p. 11)

- Practicing the third person singular affirmative form of the Simple Present.
- Practicing the third person singular negative and question forms of the Simple Present.

VOCABULARY
Verbs (SB p. 11)
Jobs (SB p. 16)

- Understanding and practicing vocabulary to describe jobs.
- Understanding and practicing vocabulary to talk about a range of jobs.

EVERYDAY ENGLISH
What time is it? (SB p. 17)

- Understanding and practicing expressions to tell the time.

SKILLS DEVELOPMENT

READING
A really good job (SB p. 14)

- Reading about a teenager from India who teaches younger children.

LISTENING
Five conversations about people (SB p. 13)
Five conversations about jobs (SB p. 16)

- Listening for key verbs in five short conversations. **CD1 27** (SB p. 115)
- Listening for key words in five short conversations. **CD1 32** (SB p. 115)

SPEAKING
Roleplay – An interview (SB p. 14)
Jobs (SB p. 16)

- Roleplaying an interview between a journalist and a student.
- Talking about friends and family and their jobs.

WRITING
Improving style – Using pronouns (SB p. 101)

- Understanding subject and object pronouns and possessive adjectives, then improving the pronoun use in a description.

MORE MATERIALS

Photocopiables – Say it! (TB p. 145)   **Tests** (Online)   **Video** (iTools and Online)

STARTER (SB p. 10)

The *Starter* activity recycles the family vocabulary from Unit 1 and allows students to use some of the jobs vocabulary they already know. Give some examples of jobs of the people in your own family and then have students continue the activity in pairs. If students ask for the names of individual jobs, give some examples that are common to the whole class, but do not let the *Starter* activity go on too long or reduce the usefulness of the *Vocabulary and listening* section on p. 16.

TWO OUTDOOR JOBS (SB p. 10)

Simple Present – *he/she/it*

⚠ **POSSIBLE PROBLEMS**

The Simple Present is the most-used tense in the English language. It is therefore important to introduce it early in the early levels of a course. In *American Headway 1*, the introduction is staged over two units. In this unit only the third person singular (including questions and negatives) is presented and practiced. All the other persons are introduced in Unit 3.

- The English language does not have many inflections. Unfortunately, this means the few that do exist cause a disproportionate amount of difficulty for foreign learners. The *-s* on the third person singular of the Simple Present is a classic example of this. Therefore we introduce it first in the hope that it will be more memorable and students will be less likely to omit it.

- The third person *-s* can be pronounced in three ways:

  /z/ comes   /kʌmz/
  /s/ works   /wɜrks/
  /ɪz/ teaches /'titʃɪz/

  The difference between /s/ and /z/ endings is practiced after the presentation texts on Andrew Johnson and Claudia Luke.

- The use of *does/doesn't* in the question and negative often seems strange to students, because of the absence of the auxiliary in the affirmative.

SUGGESTION

Before you start this unit, you can assign the vocabulary homework below in preparation for the presentation texts. This will save a lot of classroom time learning and reviewing vocabulary, and it will give you more time to focus on the grammar.

Homework prior to the lesson

Ask students to make sure they understand the following words, and if they are not sure of any meanings, to learn them for the lesson. They can use a bilingual dictionary to look up words they don't know and write the translation.

Verbs: *come, work, earn, go to the gym, play pool, research, study, walk the dog*

Nouns: *engineer, oil rig, coast, weeks off, free time, zoologist, snake, mountains, coast, oceanographer, environment*

1 Focus students' attention on the photos of Andrew and Claudia and on the text headings. Check students' understanding of *outdoor*. Elicit Andrew and Claudia's jobs (*He's an engineer. She's a zoologist.*)

Ask students *Where's he from?* and *Where's she from?* then ask them to look quickly at the texts to find the answers (*New Zealand* and *The US*).

CD1 18 Now play the recording and ask students to read and listen to the texts at the same time.

2 With weaker classes, you can go over the texts one at a time, finding the verbs with the students for the first text and then asking them to repeat the process on their own for the second.

Tell students that they should only look for verbs in the affirmative form. Ask them to work on their own to find the verbs and then check their answers with a partner before you check the answers with the class.

Answers

is   comes   lives   works   has   earns   goes   plays   teaches
researches   studies   loves   likes   walks

Ask the whole class what the last letter is (*-s*), and point out that this is the ending for the third person singular – *he/she/it* – of the Simple Present. If students ask why some verbs have *-es* or *-ies*, refer them to Grammar Reference 2.2 on SB p. 131.) Point out that the verb *have* is irregular in the *he/she/it* form – *has* and NOT **haves*.

Pronunciation

3 **CD1 19** Say the sounds and verbs in the chart as examples. Tell students they need to listen for the pronunciation of the final *-s* in each verb. Play the recording. Students listen and write the verbs in the correct place in the chart. Check the answers with the class.

Answers and audio script

/s/	likes	works	walks		
/z/	comes	goes	earns	plays	loves
/ɪz/	teaches	researches			

finishes kisses changes

Play the recording again. Students listen and repeat chorally and individually.

SUGGESTION

You can provide more pronunciation practice by having students take turns reading the texts on SB pp. 10–11 aloud in pairs. Monitor for correct pronunciation. If appropriate, ask one or two students to read a text aloud to the whole class.

Give students time to complete the sentences, working individually. Make it clear that each blank represents a word and that students sometimes need a verb in the Simple Present and sometimes the correct form of *be*. The last blank requires a negative.

CD1 20 Students listen and check their answers.

Answers and audio script
1 Andrew is an engineer. Claudia **is** a zoologist.
2 She comes from the US. He **comes** from New Zealand.
3 He lives in Scotland. She **lives** in California.
4 She works in the mountains. He **works** on an oil rig.
5 He earns £200 a day. She **earns** $75,000 a year.
6 She likes her job, and he **likes** his job, too.
7 He **goes** to the gym in his free time. She **walks** her dog. Her dog's name **is** Luna.
8 She**'s** married. Her husband's name **is** Chris. Andrew **isn't** married.

Ask students in pairs to read the sentences aloud. Monitor to check that students are producing the *-s* ending. If necessary, play the recording again and have students repeat.

This activity has students transfer the key information about Andrew and Claudia into note form, to help them prepare for the freer practice in exercise 6. Check comprehension of the categories in the chart. Elicit Andrew's and Claudia's last names as an example, and check the spelling.

Students complete the chart, working in pairs. Check answers with the class, discussing any pronunciation problems as you go.

Answers

	Andrew	**Claudia**
last name	Johnson	Luke
age	30	54
country	New Zealand	the USA
job	engineer	zoologist
salary	£200 a day	$75,000 a year
free time	goes to the gym/ plays pool	goes cycling/ walks her dog
married?	no	yes

6 The goal of this activity is to give students the chance not only to produce single sentences, but to describe Andrew and Claudia in more detail. It is both useful and satisfying for low-level students to use any and all language they know to stretch themselves beyond the language required for the question-and-answer activity.

Give students a few moments to look back at the chart in exercise 5. They then take turns closing their books and talking about Andrew and Claudia. Encourage them to prompt each other with the categories in the chart. With weaker students, you can write a few word prompts on the board.

Monitor and check for correct use of the Simple Present third person. Point out any errors in the third person *-s* ending, and any major problems with pronunciation, but also allow students to self-correct. Encourage peer correction from the other students as much as possible.

WHAT DOES HE DO? (SB p. 11)

Questions and negatives

> ⚠ **POSSIBLE PROBLEMS**
>
> Be prepared for some students to make mistakes in the use of *does/doesn't* to form questions and negatives. Try to review these forms as often as necessary. In the Simple Present and Simple Past tenses, where there is no auxiliary in the affirmative, the use of the auxiliary verbs can seem very strange. Many students feel that it would be much more logical to say:
>
> • Lives he in Paris?
> • Where lives she?
> • She not lives in London.
>
> The short answers *Yes, he does./No, he doesn't.* and common mistakes of form like **he doesn't comes* also cause problems and need to be pointed out to students.

1 To signal that you are going to introduce the question form, you can draw a large question mark on the board.

CD1 21 Play number 1 as an example and elicit the answer. Make sure students understand that *What does he/she do?* means the same as *What's his/her job?*, but that *What does he/she do?* is the more common question. Play the rest of the recording and have students read and listen, and then complete the answers.

Answers and audio script
1 What does Andrew do? He's an **engineer**.
2 Where does he come from? New **Zealand**.
3 Does he live in Scotland? **Yes**, he does.
4 Does he live in New Zealand? **No**, he doesn't.
5 He **isn't** married. He doesn't have any children.

Play the recording again and have students repeat both chorally and individually. Then have them ask and answer the questions in open pairs.

Grammar worksheet

GRAMMAR SPOT

1 Ask students to complete the sentences using the verb *live*.

Answers
Affirmative
He **lives** in Scotland.

Negative
He **doesn't live** in New Zealand.

Question
Where **does** he **live**? In Scotland.

Point out that the *-s* isn't used with the main verb in the negative and question, but appears in *does*.

2 **CD1 22** This exercise serves to further reinforce the weak and strong forms of *does* when unstressed, i.e., in affirmative sentences, the form is weak: /dəz/. However, when stressed, i.e., in a short answer or the negative, it is strong: /dʌz/, /ˈdʌznt/.

Play the recording. Students listen for the weak and strong forms of *does*/*doesn't*, then listen again and practice saying them. Drill the forms as necessary.

▶▶ Read Grammar Reference 2.1–2.2 on p. 131 together in class, and/or ask students to read it at home. Encourage them to ask you questions about it.

2 **CD1 23** Students complete the sentences, then check their answers with a partner. Play the recording and have them listen and check their answers. Students ask and answer in pairs. Monitor and check for correct stress and pronunciation. If students have problems, play the recording again and drill the questions and answers chorally and individually.

Answers and audio script
1 Where does Andrew work?
On an oil rig.
2 **Does** he work hard?
Yes, he **does**.
3 How much **does** he earn?
$**330** a day.
4 What **does** he do in his free time?
He **goes to the gym** and he **plays pool**.
5 **Does** he like his job?
Yes, he **does**.
6 **Does** he have a dog?
No, he **doesn't**.

3 Focus students' attention on the examples. Ask two confident students to demonstrate asking and answering questions about Claudia. Students continue in closed pairs. With weaker students, give them time to write out the questions before starting the pairwork. Monitor and check for correct use of third person *-s*, and correct stress and pronunciation. Discuss any common errors as a class.

Possible questions and answers
Where does she live? In California.
Does she work with her husband? No, she doesn't.
Does she like her job? Yes, she does.
Does she have a dog? Yes, she does.
What does she do in her free time? She goes cycling and walks her dog.
How much does she earn? $75,000 a year.

ADDITIONAL MATERIAL

Workbook Unit 2
Ex. 1, 3, and 4   Simple Present

PRACTICE (SB p. 12)

The dancer and the DJ

1 Focus students' attention on the photos of Chiaki Yasukawa and David Guetta. Check the pronunciation of their names and of *DJ* /ˈdi dʒeɪ/ (short for *disc jockey*, a person who plays music in a club or on the radio). Elicit any information that students know about them.

2 Give students time to read about Chiaki and David. Answer any vocabulary questions students may have and check the pronunciation of the names of people and places *Anly* /ˈæn li/, *Ibiza* /ɪˈbɪðə/ or /ɪˈbizə/, *Miami* /maɪˈæmi/, *Mauritius* /məˈrɪʃəs/, *Senegal* /ˈsɛnəgɔl/.

Focus students' attention on the example. Elicit where Chiaki comes from, then elicit a little information about David as an additional example. Divide the class into pairs. Students describe Chiaki or David to their partner. Monitor, helping as necessary. Check for correct use of *be*, *she*/*he*, *his*/*her*, and third person *-s* with the Simple Present forms. Write down any common errors to discuss as a class after the activity. Finish the activity by bringing the whole class together again, and asking one or two students to tell the others about Chiaki and David.

Asking questions

3 Divide the class into pairs and ask each pair to choose either Chiaki or David. Focus students' attention on the example question. Students work individually and write the rest of the questions about either Chiaki or David. Monitor and help as necessary. Make sure students are writing the questions correctly by having several students read them aloud. Be prepared to drill the pronunciation as necessary.

Focus students' attention on the example question and answer about Chiaki. Elicit the same question and answer about David. Students work in pairs and take turns asking and answering questions about Chiaki or David. Monitor and check for accurate question formation, and use of *he/she* and *his/her*.

Students who finish early can ask about the person they didn't choose, but don't make the activity go on too long by insisting they ask every question about both people.

Finish the activity by eliciting a few questions and answers in open pairs. Discuss any common errors as a class.

Stress and intonation

4 Demonstrate the activity by writing the following examples on the board. Drill the contrastive stress as marked below:

Chiaki's American. No, she isn't. She's Japanese.

She has three children. No, she doesn't. She has one child.

She's married. Yes, that's right.

With weaker students, highlight the use of *is* in the sentence with *be,* and *does* in the sentence with Simple Present.

CD1 24 Play the recording of the examples in the Student Book. Have students complete the second example, then listen and repeat. Encourage them to reproduce the contrastive stress accurately in the sentences where the information is corrected.

Play the recording of the rest of the sentences (3–8 below) and have the class and individual students respond. This should be quick and fun to do, so don't insist on the full correct answer if it slows down the activity – *No, he/she doesn't,* etc. is enough, especially with weaker classes.

Audio script
1 Chiaki comes from Osaka.
2 She lives in Japan.
3 She has one son.
4 She goes to the beach.
5 David's English.
6 He works all over the world.
7 He has two daughters.
8 He writes songs in his free time.

CD1 25 Play the recording, pausing after each pair of sentences to give students time to listen and to focus on the responses.

Audio script
1 A Chiaki comes from Osaka.
   B Yes, that's right.
2 A She lives in Japan.
   B No, she doesn't. She lives in Florida.
3 A She has one son.
   B No, she doesn't. She has a daughter.
4 A She goes to the beach.
   B Yes, that's right.
5 A David's English.
   B No, he isn't. He's French.
6 A He works all over the world.
   B Yes, that's right.
7 A He has two daughters.
   B No, he doesn't. He has a son and a daughter.
8 A He writes songs in his free time.
   B Yes, that's right.

CD1 24 Play the cue sentences again and have students respond. They should be able to do so more quickly and confidently this time, but with weaker classes be prepared to drill key sentences as a class.

Talking about family and friends

5 This exercise reinforces the third person -*s* with verbs in the Simple Present. Focus students' attention on the example. Students complete the sentences, working individually. Check the answers with the class, making sure students remember the -*es* ending on *watches* in number 6 and the pronunciation /ˈwɑtʃɪz/. If you want to give further pronunciation practice, have students read the complete sentences aloud, focusing on the /s/ /z/ /ɪz/ endings.

Answers
1 comes
2 lives
3 loves
4 travels
5 speaks; wants
6 watches
7 writes

6 Ask two students to read aloud the example in exercise 5 and the example response in this exercise. Students continue the matching task, working in pairs.

7 **CD1 26** Explain that students are going to check their answers against the recording and also listen for a third line in each conversation. Play conversation 1 as an example and elicit the reply *From the capital, Seoul.* Play the rest of the recording, pausing at the end of each reply. Have students check their answers and elicit the reply each time. With weaker classes, you may need to play some of the conversations again.

Refer students to **CD1 26** on p. 115. Divide the students into pairs and have them practice the dialogues. Encourage an animated delivery. If students sound flat, play the recording again as a model and have students repeat. If necessary, model some of the lines yourself, exaggerating the voice range to help students improve their intonation.

Answers and audio script

1 A My husband comes from Korea.
  B Where exactly in Korea?
  A From the capital, Seoul.
2 A My grandmother lives in the next town.
  B Does she visit you often?
  A Yes, she does. Every Sunday.
3 A My mother loves reading.
  B What does she read?
  A Detective stories.
4 A My father travels a lot for his job.
  B Where does he go?
  A He's in Tokyo this week.
5 A My sister speaks Spanish very well. She wants to learn Chinese, too.
  B Does she want to be an interpreter?
  A No, she doesn't. She wants to be a teacher.
6 A My little brother watches TV a lot.
  B What does he like watching?
  A Sports, sports, sports, and, uh, soccer!
7 A My friend, Tom writes a blog.
  B What does he write about?
  A Everything and everybody!

Listening

8 **CD1 27** This listening task consists of five short conversations. Play the recording and elicit the subject of each conversation. Check the answers with the class.

Answers and audio script

1 speaker B's sister and her studies
2 Peter's job
3 a dog
4 speaker B's friend and her level of English
5 speaker B's grandfather and his free time

CD1 27

1 A What does your sister do?
  B She's a student. She wants to be a doctor so she studies a lot.
2 A Does Peter like his new job?
  B No, he doesn't. He works very hard and he doesn't earn a lot of money.
3 A Is that your dog?
  B No, he isn't. He's my mother's. He goes with her everywhere. She loves him a lot. His name's Boris.
4 A Your friend Elena speaks English very well.
  B Yes, she does. She goes to Canada every summer.
5 A What does your grandfather do all the time?
  B Well, he watches TV a lot, but on Saturdays he plays golf with friends, and on Sundays he visits us.

9 **CD1 27** During the second listening, students have to focus on the key verbs. Explain that these are all in the Simple Present.

Play conversation 1 as an example. Elicit the other verbs (*is, wants, studies*). Play the rest of the recording and have students write the verbs they hear. With weaker students, pause the recording after each conversation to give them time to write their answers. If necessary, play selected conversations a second time if students missed any of the answers. Check answers with the class. Have students spell their answers to review the alphabet at the same time.

Answers

1 do, is, wants, studies
2 like, works, earn
3 is, goes, loves
4 speaks, goes
5 do, watches, plays, visits

10 Focus students' attention on the example questions in the Student Book. Write the name of a friend or relative on the board. Elicit a range of questions about this person from the class. Give students a moment to choose a friend or relative and write their name down. Provide any necessary vocabulary, e.g., *best friend, neighbor, (sister)-in-law*, etc.

Put students in new pairs to do the task, having them work with someone they don't know well. With weaker students, write prompts on the board to help students with the questions they can ask, e.g., *work, country/city, place of work, family, pets, free time, languages*.

Monitor and check as students do the activity, checking for question formation and third person -*s*. Don't interrupt or overcorrect as this is a fluency activity. Make a note of any common errors in the main areas of grammar and discuss them with the class after the pairwork. Finish the activity by asking one or two students to tell the class about their or their partner's friend or relative.

11 **CD1 28** This is another discrimination activity. Play sentence 1 as an example. Then play the rest of the recording and ask students to choose the sentences they hear. You can make this exercise productive by asking students to read the pairs of sentences aloud.

Answers and audio script

1 a He likes his job.
2 b She loves working.
3 b He isn't married.
4 b Does he have three children?
5 b Where does he go?

ADDITIONAL MATERIAL

Workbook Unit 2
Ex. 5   Questions
Ex. 6   Daily routines
Ex. 8   Verb + noun

Improving style

Using pronouns

This unit of the writing syllabus reviews subject pronouns and possessive adjectives, and also introduces object pronouns. Knowing how to use pronouns is an essential skill in fluent writing and it helps students understand how a text fits together.

1 Have students complete the charts, working individually before checking answers with the class.

Answers

Subject pronouns	Object pronouns	Possessive adjectives
I	me	my
you	you	**your**
he	him	his
she	her	**her**
it	it	its
we	us	**our**
they	them	their

2 Write the following sentence on the board and have students identify the subject pronoun, object pronoun, and possessive adjective:

I lend him my car every week.   *He gives me his book.*

Look at sentence 1 and the example as a class. Elicit the pronouns and other possessive adjectives in the sentence (pronouns: *I*, *him*; possessive adjective: *my*). In pairs, students continue to underline the pronouns and circle the possessive adjectives in sentences 2 and 3. Check answers with the class.

Answers

1 pronouns: I, him; possessive adjectives: her, my
2 pronouns: She, it; possessive adjective: our
3 pronouns: They, he, them; possessive adjective: their

Refer students to Grammar Reference 2.3 on p. 131.

3 Focus students' attention on the example and have them say what *she* and *me* refer back to (*girlfriend* and *I*). Look through the names in the sentences quickly and make sure that students know if they refer to a man or a woman. Have students complete the sentences, working individually. Give them time to check their answers in pairs before checking answers with the class.

Answers

2	He; them	7	her
3	it	8	He; it
4	him	9	me
5	We; us	10	She; them
6	us		

4 Ask students what they can remember about Claudia Luke (the zoologist from p. 11). Ask students to read the text quickly and find the answers to the questions. Elicit who is in the photo with her. (*a student*) .

Answers

She's a zoologist.
She works with different kinds of people.
Her husband Chris, comes from the US. He is an oceanographer.
She studies animals such as snakes and mice in their natural environment.

5 Read the first sentence of the text aloud and have students say what is wrong with it (the repetition of *Claudia* makes it sound unnatural). Focus students' attention on the example rewriting of the text and then have students continue the task. With weaker classes, elicit a longer section of the text as a whole-class activity and write the answers on the board before students complete the task individually.

Check the answers either orally or by collecting the students' written task.

CD1 29 Play the recording and let students check their answers.

Answers and audio script

Claudia Luke is American. She lives in California and she's a zoologist. She is the director of three research stations at Sonoma State University. She works outside a lot in the mountains on the coast of California. Claudia studies water and fire and how they change the natural world. She likes studying animals such as snakes and mice in their natural environment. She doesn't like studying them in the lab. Her job is very exciting and she loves teaching and working with a lot of different kinds of people, such as academics, researchers, and students. Claudia is married to Chris. He is also American and he also loves the natural world – he is an oceanographer and so he studies the oceans. In their free time Claudia and Chris often go cycling and walking with their dog, Luna. They love Luna a lot.

EXTRA ACTIVITY

Give students additional practice by asking them to write a short description of a friend or relative, or a short profile of a famous person that they admire. This can be done as a mini-project, with the students then presenting their descriptions in the form of a short talk. If you have access to a computer network, students can type their description and then upload it for other students to read. If not, you can create an area for students' written work in the classroom and display it on the walls. With weaker classes, write prompts on the board to help students plan the type of information to include, e.g. *work, country/city, place of work, family, free time*, etc.

A really good job

ABOUT THE TEXT

This activity brings together, in one text, much of the grammar that students have studied so far. It should be motivating for them to read a piece of continuous prose of this length. The section also acts as a preview of the daily routine topic in Unit 3.

The text is based on a real young Indian man, but the information has been carefully simplified and graded for Elementary students. West Bengal /bɛŋˈɡɔl/ is a state in eastern India which stretches from the Himalayas in the north to the Bay of Bengal in the south.

Encourage students to use the context in reading texts as much as possible to help them with new words. They can also pool their knowledge of vocabulary when working in groups, or, if appropriate, use a dictionary.

Students may need help with the words below in terms of meaning and/or pronunciation. You may want to pre-teach/check students' understanding of the following:

village, to be lucky, private school, rupee /ˈrupi; ruˈpi/, *bamboo hut, housework, ambition, poor.*

1 Introduce the topic by asking students: *What does a head teacher do? How old are most head teachers?* Focus students' attention on the map and the photos on pp. 14–15. Point to Babur /ˈbɑbur/ Ali and read aloud the main heading. Ask students to tell you a little about what and who they can see in the pictures, and to predict a little about Babur Ali's life. Do not insist on accuracy at this stage – use this as an opportunity for students to get into the topic and predict what they might read in the text.

Put students into pairs to talk about the information in sentences 1–8. Don't let them refer to the text at this stage.

2 Ask students to read the first paragraph quite quickly. This helps them focus on the main information and not worry about words they don't recognize. Ask students to locate Babur's region on the map on p. 14.

With weaker students, you can ask and answer some of the questions in open pairs first. Students work in closed pairs and take turns asking and answering the questions about Babur. Check the answers by having several pairs ask and answer the questions aloud. Decide according to the speed and ability of your students whether you want quick, short answers or fuller answers (see answers in parentheses below).

Answers

1 West Bengal in India. (He comes from West Bengal in India.)
2 In the small village of Bhabta. (He lives in the small village of Bhabta.)
3 No, it doesn't.
4 Because he goes to a private school. (He's lucky because he goes to a private school.)
5 1,000 rupees a year. (It costs 1,000 rupees a year.)
6 Everything that he learns. (He teaches them everything that he learns.)
7 No, they aren't.
8 Anand Shiksha Niketan School. Yes, it is. (His school's name is Anand Shiksha Niketan School.)

If appropriate, ask students for their reaction to the first part of the text. Ask if they know anyone who is young and who has a job.

3 Write the times 5:00 a.m. and 4:00 p.m. on the board and elicit the expressions *five o'clock* and *four o'clock*. Do not cover other expressions, as students will review telling the time more fully in the *Everyday English* section at the end of this unit.

Give students time to read the second paragraph. Then have two students ask and answer the questions using the example in the Student' Book. With weaker classes, you can write the key verbs on the board as prompts: *get up, go to school, travel back to his village, begin classes, stop teaching.*

Students continue to ask and answer questions. Monitor and check. Then check the answers with the class.

Answers

What time does he get up?	At five o'clock.
What time does he go to school?	At eight o'clock.
What time does he travel back to his village?	At four o'clock.
What time does he begin classes?	At five o'clock.
What time does he stop teaching?	At eight o'clock.

4 Give students time to read the last paragraph. Focus students' attention on the example and elicit the correction. Write the sentences on the board and highlight the contrastive stress:

It doesn't have sixty students. It has six hundred and fifty.

Students works in pairs to correct sentences 2–4. Monitor and check. Then check the answers with the class.

Answers

1 It doesn't have sixty students. It has six hundred and fifty.
2 It doesn't have five teachers. It has ten teachers.
3 Babur doesn't want to stop teaching. He always wants to teach poor children.
4 He doesn't want to be a doctor. He wants to go to college.

5 Ask students to look back at their answers in exercise 1. Students check if their ideas were correct.

Answers

1 5 a.m.	4 4 p.m.	7 speaks
2 mother in the house	5 the classes	8 wants
3 bus	6 likes	

Roleplay – An interview

6 This activity reinforces question formation and also gives students the opportunity to roleplay characters from the reading text.

Ask students to imagine that a journalist is visiting Babur's school and that he/she wants to interview one of the students. Elicit a few possible questions that the journalist might ask. Focus attention on the question prompts. Elicit the first question as an example (*How many students does your school have? / How many teachers are in your school?*)

Divide the class into pairs to complete the rest of the questions. Monitor and help as necessary, checking for correct question formation. With weaker students, you can do the question formation as a class, drilling the forms as necessary.

Check the answers, accepting any suitable wording for the questions.

Divide the students into A/B pairs and assign the role of journalist to the As and one of Babur's students to the Bs. Remind students to use the questions as prompts, but also to make the conversation between the journalist and students as natural as possible. Encourage the B students to give additional information in their answers. They can imagine extra details based on what they know from the text. Encourage the A students to react to the information given by the students and to sound interested.

Choose two confident students to demonstrate the beginning of the roleplay. Students then continue in closed pairs. Monitor and check for correct question formation and for good intonation. If students sound flat, model some of the roleplay yourself and have students repeat.

CD1 30 Play the recording and let students compare their conversation with the audio script. Weaker students can follow **CD1 30** on SB p. 115.

Audio script
I = Interviewer   S = Student
I Can I ask you some questions about your school?
S Yes, of course.
I How many students are in your school?
S There are 650 now.
I That's a lot. And how many teachers?
S Ten teachers.
I And what time do your classes start?
S Five o'clock every day.
I How much does it cost?
S Oh, the school is free.
I Very good! And your teacher, what's your teacher's name?
S Babur Ali. He's only sixteen.
I Sixteen! That's amazing! Is he a good teacher?
S He is very good.
I What does he teach?
S He teaches English, Bengali, history, and math.
I That's a lot of subjects. Does he work hard?
S Oh, yes, very hard. He studies all day and he teaches us every evening. He's the best teacher in the world!

SUGGESTION
Asking students to act really seems to help their pronunciation, particularly stress and intonation. You can ask pairs of students to memorize their conversation

and then act it out in front of the class. More confident students can improvise other conversations, e.g., between Babur and the journalist, Babur and another teacher, two of Babur's students.

ADDITIONAL MATERIAL

Workbook Unit 2
Ex. 7   Reading and listening

VOCABULARY AND LISTENING (SB p. 16)

⚠ **POSSIBLE PROBLEMS**
In many languages, you don't need an article (a/an) when stating a person's job. This may lead to mistakes in English *I'm hair stylist*, etc. exercise 2 provides the article in context, but students may make mistakes in less structured practice, so be prepared to highlight the correct the use of a/an + job.

Jobs

1 Focus students' attention on the pictures and elicit the names of the jobs that students already know. Elicit the correct job in picture a (nurse). In pairs, students match the rest of the pictures with the words. Let students check any new words in their dictionaries.

Check the answers and drill the words both chorally and individually as you go, paying special attention to the stress. Also, make sure that students reproduce the correct vowel sounds (see Answers below). With weaker classes, you can keep reviewing the words by saying Tell me again! What's picture a? What's picture d? etc.

Answers
a nurse /nərs/
b journalist /ˈdʒərnəlɪst/
c pilot /ˈpaɪlət/
d architect /ˈɑrkəˌtɛkt/
e lawyer

f hairstylist
g dentist
h receptionist
i taxi driver
j accountant /əˈkaʊntnt/

2 Elicit the answer to sentence 1 (hairstylist) as an example. Students work in pairs to complete the rest of the sentences. Allow students to continue to use their dictionaries, or if you have a monolingual class, you can give quick translations of any words they ask about.

CD1 31 Students listen and check their answers.

Answers and audio script
1 She's a **hairstylist**. She cuts hair.
2 He's a **pilot**. He flies from LAX airport.
3 She's a **receptionist**. She works in a hotel.
4 He's an **architect**. He designs buildings.
5 She's a **lawyer**. She works for a family law firm.
6 He's a **taxi driver**. He knows the streets of New York.
7 She's a **journalist**. She writes news stories.
8 He's a **dentist**. He takes care of people's teeth.
9 He's a **nurse**. He works in the City Hospital.
10 She's an **accountant**. She likes working with numbers.

3 **CD1 32** Play conversation 1 and elicit the job (*journalist*) as an example. Play the rest of the recording and have students complete conversations 2–5. Check the answers with the class.

Put the students in pairs to practice the conversations. Be prepared to drill selected lines if students have pronunciation difficulties.

Answers and audio script

1 A What does your brother do?
   B He's a **journalist**. He writes for *USA Today*.
   A Oh, that's a good newspaper.
2 C What does your father do?
   D He's an **accountant**. He works for a big firm in the city.
   C And your mother? What does she do?
   D She's a **teacher**. She teaches French and Spanish.
3 E Does your sister work downtown?
   F Yes, she does. She's a **receptionist**. She works at the Ritz Hotel.
   E Oh, that's near where I work.
4 G Are you a **doctor**?
   H No, I'm not. I'm a **nurse**.
   G Oh, but I want to see a **doctor**.
5 J I want to be a **pilot** when I'm big.
   K I want to be a **lawyer**. They earn lots of money.
   J **Pilots** earn a lot too, and they travel the world.

EXTRA ACTIVITIES

- Students write their own short conversations containing jobs based on the model in exercise 3.
- Students play "Twenty questions" in small groups to review the vocabulary of jobs and the Simple Present. One student thinks of a job, but doesn't say what it is. The rest of the class asks *yes/no* questions to try and find out what it is. The student answering has to say a full short answer, e.g., *Yes, it is/No, it isn't.*, *Yes, he does./No, he doesn't.* The person who guesses in less than 20 questions has the next turn. If the group cannot guess, the same student thinks of another job.

Speaking

4 Focus students' attention on the examples in the Student Book. Elicit more questions from the class about one of your friends or relatives. Students work in pairs to ask and answer questions about the jobs. If appropriate, you can set this up as a role play with students pretending to be delegates at a conference and discussing people's jobs.

Monitor and check, helping as necessary. Check for accurate use of *be*, *his/her*, third person Simple Present forms, and *a/an* + job. Don't interrupt students during the pairwork, but discuss any common errors at a later time.

ADDITIONAL MATERIAL

Workbook Unit 2
Ex. 2 and 9   Jobs

What time is it?

SUGGESTION

It is useful to have a toy or cardboard clock with movable hands for this lesson and for subsequent review of telling the time. If you don't already have one in your school, then it is very easy to make a cardboard one.

Introduce the subject of telling the time by asking *What time is it?* and *What time does the lesson start?* Initially you can accept answers in the hour + minutes form, e.g., *five thirty*, but explain that the system used in *American Headway 1* uses *after* and *to*.

NOTE

To help students learn the time in English, the clocks in exercise 1 are arranged in four groups: *o'clock/thirty*; *quarter after/to*; *minutes after*; *minutes to*. Each example has a similar time alongside to help students write the correct answers.

---

1 Focus students' attention on the first pair of clocks and elicit the missing time (*It's eight o'clock.*) Ask students to work in pairs, look carefully at the clocks and the examples provided, and write in the times.

CD1 33 Play the recording for students to check their answers.

Answers and audio script

It's five o'clock.	It's eight o'clock.
It's five thirty.	It's eleven thirty.
It's quarter after five.	It's quarter after two.
It's quarter to six.	It's quarter to nine.
It's five after five.	It's ten after five.
It's twenty after five.	It's twenty-five after five.
It's twenty-five to six.	It's twenty to six.
It's ten to six.	It's five to six.

Play the recording again. Encourage students to follow closely the stress pattern as they practice saying the times. Elicit the time of the end of the lesson.

If possible, bring a toy or cardboard clock with moveable hands to the lesson as an easy way of giving further practice. First, you can change the times on the clock, and then your students can also take turns coming to the front of the class, moving the hands, and asking *What time is it?* Alternatively, draw clocks showing different times on the board. Continue to encourage students to use accurate stress patterns.

2 This exercise introduces useful expressions for times just before or after an exact division of the clock, and for an approximate time. Focus attention on the clocks and the times.

CD1 34 Play the recording for students to listen and repeat.

Audio script

1 It's almost three o'clock.
2 It's just after five o'clock.
3 It's about two thirty.

Practice these expressions with appropriate times shown on the toy or cardboard clock, or by drawing further examples on the board. Check pronunciation and sentence stress carefully.

3 Focus students' attention on the examples. Ask *Which conversation is with a friend?* (the one with the question *What time is it?*). *Where are the people in the other conversation?* (in the street/in a public place). Drill the pronunciation chorally and individually.

Ask students to draw three or more clocks on a piece of paper. Remind them to use the expressions in exercise 2. Students practice the conversations in pairs. Monitor and check for correct pronunciation. Drill the examples again if necessary and have students repeat the pairwork.

4 **CD1 35** With weaker classes, give students time to read through the conversations first. Play conversation 1, pausing at the end, and elicit the missing words. Play the rest of the conversations without stopping. Give students time to check their answers in pairs. Play the recording again for students to check/complete their answers.

Answers and audio script

1 **A** Excuse me. Can you tell me the **time**, please?
B Yes, of course. It's **just** after **six** o'clock.
A Thank you **very** much.
2 **C** **Excuse** me. Can you **tell** me the time, please?
D I'm **sorry**. I don't have the time.
C Oh, that's OK.
3 **E** Excuse me. What time does the bus leave?
F At **ten after** ten.
E Thank you. What time is it now?
F It's **about** five after.
E Five after ten?!
F No, no, five after **nine**. You're OK. No need to hurry.
4 **G** When does this lesson **end**?
H At four o'clock.
G Oh, no! It's only **quarter** after three.

Tell students (in L1 if appropriate) to imagine that they are stopping a stranger in the street in conversations 1–3 and that they must try to sound polite. Ask two confident students to practice one of the conversations in front of the class. Students continue in closed pairs. If students sound flat or a little abrupt, play the recording as a model and drill chorally and individually. Really encourage a good imitation of the recording to help the students sound very polite.

Students can act out one or two of the conversations for the class. Keep the activity light-hearted and fun.

SUGGESTION

Try to integrate the language of telling the time into all of your lessons in a natural way. Ask students for a time check at various points in the lesson, ask about the times of their favorite TV shows, and the time schedule for local transportation.

Photocopiable Activity
UNIT 2 Say it! TB p. 145
Materials: One copy of the worksheet for each group of three of four students; dice and counters for each group.
Procedure: Explain that students are going to play a board game to practice the language from Unit 2 and review some of the language from Unit 1. Pre-teach/check *It's my/your turn. I'm/You're next, That's right/wrong, I/you go back/forward.*

• Put students into groups and hand out copies of the board game, and the dice and counters. Explain that there are different types of squares in the game – on a *Make a question* square students have to make a question from a prompt, e.g. *your teacher = married?* and they should then answer that question. On a *What's the job?* square they should give the correct job. On an *Opposites* square they should give the correct opposite adjective. On an *About you* square students have to talk about themselves.

• Explain the rules: if a student gives a correct sentence from a prompt/definition, they stay on that square, if not, they move back one. If a student asks and answers the prompt on a *Make a question* square correctly, they move forward 2 squares. The first student to reach *Finish* is the winner.

• Students put their counters on *Start* and take turns throwing the dice and moving around the board. Monitor and help as necessary. Try to encourage students to check each other's answers, but be prepared to be the final judge if there are any disputes.

ADDITIONAL MATERIAL

Workbook Unit 2
Ex. 10 What time is it?

Don't forget!

Workbook Unit 2
Ex. 11 *is/has/does*
Ex. 12 *a/an*
Grammar Reference (SB p. 131)
Word list Unit 2 (SB p. 140)
Students can translate the words, learn them at home, or transfer some of them to their vocabulary notebook.
Tests (Online)
Unit 2 Test
Video (iTools and Online)
Additional photocopiables and PPT™ presentations (iTools)

Work hard, play hard!

Simple Present (2) – *I/you/we/they* • In my free time • Social expressions (1)
VIDEO◄ Jobs

This unit builds on the theme of routines from Unit 2, but with the focus on free time and leisure activities. This creates opportunities for both controlled and personalized practice of the main grammatical goal – all other persons (those without the -s!) of the Simple Present. The skills work includes listening and reading tasks about what people do in their free time, and about different weekend routines, and speaking and listening tasks about work–life balance. This provides the opportunity to bring together and review all singular and plural forms of the Simple Present.

LANGUAGE INPUT

GRAMMAR
Simple Present (2) – *I/you/we/they* (SB p. 18)	• Practicing the *I/you/we/they* form of the Simple Present.
Questions and negatives (SB p. 19)	• Practicing the *I/you/we/they* negative and question forms of the Simple Present.
Frequency adverbs (SB p. 19)	• Expressing frequency with common adverbs.

VOCABULARY
Free-time activities (SB p. 20)	• Understanding and practicing vocabulary to talk about free time.
Verb + noun/adverb collocations (SB p. 22)	• Matching and using common collocations.

EVERYDAY ENGLISH
Social expressions (1) (SB p. 25)	• Understanding and practicing expressions in everyday situations.

SKILLS DEVELOPMENT

READING
Town and country weekends (SB p. 22)	• A jigsaw reading about how two people spend the perfect weekend.

LISTENING
Five conversations about free time (SB p. 21)	• Listening for key information in five short conversations. **CD1 41** (SB p. 116)
A talk about work–life balance (SB p. 24)	• Listening for the main ideas in a talk. **CD1 44** (SB p. 117)

SPEAKING
Role play (SB p. 19)	• Roleplaying an interview between a journalist and someone with two jobs.
Questionnaire (SB p. 24)	• Talking about work–life balance.

WRITING
Filling out forms – An application form (SB p. 102)	• Understanding the conventions of filling out forms, then comparing the information in two forms.

MORE MATERIALS

Photocopiables – How often …? (TB p. 146)   **Tests** (Online)   **Video** (iTools and Online)

- You can bring a calendar to the lesson to help with the presentation/review of the days of the week in the *Starter* section. (You can also use it to review/present months of the year in the *Vocabulary and listening* section on p. 20.)
- Assigning some vocabulary for homework before you start this unit will give you more time to focus on the grammar. It is worthwhile to get students used to taking some responsibility for the learning of vocabulary. Encourage them to write the new words in their vocabulary notebooks.

Homework prior to the lesson

1 Ask students to review/learn the days of the week in English. You can give them a handout with the phonetic script such as this:

Monday /ˈmʌndeɪ/   Tuesday /ˈtuzdeɪ/
Wednesday /ˈwɛnzdeɪ/   Thursday /ˈθɜrzdeɪ/
Friday /ˈfraɪdeɪ/   Saturday /ˈsætərˌdeɪ/
Sunday /ˈsʌndeɪ/

2 Ask students to review/make sure they understand the following words and learn them for the lesson. They can use a bilingual dictionary to look up words they don't know and write the translation.

Verbs: *stay late, sing, go to bed, eat in a restaurant, cook*

Nouns: *bookstore, singer, nightclub, apartment, band* (= music group)

Adjectives: *happy, tired*

⚠ POSSIBLE PROBLEMS

Take particular care with the pronunciation of *Tuesday* /ˈtuzdeɪ/ and *Thursday* /ˈθɜrzdeɪ/ which students can easily confuse because they sound very similar. Also, the pronunciation of *Wednesday* /ˈwɛnzdeɪ/ can be a problem because of the spelling, and the consonant cluster /nzd/ that results from it being pronounced as two syllables, not three.

STARTER (SB p. 18)

1 If you didn't ask your students to review/learn the days of the week for homework, use a calendar to present the days. (Alternatively, write the days on the board in abbreviated form, e.g., *Mon., Tues.*, etc). Ask *What day is it today?* Go over the days of the week with the whole class, having students repeat both chorally and individually. Then have one student after another say the days aloud in order very quickly until students can say them correctly without hesitation.

To give further practice with the days of the week and the alphabet, ask one or two students to say the days of the week in order, and then to spell each one. This will take less time if you have assigned the above for homework.

2 Elicit the weekend days and ask students which days of the week they are busy. Ask students to give reasons.

Simple Present – *I/you/we/they*

See the notes on *Homework prior to the lesson* in *Suggestions*, opposite. Having students preview vocabulary will help maintain a lively pace in the grammar presentation.

This section introduces the first person singular of the Simple Present. This should present few problems for students, as they have already seen the *he/she/it* form in Unit 2.

1 **CD1 36** Focus students' attention on the photos and the title of the text. Elicit basic information: *What's her name? (Claire). Where is she in the photos? (in a bookstore and on a music poster).* Focus students' attention on the questions in exercise 1. Ask students to close their books and then play the recording through once. Elicit the answers to the gist questions. *Where does she live? How old is she? What are her 2 jobs?*

Answers
She lives in New York City.
She's 24.
She works in a bookstore and she's a singer.

2 Students open their books. Focus students' attention on the example in the text about Claire. Elicit which verbs in the box are negatives (*don't do, don't go*). Students complete the rest of the text with the verbs.

CD1 36 Give students time to compare their answers in pairs before playing the recording as a final check.

Reading aloud is a way of reinforcing new language in a way that all students find accessible. Ask a confident student to read aloud the first paragraph. Put students in pairs to read aloud alternate paragraphs. Monitor and check for accurate pronunciation. Be prepared to drill selected sentences either from the recording or by modeling the sentences yourself.

Answers and audio script
Claire's two jobs
"Hi, I'm Claire Higgins. I'm 24 years old and I live in New York City. I'm always very busy but I'm very happy. From Monday to Friday I **work** in a bookstore, the Strand Bookstore in Manhattan. Then on Saturdays I **have** another job, I'm a singer with a band. It's great because I love books and I **love** singing.
On weekdays I usually **finish** work at 6 o'clock, but sometimes I **stay** late, until 9 or 10 o'clock at night. On Saturday evenings, I **sing** in nightclubs in all parts of the city. I **don't go** to bed until 3 or 4 o'clock in the morning. On Sundays I **don't do** much at all! I often **eat** in a little restaurant near my apartment. I never **cook** on Sundays. I'm too tired."

Questions and negatives

3 You can signal that you are going to focus on questions by drawing a large question mark on the board.

CD1 37 Play number 1 as an example. Play the rest of the recording and have students complete Claire's answers.

Play the recording again or model the questions and answers yourself. Practice the questions and answers in open pairs to correct any mistakes. Take particular care with these aspects of pronunciation:

Sounds

weak vowel sound /də/ in the question
strong vowel sound /du/ in the short answer

Do you like your job?   *Yes, I do.*
/də yə laɪk yər dʒɑb/   /yɛs aɪ du/

Stress and intonation

The intonation rises at the end of *Yes/No* questions and falls at the end of short answers and *wh-* questions.

Do you like your job?   *Yes, I do.*

Where do you live?

SUGGESTION

With weaker students or if students ask why *do* and not *does* is used in questions with *you*, go over the Grammar Spot with the class before students do the Role play section.

Role play

SUGGESTION

If you have access to video equipment, you can record students doing the interview.

4 Set up this task as an interview, rather than just straight question and answer practice. If possible, move the desks to create a more relaxed setting and have students use a classroom object as a microphone prop. Pre-teach/check understanding of the language for greetings and thank yous: *Nice to meet you. Thank you very much. My pleasure.* /ˈplɛʒər/), and the use of *because* in replying to *why* questions.

Tell students to read the text on p. 18 quickly, but then to cover it and try to remember the information about Claire's life. This will help the role play sound more natural. With weaker students, go over the questions as a class first and elicit the full form of each question.

Demonstrate the activity by having two students ask and answer the first two questions for the class. Students then work in closed pairs and roleplay the interview. Give students time to change roles so that everyone practices

the question formation. Go around the class and check for correct question formation and correct use of strong and weak forms in the pronunciation of *do*.

CD1 38 Play the recording and have students compare their answers. You can refer students to **CD1 38** and highlight the use of frequency adverbs (*often, usually, sometimes, always, never*) in the conversation before students look at the Grammar Spot for reinforcement of the grammar point.

Audio script

I = interviewer   **C** = Claire

I   Hi, Claire. Nice to meet you.
C   Nice to meet you, too.
I   Now, I hear you often sing in nightclubs here in New York City.
C   That's right. I love singing.
I   And how old are you, Claire?
C   I'm 24.
I   And do you live in New York?
C   Yes, I do. I live downtown near the river.
I   And where do you work?
C   I work in a bookstore. The Strand Bookstore in Manhattan.
I   Mm. What time do you finish work?
C   Well, I usually finish at 6 o'clock but sometimes I stay late, until 9 or 10 o'clock, but I always finish at 6 on Saturdays because I sing in the evening.
I   How many jobs do you have?
C   Just two! The bookstore and singing.
I   And do you like your jobs?
C   Oh, yes! I love them both.
I   Why do you like them?
C   Because I love singing and I love books. I'm lucky. I love my work.
I   What do you do on Sundays?
C   I don't do much at all. I often eat in a little restaurant near my apartment.
I   Do you sometimes cook on Sundays?
C   Never! I'm too tired.
I   I understand that! Thank you very much for your time, Claire.
C   My pleasure.

GRAMMAR SPOT

1 Ask students to complete the chart with the affirmative and negative forms. Check the answers.

Answers Simple Present	Affirmative	Negative
I/you	work	don't work
he/she/it	**works**	**doesn't work**
we/they	**work**	**don't work**

Ask students to focus on the affirmative forms in the chart. Ask them which have a different form (*he/she/it*) and how they are different (they end in *-s*).

Ask students to focus on the negative forms in the chart. Ask them how the *I/you/we/they* forms are different from the affirmative forms (they use the auxiliary *don't*). Ask students to focus on the *he/she/it* forms and ask them how they are different from the other negative forms (they use the auxiliary *doesn't*).

2 Ask students to complete the questions and answers. Check the answers with the class.

> **Answers**
> Where **do** you work?
> Where **does** she work?
> **Do** you work in New York? Yes, I **do.**
> **Does** he work in New York? No, he **doesn't.**

Ask students which auxiliary verb is used in questions with *I/you/we/they* (*do*) and which with *he/she/it* (*does*). Remind students that questions can begin with a question word, or have no question word and the answer *Yes/No*. Ask students to give you examples of each type of question from the chart.

> **SUGGESTIONS**
> * Ask a few questions to review the third person:
>   *Where does Claire live? (In New York.)*
>   *How old is she? (Twenty-four.)*
>   *What does she do? (She works in a bookstore and she's a singer.)*
>   *Does she like her jobs? (Yes, she does.)*
>   *What time does she finish work? (She usually finishes work at six o'clock.)*
> * You can do exercise 4 in the Workbook to introduce adverbs of frequency before you do the next exercise.

3 Students find the adverbs of frequency in the text about Claire. To reinforce the meaning, refer students to the percentage chart in Grammar Reference 3.2 on p. 132.

> **Answers**
> I'm **always** very busy …
> On weekdays I **usually** finish work at 6 o'clock …
> … but **sometimes** I stay late …
> I **often** eat in a little restaurant
> I **never** cook on Sundays.

▶▶ Read Grammar Reference 3.1–3.2 on pp. 131–2 together in class, and/or ask students to read it at home. Encourage them to ask you questions about it.

> **EXTRA ACTIVITIES**
> * Student A describes their routine as if they do a certain job and the rest of the class has to guess what the job is. They can ask *Yes/No* questions.
> * Student A describes their routine as if they were a famous person (politician, actor, singer, etc.) and the rest of the class has to guess who they are pretending to be. They can ask *Yes/No* questions. (You can provide index cards with information about people who are often in the news.)

Listening and pronunciation

5 **CD1 39** Play number 1 as an example. Play the rest of the recording and students choose the sentences they hear. Play the recording again. Pause after each sentence and ask students to discuss the answer with a partner before you establish the correct one. You can make this exercise productive by asking students to read the pairs of sentences aloud.

> **Answers and audio script**
> 1 **a** Claire, why do you like your job?
> 2 **b** Where do you live in New York?
> 3 **a** What do you do on Tuesday evenings?
> 4 **b** He really loves singing.
> 5 **b** She eats a lot.
> 6 **b** What does she do on Sundays?

PRACTICE (SB p. 20)

Talking about you

1 Focus students' attention on the example. Then ask students to match the rest of the questions and answers, working individually. Students who finish early can then check their answers with a partner.

CD1 40 Play the recording and have students check their answers. As preparation for the next activity, ask students to listen and repeat the questions and answers chorally and individually. Take particular care with intonation.

> **Answers and audio script**
> 1d What time do you get up?
>   At about 7 o'clock on weekdays.
> 2b Where do you go on vacation?
>   To Thailand or Hawaii.
> 3e What do you do on Sundays?
>   I always relax.
> 4c When do you do your homework?
>   When I get home.
> 5a Who do you live with?
>   My parents and brothers.
> 6h Why do you like your job?
>   Because it's interesting.
> 7f How do you travel to school?
>   Usually by bus.
> 8g Do you go out on Friday evenings?
>   Yes, I do sometimes.

2 This activity practices the first and second persons only. Demonstrate the activity by having a pair of students ask and answer the first question for the class. Remind students to have the whole question ready before they speak.

Students work in pairs to ask and answer the questions in exercise 1. Go around and check as students do the activity, listening for correct intonation. Students who finish early can be encouraged to ask similar questions, but with different days or question words, e.g., *Do you go out on Saturday evenings? Where do you do your homework?*

3 This activity practices the third person singular as well as the other persons. It also pulls the class together after the pairwork. Focus students' attention on the examples in the Student Book. Then ask a few individuals to tell the rest of the class about themselves and their partner. If necessary, remind students they need to use the third person -s when talking about their partner. (Unless you have a small class, it will take too long to give everyone a turn.)

Affirmatives and negatives

4 This exercise reviews the verb *to be* as well as other verbs in the Simple Present. The exercise can be assigned for homework, but it can also be fun if done orally and at a quick pace with the whole class. Focus students' attention on the examples and then have students complete the exercise orally. They can then write their answers as reinforcement of the grammar point.

> **Answers**
> 3 She speaks Spanish.
> 4 They don't want to learn English.
> 5 We aren't tired and we don't want to go to bed.
> 6 Roberto doesn't like watching football on TV, but likes playing it.
> 7 I don't work at home because I don't have a computer.
> 8 Amelia is happy because she has a new car.
> 9 I go to bed early.
> 10 He doesn't go to bed early.

5 Focus students' attention on the examples. Then write two false sentences, one about yourself and one about a student, for the class to correct. Give students time to write their sentences. Students read aloud their sentences for the rest of the class to complete. With larger classes, have students work in small groups. If necessary, highlight the use of contrastive stress when correcting information:

I'm a doctor.   *You aren't a doctor. You're a nurse.*

Yuko has two children.
She doesn't have two children. She has three children.

ADDITIONAL MATERIAL

Workbook Unit 3
Ex. 1   Days of the week
Ex. 2–4   Simple Present

VOCABULARY AND LISTENING (SB p. 20)

In my free time

> **SUGGESTIONS**
> • You can bring a calendar to the lesson to help with the presentation/review of the months of the year in exercise 1.
> • If you have access to a class set of dictionaries, bring them to this class to help students with the vocabulary work.

> • It will save time in the lesson if you ask your students to review/check their understanding of the names of seasons and months for homework before the lesson. You can give them a handout with the phonetic script such as this:
>
> **Seasons**
> spring /sprɪŋ/   fall /fɔl/
> summer /'sʌmər/   winter /'wɪntər/
> **Months**
> January /'dʒænyu͵ɛri/   July /dʒʊ'laɪ/
> February /'fɛbyu͵ɛri/   August /'ɔgəst/
> March /mɑrtʃ/   September /sɛp'tɛmbər/
> April /'eɪprəl/   October /ɑk'toʊbər/
> May /meɪ/   November /noʊ'vɛmbər/
> June /dʒun/   December /dɪ'sɛmbər/

> ⚠ **POSSIBLE PROBLEMS**
> Students often confuse the months *March* and *May*, and *June* and *July*. They are likely to need help with the vowel sounds and word stress in the seasons and months, particularly: *January* /'dʒænyu͵ɛri/, *February* /'fɛbyu͵ɛri/, *April* /'eɪprəl/, and *August* /'ɔgəst/. Be prepared to drill the months and seasons as a class, repeating as often as necessary until students feel confident using the words.

Students have already seen *like/don't like + -ing* and practiced it in simple contexts. This section extends the vocabulary of free time activities and gives a reminder of the form in the Caution Box on p. 21.

1 Ask students to look at the pictures and see if they can identify the seasons. Ask students to work in pairs and answer the questions in exercise 1. They will find this easier if you assign the seasons and months for homework (see *Suggestions* above). Monitor, noting any problems with pronunciation and confusion with the months of the year.

If your students had no difficulties with the questions in exercise 1, briefly go over the answers as a class, highlighting any specific problems you noted earlier. If necessary, do further spot checks by asking: *What's before/after September?* etc. *When's your birthday?* (Make sure that students give only the month in their answers, not the actual date.)

If your students had problems with the questions in exercise 1, use a calendar or write abbreviations of the months on the board to present the key language again. Go over the seasons and months. Say them first yourself and ask students to repeat each one in order, both chorally and individually. Repeat the months and seasons a few times, making it fast and fun if you can. Then ask students the questions in exercise 1 again, checking for accurate pronunciation.

2 In pairs or small groups, students look at the photos and match as many as they can with the names of the activities. If possible, students look up any new words in their dictionaries. Encourage them to write any new words in their vocabulary notebooks.

Check the answers with the class, going over any pronunciation problems as you go.

Answers

m	playing golf
d	going to the movies
c	listening to music
e	swimming
b	watching TV
l	going to the gym
q	windsurfing
h	playing computer games
n	cooking
k	playing tennis
a	playing cards
p	skiing
f	dancing
i	sailing
o	running
g	reading
j	cycling

Ask the questions about seasons and activities, focusing on the example sentences. Students work in pairs or small groups to compare their ideas.

Possible answers
Summer activities: golf, swimming, windsurfing, tennis, sailing, cycling.
Winter activities: skiing
More than one season: dancing, watching TV, going to the gym, cooking, playing cards, listening to music, running, reading, going to the movies, playing computer games

Focus students' attention on the information about *like + -ing*. Write *I like …* and *I don't like …* in exercise 3. Elicit a few true sentences from the class, making sure students use an *-ing* verb form rather than a noun.

Read Grammar Reference 3.3 on p. 132 together in class, and/or ask students to read it at home. Encourage them to ask you questions about it.

Listening

3 **CD1 41** Tell students that they are going to listen to five conversations about what people like doing in their free time. This script includes the key language from this section and recycles vocabulary that students have already learned, so students should not have problems completing the task. Point out that some of the speakers talk about more than one activity, but may not say when they do each one. The information for *When do they do it?* can be seasons, months, days, or parts of a day. With weaker students, remind them that they don't need to understand every word, just to pick out the key information to complete the chart.

Play conversation 1 as an example. Then play the rest of the recording and have students complete the chart. Students compare their answers in pairs. Play the recording again to let students complete/check their answers. Check the answers with the class, making sure students use *like + -ing* correctly.

Answers and audio script

	What do they like doing?	When do they do it?
Andy	playing tennis	usually summer, spring and fall if sunny
Roger	skiing	January
Linda	going to the gym, swimming	every morning
Ben/Josh	windsurfing	every summer
	playing golf and football	–
	watching sport on TV	–
	playing computer games	after school
Brian	watching TV	–
	playing cards	winter
Sandra	watching TV	–
	playing cards	summer, on vacation

CD1 41

1 Andy
A   I play tennis a lot. I'm not very good, but I like playing.
B   When do you play?
A   Oh, usually in the summer, but sometimes in spring and fall if it's sunny.

2 Roger
R   My favorite sport is skiing. I go skiing with my family every year. We all love it.
B   When do you go?
R   Always in January. We go to Canada.
B   And are you a good skier?
R   I'm OK. My wife's good, the kids are really good – but I'm just OK.

3 Linda
B   Do you go to the gym every day?
L   Yes, I do, every day, every morning before work.
B   And do you go swimming there?
L   Yes. I swim every morning too. Do you go to the gym?
B   Well, uh, no, I don't. I like my bed in the morning!

4 Ben and Josh
B   You like a lot of sports, don't you?
B&J Oh yeah, my favorite is windsurfing. Me and my brother go to surf school every summer and …and we play golf and soccer, of course.
B   All outdoor sports?
B&J Uh, no, we watch sports a lot on TV …and we play computer games after school.
B   So, not a lot of time for homework?
B&J Well. …

5 Sandra and Brian
S   In winter we love evenings at home.
B   What do you do? Watch TV?
S   Well, yes, sometimes. We like all the cooking shows. I love cooking.
B   Oh, we love those shows too, but we often play cards on winter evenings.
BR We like cards too, but we only play when we're on vacation in the summer. It's a "vacation thing" in our family.
B   What do you play?
BR Well, usually we play …

If you have time, you can play the recording again and have students tell you any other information they understood. This can help to build confidence.

4 Choose a student and give examples of what you think he/she likes doing. Focus students' attention on the examples in the Student Book. Then ask students what they think you like doing. Elicit one or two examples, but don't confirm or deny anything at this stage.

Ask students to continue in groups, making a list of activities. Students can choose activities from the Student Book and also ask you for other vocabulary as necessary.

Students ask you questions to find out if they were correct about what you like, following the example in the Student Book. (Students are often interested in finding out about their teacher, but keep this fairly short to allow time for the personalized stage.) Be prepared to drill key sentences if students have problems with stress and intonation.

Talking about you

5 First, build a dialogue with two students, using the example in the Student Book and the possible follow-up questions. Then tell the students some true things about yourself, encouraging them to respond to your likes and dislikes as in the example.

Students continue in pairs or small groups. Monitor and help as necessary. Make sure that students are using the -ing form correctly.

Finally, ask a few students in the class to share their and their partner's responses with the class. This gives further practice with the different forms of the Simple Present.

EXTRA ACTIVITIES

- Ask students to do some independent vocabulary research by looking for other activities which are not in the Student Book. They can look them up in a bilingual dictionary, or on the Internet, as well as pooling their knowledge in groups. Students can then exchange the new vocabulary in a later lesson, including both spelling or pronunciation. They can act out the words or give simple descriptions to help with meaning.

- Students interview each other to find out when the best month/season is for a certain activity in their country: *When's the best month for (skiing, walking, swimming, shopping, visiting your city,* etc.)?

- Students write a description of how their home area changes from season to season. Have them include information on the weather, the activities people do, and the number of visitors.

ADDITIONAL MATERIAL

Workbook Unit 3
Ex. 5 Free time activities
Ex. 6 Listening

WRITING (SB p. 102)

Filling out forms
An application form

The writing syllabus continues with a focus on filling out forms. The context is an application form for a sports and recreation center, and students review the language of talking about what they like doing.

Introduce the topic by asking *What types of forms do people fill out?* (applications for a job/course/bank account/ organization or society; booking forms for hotels/vacations; income tax/voting/medical forms; feedback on objects/ services, etc.) Ask *How often do you fill out a form? What for? Do you usually fill out a paper form or do the application online?* Elicit a range of answers from the class.

1 Focus students' attention on the categories on the form. Students learned a lot of the personal information categories in Unit 1, but you may need to check their understanding of the following: *title, mm/dd/yy = month/ day/year, zip code.* Make sure they understand *spa* and *exercise classes* from the *Health & fitness* section.

Ask a few comprehension questions about Lena, e.g., *What nationality is she?* (Australian) *Where does she live?* (Chicago) *How do you spell her first name?* (L - E - N - A) *Does she have a cell phone?* (Yes, she does.), etc.

Focus students' attention on the sentence starters in the box. Elicit one or two examples of complete sentences. Then let students continue in pairs. Monitor and check for correct use of *to be*, third person singular of the Simple Present, and *like + -ing.* Discuss any common errors as a class.

2 Give students time to complete the form. Monitor and help as necessary. Then put students in new pairs. Try to have students work with someone they don't know very well.

Focus students' attention on the example. Elicit one or two further examples from the class. Highlight the stress patterns if necessary, e.g.,
I like swimming, but Natalia doesn't.
We both like going to the gym.

Give students time to continue in their pairs. Monitor and help as necessary, but don't interrupt to correct students. Discuss common errors after the pairwork.

3 Discuss as a whole class which activities are popular.

EXTRA ACTIVITY

Ask students to find examples of forms in English, either printed or on the Internet. Students can use them to reinforce the language of personal information by roleplaying new characters in different situations, e.g., making reservations for a vacation, joining a club, giving feedback on a product or service, etc.

Photocopiable Activity

UNIT 3 How often …? TB p. 146

Materials: One copy of the worksheet for each student.

Procedure: You can reinforce the Simple Present and leisure activities from this unit, and also review frequency adverbs from the Workbook with the photocopiable activity on TB p. 146.

- Briefly review the expressions of frequency from Workbook p. 16. Hand out the questionnaires and have students complete the questions, using their own ideas for questions 9 and 10.
- Divide the class into pairs and have students interview each other, and write their partner's answers.
- Then put two pairs of students together and have them compare answers and find the relevant activities.
- Students share their partner's answers with the class.

READING AND SPEAKING (SB p. 22)

Perfect weekends

> **ABOUT THE TEXT**
>
> This is the first "jigsaw" reading in the course and so will need careful setting up. The "jigsaw" technique integrates reading and speaking skills by having students read one of two texts and then working in groups to exchange information in a speaking phase. It's important to remind students to read only their text and to get information about the other text via speaking. If necessary and possible, give the instructions for the jigsaw reading in L1.
>
> The theme of the section is "My perfect weekend" and the texts describe the weekend routines of a musician and a famous business person.
>
> Jamie Cullum /ˈdʒeɪmi ˈkʌləm/ is an English jazz pianist and songwriter. Although primarily a pianist, he also plays guitar and drums. He has released a number of successful CDs and has won several awards for his music. (There is an extract from one of his songs in exercise 7 of this section.) He is married to food writer and former model, Sophie Dahl, whose grandfather was the children's author, Roald Dahl. In his text, he mentions Portobello Market, an antiques market in West London.
>
> Bobbi Brown /ˈbɑbi braʊn/ is a professional makeup artist and a very successful businessperson. She has written 8 books about makeup and beauty. She has her own line of cosmetics that are sold internationally. She also launched a campaign to empower women and girls through job skills and education.
>
> These texts have been written to demonstrate the grammar taught in this and previous units (Simple Present for routines, frequency adverbs, and *like + -ing*).

Encourage students to use the context to help them with new vocabulary and to pool knowledge with other students. With weaker classes or if you are short on time, ask students to make sure they understand some of the following vocabulary before the lesson:

Homework prior to the lesson

Jamie Cullum: *song-writer, pianist, model, cookbook writer, market, to make breakfast, kitchen, postcards, foreign movies, play cards, roast chicken, nan* (informal for *grandmother*)

Bobbi Brown: *founder, CEO, cosmetics, suburb, barbecuing, yoga, hip hop, exchange students, sneakers, backyard, farmers' market*

1 **CD1 42** This exercise reviews and extends common verb + noun/adverb collocations. Focus students' attention on the example, then have students complete the task, working in pairs. Point out that some of the verbs have more than one answer.

Play the recording and have students check their answers. Elicit the wording of the complete sentences, checking pronunciation as necessary.

> **Answers and audio script**
> 1 I often **watch TV**.
> 2 I sometimes **watch French movies**.
> 3 I always **listen to music** in the car.
> 4 I don't **play the piano**.
> 5 I sometimes **play cards** with friends.
> 6 I **go dancing** a lot.
> 7 I **go shopping** every Saturday.
> 8 I **get up late** on Sundays.
> 9 I often **cook dinner** for my friends.

2 Focus students' attention on the photos. Check pronunciation of the names (see *About the text* above). Ask students if they recognize the people and elicit any information they know about each person. Give students a minute to read the introduction to each text. Elicit the answers to the questions.

> **Answers**
> Jamie Cullum is a songwriter and jazz pianist. He enjoys going to markets, French movies, and playing cards on weekends.
> Bobbi Brown is the founder and CEO of Bobbi Brown cosmetics. She enjoys barbecuing, doing yoga, and listening to hip-hop on weekends.

3 Put students into two groups, A and B. (With larger classes, you may need to have multiple sets of the two groups.) Assign a text to each group and remind students to read only their text:

Group A – Jamie Cullum

Group B – Bobbi Brown

Have students read their text quickly, asking others in their group for help with vocabulary if you didn't pre-teach the items listed in *About the text*. Monitor and help with any questions.

4 Give students time to read the questions. Answer any questions they may have. Have them work in their groups and answer the questions about their text, writing down the answers to each one. Monitor and help as necessary. The answers for each group are provided below for reference, but don't check the answers with the whole class at this stage.

Answers
Jamie Cullum
1 He likes to stay at home in London.
2 He likes to be with his wife and his brother.
3 He goes dancing/to a club.
4 He likes getting up late, making breakfast, and playing the piano.
5 He goes shopping in Portobello Market.
6 Yes, he does.
7 He sleeps late, cooks Sunday dinner, and calls his parents and his nan.
8 Yes, he does.

Bobbi Brown
1 She likes to stay at home in New Jersey.
2 She likes to be with her family.
3 She usually stays at home and cooks outside.
4 She likes getting up at 7:00 a.m., drinking coffee, reading the newspaper, and exercising.
5 She goes shopping at the farmers' market in the summer or at a store in the winter.
6 Yes, she does.
7 She goes for a walk.
8 Yes, she does.

SUGGESTION
You might want to provide any language students can use for the information exchange, e.g.,

Do you want to start?
You next.
Sorry, I don't understand.
Can you repeat that, please?

5 Re-group the students, making sure there is an A and a B student in each pair. Demonstrate the activity by having a pair of students talk about the person in their text. Students continue talking about the answers to the questions in exercise 4 and exchanging the information about their person. Monitor and help. Also check for correct use of the Simple Present, frequency adverbs, and *like + -ing*. Write down any common errors, but discuss them with students them at a later stage. Bring the whole class together for students to share their answers. Encourage students to expand on their answers where applicable.

Answers
Both Jamie and Bobbi work and travel a lot. They both like being with their family and friends, music, and cooking.
Jamie likes to go out dancing on Friday nights, but Bobbi likes staying at home and relaxing. Jamie plays his piano, but Bobbi listens to hip-hop. Jamie watches movies, but Bobbi reads the newspaper. Jamie sleeps late, but Bobbi doesn't.

Speaking

6 This is a simple guessing game to give further practice in talking about free-time activities. Write down two things you like doing on a small piece of paper, but don't tell students your choice. Students write down their activities, also keeping them a secret from the rest of the class. Remind them *not* to write their name anywhere on the paper.

Collect the papers and then hand them out to different students at random. Focus students' attention on the example in the Student Book. Students read aloud the activities on their paper to the class and then try to guess the name of the student. With larger classes, students can play in groups.

Bring the students back together to decide on the most popular weekend activities in the class.

7 **CD1 43** This is an extract from a song by Jamie Cullum called *20-Something*. Play the recording and let students just listen. Play the recording again if necessary. Then elicit a range of reactions to the song and to Jamie Cullum's music in general.

ADDITIONAL MATERIAL

Workbook Unit 3
Ex. 7 Reading

SPEAKING AND LISTENING (SB p. 24)

Your work–life balance

This section focuses on one of the much-debated questions of modern life: how to achieve a balance between career and home life. Students read and complete a questionnaire on work–life balance, and then discuss their answers. Students then listen to a talk by an expert on work–life balance, and the section finishes with a short Writing section in which students write about their partner.

1 Introduce the topic by writing the name of the questionnaire on the board *Do you live to work or work to live?* Check comprehension: *Is your work the most important thing to you? Or do you work just to earn money to live?* Ask students in which category they think they belong.

Check comprehension of *relax on weekends* and *have trouble sleeping*. Focus students' attention on the questionnaire. Students answer the questions and complete the *Me* column about themselves. Then have them calculate their score and read the answer key. Elicit who thinks they have a good work–life balance and why.

2 Focus students' attention on the examples in the Student Book. Have students practice the questions and answers as a class. Then have individual students ask you the questions so that they can complete the T section of the questionnaire. With weaker classes, be prepared to drill some of the questions with the class to ensure good pronunciation. Have students figure out your score. You can say whether you agree with it or not.

Ask the whole class to stand up and mingle to do the next part of the activity (if there is enough space to do so!). Tell them to take turns with two other students asking and answering the questions.

Divide the students into small groups, and have them compare their scores before reporting back to the class. Elicit a range of scores from the class to establish which students have a good work–life balance.

CD1 44 Tell students they are going to hear a medical doctor talk about work–life balance. The recording is in the form of a talk, so Dr. Hall's voice is the only one they will hear. Pre-teach/check students' understanding of: *structure, everyday life, balanced, bad for your health.* Give students time to read the questions, then play the recording through once. Give students time to exchange the information they understood and compare their answers. Play the recording again so that students can listen for any information they missed.

Check answers with the class.

Answers and audio script

1 Work gives us money to live, and it gives structure to our everyday lives.
2 "Play" is important for a happy, balanced life. It's important to find time to relax with friends and family. It's not good to think about work all the time.
3 If you take your work home, you also take your problems home, so you never relax.
4 Life is more than work.

CD1 44

Of course, work is important for us all, it gives us money to live, it gives structure to our everyday lives. But for a happy, balanced life it's also important to "play" sometimes. It's important to find time to relax with friends and family. It's not good to think about work all the time. I know from my work as a doctor that it's sometimes difficult *not* to take your work problems home – but if you take your problems home, you never relax, and it's difficult for your family and bad for your health. Don't live to work, work to live! Life is more than work.

What do you think?

The goal of this activity is to encourage some free discussion. Don't worry if the activity turns out to be quite short. Ask the questions to the whole class. Encourage students to join the discussion and talk about their experiences and opinions.

Writing

5 This part of the activity is designed to review the third person singular again along with the other forms. (It can be assigned for homework or done in class.)

Focus students' attention on the examples in the Student Book. Also highlight the use of the auxiliary *does* to avoid repeating the main verb, e.g., *I don't relax on weekends, but Leyla does.* Point out that we don't say *I don't often take work home, but Sofia takes,* or … *Sofia yes.*

Students use the information they have collected to write and compare themselves with another student. Then ask one or two students to read what they have written aloud for the others to comment on.

EXTRA ACTIVITIES

- You can "test" how much students can remember about each other's lives by using the ideas in the *Do you live to work or work to live?* questionnaire. Collect the questionnaires and read aloud students' answers. Ask the class to guess who is being referred to.

- Students imagine they have a very extravagant and luxurious lifestyle and interview each other, practicing *wh-* and *Yes/No* questions, e.g.,

Where do you work?	*I don't work!*
What time do you get up?	*About 11 o'clock.*
Where do you live?	*In a very big house in Paris.*
Do you like cooking?	*No, I never cook. I have a chef.*
Do you have a busy life?	*Of course! I go shopping every day and I go to parties every night!*

EVERYDAY ENGLISH (SB p. 25)

Social expressions (1)

This is the first of two sections that focus on social expressions. The second is in Unit 10. The conversations introduce and practice expressions for day-to-day conversational exchanges.

1 Focus students' attention on the photos and ask the questions to the whole class. Encourage students to speculate about where he is and who the other people are.

2 Focus students' attention on the first lines of the conversations. Ask students who the speakers are. Ask students to relate each of the conversations to the correct picture.

Answers

1 his host family
2 Hakan
3 his teacher
4 Hakan
5 Hakan
6 the woman who works in the coffee shop
7 Hakan
8 another student
9 his host family

---

3 **CD1 45** Focus students' attention on the example. Ask students to work in pairs and match the second lines of the conversations with the lines in exercise 2.

Then play the recording for students to check their answers.

Answers and audio script

1 **A** Bye! Have a nice day!
  H Thanks. You too. See you later.
2 **H** I'm sorry I'm late. The traffic's very bad this morning.
  B That's OK. Come and sit down.
3 **B** What's the matter, Hakan? Do you have a problem?
  H Yes, I don't understand this exercise.
4 **H** Can I open the window? It's really warm in here.
  B Sure. Good idea. It is hot in here, isn't it?

---

5 **H** Can you help me? What does *bilingual* mean?
  B **It means *in two languages*.**
6 **C** Do you want a macchiato?
  H **Excuse me? Can you say that again?**
7 **H** Excuse me! Is this seat free?
  D **Yes, it is. Please sit down if you want.**
8 **E** *Fala Português?*
  H **I'm sorry. I don't speak Portuguese.**
9 **A** Hi, Hakan! How was your day?
  H **Good, thanks. Really interesting. How about yours?**

4 Focus students' attention on the example conversation. Ask two students to read it aloud. Put students in pairs to practice the conversations. With larger classes, you may need to allocate just two different conversations to each pair so that the activity doesn't go on too long. Monitor and help as necessary. If students have pronunciation problems, play sections of the recording again. Students listen and repeat, paying special attention to stress patterns and intonation, following the model as closely as possible.

Students practice the conversations with a partner then try to continue them. With weaker students, you can brainstorm ideas as a class and write key lines on the board. Remind students to try to use the appropriate stress and intonation.

CD1 46 Play the recording, pausing at the end of each conversation to give students time to compare their version.

If you have time, students can memorize one of the conversations and act it out for the rest of the class. Acting out dialogues can improve their pronunciation considerably.

Audio script
1 **A** Bye! Have a nice day.
  B Thanks. You too. See you later.
  A OK. At about four o'clock?
  B Well, uh … school doesn't finish until four.
  A Oh, OK! See you about 4:30, then!
2 **H** I'm sorry I'm late. The traffic's very bad this morning.
  B That's OK. Come and sit down.
  H Thanks.
  B We're on page 28.
3 **B** What's the matter, Hakan? Do you have a problem?
  H Yes, I don't understand this exercise.
  B Don't worry. I'll help you with it.
  H Oh, thank you very much.
4 **H** Can I open the window? It's really warm in here.
  B Sure. Good idea. It is hot in here, isn't it?
  H Very. Thanks a lot.
  B That's all right. I think we all need some fresh air.
5 **H** Can you help me? What does *bilingual* mean?
  B It means *in two languages*.
  H Oh, right, of course. I need to buy a bilingual dictionary!
  B Yeah, that's a very good idea!
6 **C** Do you want a macchiato?
  H Excuse me? Can you say that again?
  C A macchiato. Do you want a macchiato?
  H Sorry. What is a "macchiato"?
  C It's a strong white coffee.
  H Uh – yes, OK. Fine. I'll try one. Thank you.

7 **H** Excuse me! Is this seat free?
  D Yes, it is. Please sit down if you want.
  H Thanks very much. That's very nice of you.
  D No problem. Are you a new student?
  H Yes, I am.
  D Are you having a good time?
  H Yes. It's getting better, thanks.
8 **E** *Fala Português?*
  H I'm sorry. I don't speak Portuguese.
  E Oh! That's OK. It doesn't matter.
  H Can I help you?
  E No. Don't worry. I need some help with my homework, but I can do it.
  H All right.
9 **A** Hi, Hakan. How was your day?
  H Good, thanks. Really interesting. How about yours?
  A Oh, not bad. Just another day at work.
  H Well, tomorrow's the weekend.
  A Yes, thank goodness!

SUGGESTIONS

- Students can think of other situations when these expressions would be useful and write or act out parallel conversations.
- Encourage students to use these expressions in class whenever appropriate, e.g., apologizing for being late, asking to open the window, checking what a new word means, etc. You can put key phrases on a classroom poster.

ADDITIONAL MATERIAL

Workbook Unit 3
Ex. 8–9 Everyday English

Don't forget!

Workbook Unit 3
Ex. 10 *am/is/are* or *do/does*?
Ex. 11 *a/an* or no article?
Ex. 12 Prepositions
Grammar Reference (SB pp. 131–2)
Word list Unit 3 (SB p. 140)
Students can translate the words, learn them at home, or transfer some of them to their vocabulary notebook.
Tests on (Online)
Unit 3 Test
Video (iTools and Online)
Additional photocopiables and PPT™ presentations (iTools)

4 Somewhere to live

There is/are • some/any/a lot of • this/that/these/those • Adjectives • Numbers and prices

VIDEO A new home

The theme of this unit is places. Students describe their own home, a famous building in their country, and where they live. There is a reading text about the White House, the US president's home and workplace. This text reinforces the language of the unit and, hopefully, students will be interested in finding out about this famous place. There is a *Vocabulary and Listening* section to extend students' range of adjectives and adverbs.

LANGUAGE INPUT

GRAMMAR

There is/are (SB p. 26)
some/any/a lot of (SB p. 28)
this/that/these/those (SB p. 28)

- Practicing there *is/are* to describe places and facilities.
- Practicing *some/any/a lot of* to talk about indefinite quantity.
- Practicing *this/that/these/those* to identify objects.

VOCABULARY

Adjectives for *good* and *bad* (SB p. 32)
Adverb + adjective (SB p. 32)

- Understanding and practicing adjectives with positive and negative meanings.
- Using adverbs to make adjectives stronger/not as strong.

EVERYDAY ENGLISH

Numbers (SB p. 33)
Prices (SB p. 33)

- Understanding and practicing the language of numbers and prices.

SKILLS DEVELOPMENT

READING

America's most famous address (SB p. 30)

- Reading about the home and office of the US president.

LISTENING

What's in your bag? (SB p. 29)
Five conversations giving descriptions (SB p. 32)

- Listening for key words in a short monologue. **CD1 54** (SB p. 118)
- Listening for key information in five short conversations. **CD1 57** (SB p. 118)

SPEAKING

Location, location, location (SB p. 27)

- Exchanging information to describe an apartment.

WRITING

Describing your home – Linking words *and, so, but, because* (SB p. 103)

- Understanding linking words, then writing a description of your home.

MORE MATERIALS

Photocopiables – Numbers and prices (TB p. 147)   **Tests** (Online)   **Video** (iTools and Online)

STARTER (SB p. 26)

- Students may need help with pronunciation of some of the key words in this section: *sofa* /'soufə/, *DVD* /ˌdi vi 'di/, *bookshelves* /'bʊkʃɛlvz/, *sidewalk* /'saɪdwɔk/, *traffic lights* /'træfɪk laɪts/, *refrigerator* /rɪ'frɪdʒəreɪtər/, *oven* /'ʌvn/

  You will also need to highlight the stress on the compound words: washing machine

  Note that students may also need help with the stress patterns of the words in the vocabulary box in *Starter*. If you think students will be unfamiliar with the idea of word stress, you can use international words such as *computer*, *Internet*, *telephone* to show students how words have both stressed and unstressed syllables.

- Students may ask about the difference between *a stove* and *an oven*. Explain that *a stove* is typically on top of the kitchen counter and has circular burners for cooking food on top. *An oven* is typically built into a wall or under the kitchen counter and has a door that has a hinge on the bottom. It is basically a heated box. Food is put inside to cook.

SUGGESTION
Homework prior to the lesson

Ask students to look up the following words in their dictionary, and write them in their vocabulary notebook.

sofa DVD player drugstore stove bookshelves post office sidewalk traffic lights refrigerator oven mirror living room shower carpet dining room

1 Focus students' attention on the vocabulary and ask them to give two or three examples of correct words to go in the *living room* column. Put students in pairs and have them continue to categorize the vocabulary.

2 **CD1 47** Play the recording and have students check their answers. (Note that these are the most usual answers, but other combinations may be possible, e.g., a table in the living room.)

Drill the pronunciation of the words chorally and individually, using the recording or modeling the words yourself. Check pronunciation of the words in *Possible problems* above in particular.

Answers and audio script

living room	kitchen	street
sofa	stove	bus stop
DVD player	refrigerator	post office
armchair	table	café
bookshelves	oven	sidewalk
mirror		drugstore
	other room	traffic lights
	washing machine	

AN APARTMENT TO RENT (SB p. 26)

There is/are – prepositions

Students often confuse *It's a …* with *There's a … .* The difference is that *It's a …* defines something and gives it a name. *There's a …* expresses what exists. This is quite a subtle area, and we don't suggest that you explore it with students unless absolutely necessary, using translation as a support. Using *there is/are* in context is often the best way to help students understand the concept.

Learners sometimes confuse *there* and *their*. For such a short structural item, there are also a lot of pronunciation problems:

- Many nationalities have difficulty with the sound /ð/.

- In *There are* and the question forms, the *r* is pronounced as a linking sound when the following word begins with a vowel.

- Students may need help with the intonation in questions. Encourage students to start "high" and fall, ending with a rise in *yes/no* questions.

It is worth working on these pronunciation areas, but not to the point of exhaustion!

1 **CD1 48** Focus students' attention on the photo of Josie and Emily. Ask *Where are they?* (in a café/restaurant). Read the instructions for exercise 1 as a class. Check students' understanding of the situation by asking *Who's Josie?* (the woman with the laptop) and *Who's Emily?* (the woman with the cup). If necessary, you can briefly review/check student's understanding of the names of the main rooms/parts of a house or apartment: *living room, bedroom, kitchen, bathroom,* and *yard*.

Focus students' attention on the examples. Give students time to read the rest of the conversation. Play the recording once without stopping. Play the recording again if necessary to let students complete/check their answers.

Ask students *Is Josie interested in the apartment?* (Yes, she is.) *What does she say about it?* (It sounds great.)

Put students in pairs to practice the conversation. If students have problems with the pronunciation, highlight the linking in *there is* and *there are*:

There's a/an …

There are …

Answers and audio script

J = Josie   E = Emily

J Here's an apartment on Franklin Street!
E Is it nice?
J Well, there's a big living room.
E Oh, that's good.
J And there are two bedrooms.
E Great! What about the kitchen?
J **There's** a new kitchen.
E Wow! How many bathrooms **are there**?
J Uh … **there's** just one bathroom.
E **Is there** a yard?
J No, **there isn't** a yard.
E That's OK. It sounds great!

Focus students' attention on the chart and on the examples of *there is/are* in exercise 1. Have students complete the chart, using contracted forms where they can. Check the answers with the whole class. In a monolingual class, you might want to ask for a translation of *There's* and *There are*.

If students have questions about the use of *any*, explain that it is used with plural negative sentences, but do not go into a long grammatical explanation at this stage. (*Some/any* is covered in the next presentation *A new apartment*.)

Answers

Affirmative	There is a washing machine. There **are** two bedrooms
Negative	There **isn't** a yard. There aren't any carpets.
Question	**Is there** a dining room? How many bathrooms **are there**?

▶▶ Read Grammar Reference 4.1 and 4.2 on p. 132 together in class, and/or ask students to read it at home. Encourage them to ask you questions about it.

2 Call out the following words and have students point to the objects in the photo of the living room on Franklin Street: *sofa, ottoman, armchair, bookshelves, window, plant*.

Read the example sentences as a class. Check that students understand the use of singular and plural. Ask *Why "There's?"* (singular) and *Why "There are?"* (plural).

Drill the sentences, checking for accurate linking between *There's a/an …* and *There are …* . Point out that with plural nouns students need to say the exact number.

Students then work in pairs to produce more sentences. Monitor and check for correct use of *there is/are*.

Bring the whole class together again to check the answers. Correct mistakes carefully.

Possible answers
There's a sofa. There's an ottoman. There's a plant. There are two armchairs. There are two windows. There are five bookshelves.

3 **CD1 49** You can signal that you are going to introduce the question forms by drawing a large question mark on the board.

Focus students' attention on the incomplete questions and sets of prompt words. Make sure students realize that the first set is singular and the second and third sets are plural.

Have a pair of students ask and answer the example question in open pairs. Elicit an example from the other sets of prompts, e.g., *How many bedrooms are there? Are there any pictures?*

Drill the questions and answers. Then have students work in closed pairs to ask and answer the questions. Monitor and help as necessary. Check for accurate pronunciation (sounds, linking, and stress).

Play the recording and have students check their answers. If students had problems with pronunciation during the pairwork, play the recording again and have them repeat. Drill key sentences to ensure accurate pronunciation. Students then practice the questions and answers again.

Answers and audio script
Is there a shower?
Yes, there is.
Is there a washing machine?
Yes, there is.
Is there a refrigerator?
Yes, there is.
Is there a dining room?
No, there isn't.
How many bedrooms are there?
Two.
How many bathrooms are there?
One.
How many armchairs are there?
Two.
Are there any pictures?
No, there aren't.
Are there any bookshelves?
Yes, there are.
Are there any carpets?
No, there aren't.

Prepositions

4 **CD1 50** This exercise practices/reviews prepositions. If you think the prepositions will be new to your class, you will need to present them first. Do this very simply, perhaps using classroom objects, such as a book or chair (*The book is on the desk*), or the students themselves (*Juan is next to Maria*), etc. Highlight the difference between *next to*, *across from*, and *under* by using gestures.

Refer students to the picture of Franklin Road. Pre-teach/ check students' understanding of *bench*. Ask students to work in pairs to fill in each blank with a preposition.

Play the recording and check the answers. You can practice the prepositions further by using your classroom layout and/or the area near your school.

Answers and audio script
1 The apartment's on Franklin Street.
2 It's **above** a drugstore on the second floor.
3 The drugstore is **next to** a clothing store.
4 There's a cell phone store **across from** the clothing store.
5 There's a post office **near** the apartment.
6 The bus stop is **outside** the drugstore.
7 There's a bench **under** a tree.

PRACTICE (SB p. 27)

Location, location, location

1 Read the instructions as a class. Divide the students into A/B pairs. Make sure they understand that they each have a different advertisement (or ad) for an apartment and that they need to ask and answer questions to find out more information about each apartment. Remind students not to look at each other's information.

Teach/check students' understanding of the meaning of *floor* (*on the first floor, second floor*, etc.) Focus students' attention on the examples and demonstrate the activity with a pair of students. Allow students enough time to complete the information exchange.

When students have finished, have them compare their advertisements and see how well they provided their partner with the key information. Ask students which apartment they would like to rent and why. Elicit a range of responses.

2 **CD1 51** Ask students to look at the advertisement on p. 145. Read the instructions as a class. Pre-teach/check students' understanding of *town center, view*, and *fire place*. Focus students' attention on the example and highlight the contrastive stress used when correcting mistakes:

There aren't four bedrooms! There are only three!

Play the recording. Students listen and shout "Stop!" when they hear a mistake.

Answers and audio script

These are the mistakes:

1 There are only three bedrooms.
2 It has only one bathroom.
3 The kitchen is small.
4 There's no dining room.
5 The apartment is on the third floor.
6 There is only one sofa.
7 There are no pictures on the wall.
8 There is no TV.
9 There is no DVD player.

CD1 51

The apartment is near the center of town. It has four bedrooms, a nice living room with views of the town, and two bathrooms. The kitchen is very big, and there's a dining room next to it.
The apartment is on the second floor. In the living room there are two sofas and an armchair. There are a lot of pictures on the wall. There's a carpet in front of the fire place, and there's a TV and a DVD player. There's a table in front of the sofa.

---

3 Demonstrate the activity by drawing a simple plan of your home on the board. Describe what's in your home. Do this in as natural a way as possible, but do not give too much extra detail like size, color, etc., as the main focus here is the vocabulary of furniture and appliances, and the prepositions.

Give students time to draw their plan. Divide the class into pairs and have students continue the activity working in pairs. Monitor and help as necessary. Check for correct use of *there is/are* and the prepositions of place, and write down any common errors. Don't interrupt or overcorrect grammar mistakes, as the emphasis here is on fluency. You can discuss corrections at a later stage.

Bring the class back together and ask for any interesting examples that students exchanged.

ADDITIONAL MATERIAL

Workbook Unit 4

Ex. 1   Rooms and things in the house
Ex. 2   *there is/are*
Ex. 3   Prepositions

A NEW APARTMENT (SB p. 28)

some/any/a lot of

In this section, *some* and *any* are presented with mainly count nouns (*plates, glasses, clothes*, etc). In Unit 8, they are presented with both count and noncount nouns. Students also practice *a lot of* with count nouns.

⚠ **POSSIBLE PROBLEMS**

Some as a concept has a tangible meaning, i.e., a certain, unspecified number of (something). The same cannot be said of *any*. It is a determiner used often (but not exclusively) in questions and negatives. We suggest you do not go into the deeper areas of *any* expressing fundamentally negative ideas. This is unnecessary, and difficult for elementary-level students.

Some also presents problems of pronunciation with its weak form /səm/.

In affirmative sentences, we usually use *a lot of* rather than *much* or *many*, e.g., *She has a lot of CDs.* (NOT *She has many CDs.) *She has a lot of homework.* (NOT *She has much homework.) Students may need help with this usage, and with the weak forms and linking in the pronunciation /ə ˈlɑtəv/.

---

1 **CD1 52** Refer students back to the photo on p. 26 and ask students to point to Josie. Ask *What does she want?* (a new apartment). Refer students to the photo with exercise 1 and tell them this is Josie's new apartment.

Use the photos on pp. 28–9 to pre-teach/check students' understanding of the key vocabulary: *clothes, mugs, towels* /ˈtaʊəlz/, *teakettle* /ˈti kɛtl/, *lamp*.

Focus students' attention on the examples. Check that students understand the use of X's and checks to cue the answers (two checks = *some*; four or five checks = *a lot of*; X = *not any*). Drill the sentences chorally and individually. Don't go into an explanation of *some/any* and *a lot of* at this stage, but with weaker classes, you can copy the checks and X's onto the board and drill more examples of *She has some/a lot of …* and *She doesn't have any …* .

Put students in pairs to continue the activity. Monitor and check for correct use of *have, some/any*, and *a lot of*, and for accurate pronunciation.

Play the recording for students to check their answers. If necessary, play selected sentences again, drilling chorally and individually.

Answers and audio script

1 She has some plates.
2 She has a lot of clothes.
3 She doesn't have any glasses.
4 She has some pictures.
5 She doesn't have any mugs.
6 She has a lot of shoes.
7 She doesn't have any towels.
8 She has some cups.

1 Look at Grammar Spot question 1 as a class. Allow students time to think before checking the answer.

2 Have students work in pairs to answer question 2. Check the answers with the whole class.

Answers
1 *Five plates* gives us the exact number. *Some plates* doesn't give us the exact number. *A lot of* means "a big number of."
2 We use *some* in affirmative sentences. We use *any* in negative sentences and questions.

▶▶ Read Grammar Reference 4.3–4.4 on p. 132 together in class, and/or ask students to read it at home. Encourage them to ask you questions about it.

this/that/these/those

2 Focus students' attention on the *Things to buy* list. Make sure that students understand these are things Josie doesn't have in her apartment. Elicit examples of what she still needs to buy. Check for the accurate use of *some*.

Answers
She needs some glasses and some towels.
She needs a lamp, a teakettle, and some mugs.

3 **CD1 53** Explain that Josie and Emily are shopping for things for Josie's new apartment. Point to the man in photos 1 and 3. Ask *Who's he?* (the salesperson).

Students listen to the conversations and fill in the blanks. Have them check their answers in pairs, then play the recording again if necessary. Check the answers.

Put students in pairs to practice the conversations. Encourage a lively intonation and enthusiastic delivery. If students sound flat, play selected conversations again and get students to repeat.

Answers and audio script
J = Josie   A = Salesperson   E = Emily
1 J How much is **this** lamp, please?
  S It's $45.
2 J I like that **picture**.
  E Yes, it's cool!
3 J How much are these **glasses**?
  S They're $15.
4 J I love those **towels**!
  E They're great!
5 J Look at **those flowers**.
  E They're beautiful!
6 J Do you like **this teakettle**?
  E Yeah, it's a great color!
7 J How much are **these mugs**?
  S $5 each.
8 J Look at **that coat**!
  E You don't need any more clothes

Read the chart with the class. Elicit further nouns that can go with each of the words.

▶▶ Read Grammar Reference 4.5 on p. 132 together in class, and/or ask students to read it at home. Encourage them to ask you questions about it.

SUGGESTION

If students have difficulty with the use of *this/that/these/ those*, use the classroom environment to reinforce the language. Choose objects near to you to demonstrate *this/these*, e.g., *This is my desk. I like these posters* and objects that you have to point to to demonstrate *that/ those*, e.g., *That CD player is new. We use those books.* Give students objects to hold, or point to objects and have students say sentences using *this/that/these/those*.

PRACTICE (SB p. 29)

In our classroom

Note that there are a couple of examples of *some/any* with noncount nouns, but there's no need to go into an explanation of noncount nouns at this stage.

1 Focus students' attention on the example. Students work in pairs or small groups to fill in the blanks.

Check the answers by having students read aloud the complete sentences.

Answers
1 I have a dictionary and some books on my table.
2 There aren't **any** French students in our class.
3 Do we have **any** homework tonight?
4 I need **some** help with this exercise.
5 Is there **a** test next week?
6 There are **some** difficult exercises in this book, but we have **a** very good teacher.

SUGGESTION

If your students need more practice with *some/any*, you can have them write more true sentences about their own classroom.

2 Focus students' attention on the examples. Have students work in pairs/small groups and describe the classroom. If necessary, write word prompts on the board to help generate a range of forms of the target grammar, e.g., *television, DVD player, flowers, photos,* etc.

What's in your bag?

3 **CD1 54** Focus students' attention on the photo of Christina. Have students say how old they think she is and what her job is.

Read the instructions as a class. Give students time to read the list of items. Answer any questions about the vocabulary.

Play the recording. Students record their answers with a (✓) or a (✗).

> **Answers and audio script**
>
> | ✓ | a phone | ✓ | glasses |
> |---|---|---|---|
> | ✗ | a notebook | ✗ | a comb |
> | ✓ | a lipstick | ✗ | stamps |
> | ✗ | a phone charger | ✓ | keys |
> | ✓ | pens | ✓ | a wallet |
>
> **CD1 54**
> What's in my bag? Well, there's my phone, and my wallet, of course. I have some pens. I always have some pens. A blue one, and a red one. And there are my glasses. I need them for driving. And I have a lipstick … Oh, and keys. I have some keys, my house keys and my car keys. And that's all!

4 Put students into pairs to say what Christina has and doesn't have. Monitor for correct use of *some* and *any*. Be prepared to go over the difference between them again if necessary.

5 Focus students' attention on the examples and have students read them aloud.

With weaker students, brainstorm items that people often carry before students start the pairwork, e.g., *an umbrella, tissues, brush, comb* /koʊm/, *driver's licence, ID card*, etc.

Have students practice the questions in open pairs, highlighting the stress to ensure good rhythm. Students then continue working in closed pairs. Monitor and help as necessary, providing any vocabulary students may need.

Ask one or two students to say what is in their or their partner's bag. Try not to be over-curious, as some students may consider it too personal.

Check it

6 Elicit the answer to number 1 as an example. Students work in pairs and complete the exercise.

> **Answers**
> 1 Do you have a dictionary?
> 2 Here are some photos of my children.
> 3 I have a lot of books.
> 4 Pete, this is Dave. Dave, this is Pete.
> 5 I don't have any money.
> 6 Look at those people over there.

ADDITIONAL MATERIAL

Workbook Unit 4

Ex. 4 *some/any/a lot of*
Ex. 5 *this/that/these/those*

READING AND SPEAKING (SB p. 30)

America's most famous address

> **NOTE**
> At the end of this section, there is a speaking activity about a famous building in the students' own country. If you think your students may not have the knowledge to do this task without preparation, have them research a building for homework. They can also write down any useful vocabulary they may need to describe the building.

> **ABOUT THE TEXT**
> The text gives a description of the White House, both in terms of the building and its function as the US president's home and workplace. The White House is located in the US capital, Washington DC. (This stands for "District of Colombia" and means that Washington is a special area that is not contained in any of the 50 US states.) It was named after George Washington (1732–1799), the first president of the US.
> People/Places mentioned in the text are:
> - Queen Victoria (1819–1901), British queen from 1837 until her death, a reign of 64 years; President Reagan /reigən/ (1911–2004), US president from 1981 to 1989; the First Lady, the title given to the wife of the US president.
> - the West Wing, where the staff offices are located, including the Oval /ˈoʊvl/ Office, the official office of the president; the East Wing, where offices of the First Lady and her staff are located; the Press Room for dealings with the media.
> - the Queen's bedroom, the Lincoln /ˈlɪŋkən/ Bedroom, where special guests stay; the East Room, where the president meets special guests; the State Dining Room, used for receptions and entertaining.
>
> Encourage students to use the context to help them with new vocabulary and to pool knowledge with other students. With weaker classes or if you are short of time, ask students to look up some of the following vocabulary before the lesson: *private home, birthday party, wedding, built, to govern, guest, staff, fireplace, curtains, furniture* /ˈfərnɪʃər/, *gift, elevator, jogging track, billiard room, bowling alley, library*.

1 Focus students' attention on the photos and elicit examples of what is shown.

> **Answers**
> The outside of the building and park area round it, visitors standing in line to see the White House, an old image of the White House from the 19th century, the president's office/Oval Office

2 This activity helps students think about what they know about the topic of the text and serves as a prediction exercise.

Pre-teach/check students' understanding of *government offices* and *open to the public*. Focus students' attention on the example. Ask students to work in pairs and decide on their answers to the rest of the questions.

3 Set a time limit of about three minutes to encourage students to read quickly. Tell them not to worry about words they do not recognize and just to focus on finding the answers.

Check the answers with the class. You can have students correct the false answers. Ask students if they found any of the answers surprising.

Answers
1 T   2 F   3 F   4 T   5 T   6 T

4 Give students time to read the questions. Answer any vocabulary questions they have. Elicit the answer to question 1, then have students complete the task, working in pairs.

Check the answers with the whole class. Decide according to the speed and ability of your students whether to accept short answers or whether you want fuller answers (given in brackets).

Answers
1 Where the US president works and lives. (The White House is the place where the US president works and lives.)
2 On the third and second floors. (The president lives on the second and third floors.)
3 In the Oval Office. (The president works in the Oval Office.)
4 In the Queen's Bedroom or the Lincoln Bedroom. (They stay in the Queen's Bedroom or the Lincoln Bedroom.)
5 Three large windows (behind the president's desk) and a fireplace (at the other end). (There are three large windows (behind the president's desk) and a fireplace (at the other end).)
6 New curtains, new furniture, and a special new carpet. (Each new president chooses new curtains, new furniture, and a special new carpet.)
7 Nothing/It's free.
8 250 (150 people work for the President and the presidential family and another 100 take care of the building day and night.)
9 Play tennis, go jogging, go swimming, watch a movie, play billiards, go bowling, and read. (He can play tennis, go jogging, go swimming, watch a movie, play billiards, go bowling, and read.)

5 Briefly review how to say the numbers in the box. Focus students' attention on the example and then have students continue the task, working in pairs.

Check the answers with the class.

Answers

50	there are fifty states in the US.
317 million	the number of people in the US/the population of the US
6,000	the number of people who visit the White House each day
132	the number of rooms in the White House
35	the number of bathrooms in the White House
five	the number of kitchens in the White House
six	the number of floors in the White House
140	the number of guests that can eat in the State Dining Room

Language work

6 This activity practices the use of *Is/Are there …?* and short answers. Focus students' attention on the examples. With weaker students, briefly review the use of *is* for singular objects (*movie theater*) and *are* for plural (*offices*).

Students ask and answer the example questions and answers in open and closed pairs. Make sure that students can reproduce the correct stress patterns. Drill the pronunciation of the list of things students have to ask about.

Students continue to ask and answer questions about the things in the list. Monitor and check for accurate use of *Is/Are there …?* and that students use *a lot*, not *a lot of* in short answers, e.g., *Yes, there are a lot of.* Check the answers with the whole class, and discuss any common errors.

Answers

Is there a movie theater?	Yes, there is.
Are there many offices?	Yes, there are a lot.
Are there many bathrooms?	Yes, there are (35).
Is there a swimming pool?	Yes, there is.
Is there a library?	Yes, there is.
Are there any elevators?	Yes, there are (three).
Is there a tennis court?	Yes, there is.
Is there a vegetable garden?	Yes, there is.

7 Have students brainstorm a few rooms in a house and write a list on the board. Elicit possible actions for each room, e.g., *make dinner – kitchen*.

Focus students' attention on exercise 7 and have students match the verbs and the places. Check the answers with the class.

If appropriate, elicit other true sentences for each of the rooms, e.g., *We listen to music in the living room.*

Answers
sleep – bedroom   take a shower – bathroom   relax – living room
eat – dining room   work – office   read – library
grow vegetables – garden

Project

See *Note* at the start of this section. Give an example of a building from your own country. Try to do this as naturally as possible, using some of the following language:

The (building) is in/near/in the center of …

It is a museum/palace/government building/station/ office block.

People go there to meet their friends/take photos/relax/ look at the architecture/get married.

I like/don't like it because …

With weaker students, write some of the above language on the board as prompts.

Divide the class into small groups to talk about their chosen building. Monitor and help as necessary. The goal here is for students to personalize the topic, so do not interrupt or overcorrect.

EXTRA ACTIVITY

Students turn their work on famous buildings into a mini-project. If you have access to computers, this can be produced with researched photos and uploaded onto the class/school network. Alternatively, students produce their work on paper and display it on the classroom wall/noticeboard.

Workbook Unit 4
Ex. 6   Reading

WRITING (SB p. 103)

Describing your home

Linking words *and, so, but, because*

Being able to link ideas is an essential skill for students. It's important to give a good grounding in understanding and using linkers, and so the writing syllabus continues with a focus on key linking words and correct punctuation for elementary students.

1   Focus students' attention on the chart. Have students read the words in each column. Point out the comma before *so* and *but* and the absence of one before *and* and *because*. Elicit an example with *and*: *I love my new apartment and I like your apartment, too.* Students continue making sentences. Check the answers with the class.

> **Answers**
> I love my new apartment and I like your apartment, too.
> I love my new apartment, so please come and see it soon.
> I love my new apartment, but unfortunately there isn't a yard.
> I love my new apartment because it's very beautiful.

2   Give examples based on where you live, e.g., *I like my apartment and I love the park near it/so I want to stay there/but it's very expensive/because it's got a lot of space.*

Students write similar sentences about where they live. You can ask one or two students to read their sentences to the class.

3   Focus students' attention on the example and then have students complete the sentences, working individually. Give them time to check their answers in pairs before checking the answers with the whole class.

> **Answers**
> 2 but   3 because   4 so   5 because   6 but   7 and   8 so

4   **CD1 55** Focus students' attention on the photo and elicit basic information (*Her name's Megan. She has a new apartment.*) Pre-teach/check students' understanding of *to face south.* Elicit the first linking word in the text (*so*) and then have students continue the task.

Play the recording and have students check their answers.

> **Answers and audio script**
> | 1 | so | | 7 | but |
> | 2 | but | | 8 | because |
> | 3 | and | | 9 | but |
> | 4 | because | | 10 | so |
> | 5 | and | | 11 | but |
> | 6 | so | | 12 | because |

> **CD1 55**
> My new apartment is near the center of town, so I often walk to work. It's not very big, but it's very comfortable! There's just one bedroom, a living room, and a pretty big kitchen with a table in the center. This is good because I love cooking, and I can invite my friends to dinner. The living room has one big window. It faces south, so it's always very sunny. I have two comfortable, old armchairs, but I don't have a sofa because the room is pretty small.
>
> There isn't a yard, but there's a small balcony outside my bedroom. I want to put a chair there so I can sit in the sun on summer afternoons.
>
> I love my new apartment for many reasons: the big kitchen, the sunny living room, but most of all I love it because it's my first home!

5   Set up the activity by answering the questions in exercise 5 about where you live. Then give students time to write notes about their home, using the questions as prompts. Divide the class into pairs and have students exchange information about their homes, using the questions in the exercise and their notes.

Write a paragraph plan from the questions in exercise 5 for students to follow when they write their own description:

Paragraph 1:	Where is it?
	Is it old or new?
	How many rooms are there?
	Is there a yard?
Paragraph 2:	Who do you live with?
Paragraph 3:	Do you like it? Why?
	What is the best thing?

With weaker classes, go back to the model text in exercise 4 and have students underline the key structures they will need to use, e.g., *My (apartment) is …*, *there's …*, etc.

6   Give students time to write their descriptions in class or assign it for homework. Students read their descriptions to each other. Encourage students to ask each other questions.

When you check the students' descriptions, point out errors, but allow students to correct them themselves. Try to limit correction to major problems to avoid demoralizing students. If possible, display the students' descriptions on the classroom wall or noticeboard.

VOCABULARY AND LISTENING (SB p. 32)

Adjectives for *good* and *bad*

This section is designed to extend students' vocabulary range. It's common for elementary students to rely on a small bank of basic adjectives, such as *good, bad,* and *nice.* It is important for them to be encouraged to understand and use a wider range of vocabulary, particularly in the language of giving opinions.

> **SUGGESTION**
>
> It is worth checking from time to time to see how students are progressing with their vocabulary notebooks. Are they still adding to them? Have they started a new one? Do they try to review regularly? Have they thought of new ways of organizing their notebooks?

Students shouldn't have too many problems with the meaning of the adjectives, as many of them are similar in other European languages. However, be prepared to help with the word stress and vowel sounds in some of the words:

awful /'ɔfl/
amazing /ə'meɪzɪŋ/
wonderful /'wʌndərfl/
fantastic /fæn'tæstɪk/
fabulous /'fæbyələs/
horrible /'hɔrəbl; 'hɑrəbl/
terrible /'tɛrəbl/

1 Write *good* and *bad* on the board and elicit any words with similar meanings that students know. Focus students' attention on exercise 1 and on the example. Give students time to categorize the words, working individually.

Check the answers, drilling any words students have problems with.

Answers

good	bad
excellent	terrible
amazing	horrible
terrific	awful
great	
fabulous	
wonderful	
fantastic	

2 **CD1 56** Focus students' attention on the examples. Remind students of the system of highlighting the word stress. Use the examples to point out that the stress can fall on different parts of different words and that it's a good idea for students to mark the stress when they write new words in their vocabulary notebooks.

Focus students' attention on the arrows. Remind students that these indicate the rise and fall of the voice within the sentences.

Play the recording. Reinforce the intonation by drawing the pattern in the air with your hand.

Play the recording again. Have students repeat, paying special attention to the intonation. If students sound flat, exaggerate the intonation pattern, and then have students repeat the sentences again.

Model pronunciation of the sentences again, replacing the adjectives with others from exercise 1. Have students repeat chorally and individually, making sure they use the correct intonation patterns.

3 **CD1 57** Tell students they are going to hear six short conversations. Give students time to look at the nouns and adjectives. Answer any questions about vocabulary.

Play conversation 1 as an example. Then play the rest of the recording and have students complete the task. Only play the recording a second time if students missed a lot of the answers. If appropriate, elicit any further information that students understood, e.g., the location of the apartment, the color of the shoes, etc.

Refer students to **CD1 57** on p. 118. Put students into pairs to practice the conversations. Remind them to think about the intonation of the sentences with adjectives. Monitor and check. If students sound flat, play key lines of the conversations again and have students repeat chorally and individually. Students then repeat the closed pairwork.

Answers and audio script

Alice's new boyfriend – great
Ben's new apartment – fantastic/fabulous
the weather – horrible/terrible
the meal – excellent
new shoes – great/amazing
the new teacher – awful

CD1 57

1 A Do you know Alice has a new boyfriend?
   B Really? Is he nice?
   A Yeah! He's great!
   B Ooh! What's his name?
   A James.
   B Good for Alice!
2 C Ben has a new apartment.
   D Wow! Where is it?
   C In the center of town.
   D Is it nice?
   C Oh, yes. It's fantastic! The living room is fabulous!
3 E What a horrible day!
   F Yes, it is! Rain, rain, rain. It's terrible weather at the moment.
   E Oh, well! Tomorrow's another day!
4 G Mmm! This is an excellent meal!
   H Thank you! I'm glad you like it.
5 I I love your new shoes! They're great!
   J They're nice, aren't they? They're Italian.
   I The color's amazing! Red! Wow!
6 K We have a new teacher. Her name's Nancy.
   L Is she nice?
   K No, she's awful! I don't like her.
   L Why?
   K I don't understand her. She talks and talks and talks all the time!

4 Focus students' attention on the conversation starters. With weaker classes, elicit possible adjectives for each question. You can also elicit whole lines for some of the conversations.

If possible, put students in new pairs to do this activity. Give them time to think about ways of continuing the conversations. Monitor and help as necessary. Check for correct pronunciation of the adjectives and for lively intonation. Drill key lines if necessary and let students practice again.

Adverb + adjective

This section practices common modifiers of adjectives. This is a regular feature of language, particularly in speaking, and will help elementary students further improve their range of expression.

5 Focus students' attention on the pictures and the explanations. Elicit sentences using each of the words/phrases. Check the sentence stress, e.g.,

My trailer isn't very big.
My mother's house is big.

My boss's house is very big.
Our new office building is really big.

Point out that in a sentence *not very ...* is usually contracted, e.g., *She isn't very old*, but students will also hear *She's not very old*.

6 **CD1 58** Tell students they are going to hear five short conversations. They need to listen to the key information to complete the chart, but they don't need to understand every word. Pre-teach/check students' understanding of *jeans*, *make* (noun), *smart*, and *intelligent*. Write the proper nouns on the board to help students with spelling: *Angela*, *Tom*, *Peter*, *Maria*.

Play conversation 1 as an example. Then play the rest of the recording and have students complete the task. Remind them to include the phrases *not very/very/really* + adjective in their answers where relevant. Only play the recording a second time if students missed a lot of the answers. If appropriate, elicit any further information that students understood, e.g., the type of car, the make of jeans, etc.

Refer students to **CD1 58** on p. 118. Put students into pairs to practice the conversations. Remind them to think about the intonation of the sentences with adjectives. Monitor and check. If students sound flat, play key lines of the conversations again and have students repeat chorally and individually. Students then repeat the closed pairwork.

Answers and audio script

What/Who are they talking about?	How do they describe it?
1 Angela's car	really expensive, very fast
2 Tom's house/money	really beautiful, very big, very rich
3 jeans	really nice, not very expensive
4 Peter's new girlfriend	pretty, not very old
5 Maria	very smart, really intelligent, not very nice

CD1 58

1 A Look at Angela's car! It's a Mercedes!
  B Wow! They're really expensive! Is it fast?
  A Very fast.
2 C Does Tom have a lot of money?
  D Well, he has a really beautiful house with a very big yard, and a swimming pool.
  C Mm. He's very rich, isn't he?
3 E Do you like my new jeans?
  F Yeah! They're really nice! What make are they?
  E They're Prada.
  F How much were they?
  E They weren't expensive. Well, not very expensive.
4 G Look! That's Peter's new girlfriend!
  H Oh! She's pretty. How old is she?
  G 28.
  H Wow! That's old!
  G 28? She isn't very old!
5 I Maria's very smart, isn't she?
  J Oh, yes. She's really intelligent. She knows everything.
  I Do you like her?
  J No, not really. She isn't very nice to talk to.
  I No, I don't like her either.

7 Focus students' attention on the questions in the Student Book and the example conversation. Have students read it aloud chorally and then practice it aloud in open pairs. With weaker students, elicit possible adjectives for the other conversations:

  school: small/not very big/dark/messy/old/new
  apartment: small/not very big/dark/old/new

Then have students continue the conversations in pairs.

ADDITIONAL MATERIAL

Workbook Unit 4
Ex. 7 Listening

EVERYDAY ENGLISH (SB p. 33)

Numbers

The functional syllabus continues with a focus on numbers up to one million, ways of reading different numbers, and understanding and talking about prices.

> ⚠ **POSSIBLE PROBLEMS**
>
> Most students will need regular practice to be able to produce numbers spontaneously. They often have problems distinguishing *-teen* and *-ty* numbers because of the different stress:
>
> *fifteen*   *fifty*
>
> There is also a set of "rules" for saying different categories of number:
>
> **Fractions:** When a fraction follows a whole number, we use *and*, e.g., 1½ = *one and a half*, 2¼ = *two and a quarter*.
>
> **Decimals:** We use a point (.), not a comma, in decimals. The stress falls on the last figure, e.g., 1.75 = *one point seven five*.
>
> **Phone numbers:** We usually give phone numbers using single figures 0–9, and 0 is pronounced "oh." Longer numbers are grouped into series with a pause in between. The intonation is rise, rise, fall, e.g.,
>
> 607 555 3425 = *six oh seven, five five five, three four two five*
>
> **Prices:** We express prices in dollars and cents, or in just simple numbers, e.g., *two dollars and fifty cents*, or, *two-fifty*. When the words *dollars* and *cents* are used, they are joined by *and*.

1 Briefly review numbers 1–20 by having students count around the class. Repeat until they can say the numbers accurately without hesitation. Then have students count aloud to 100 in tens, to review *twenty*, *thirty*, etc. Drill the words and deal with any pronunciation problems as necessary.

Focus students' attention on the photos and elicit the correct numbers. Point out that in numbers such as *215* we say *two hundred and fifteen*, NOT *two hundreds and fifteen*. Point to the pictures in random order and elicit the numbers again. Repeat, getting faster and faster until students can say all the numbers with confidence.

2 **CD1 59** Elicit the first line of numbers with the whole class. Then put students in pairs to continue saying the numbers. Monitor and check.

Play the recording and let students check their answers. Students practice the numbers again. If students have problems, play the recording or model the numbers yourself and have students repeat chorally and individually.

Answers and audio script
eight   ten   twelve   fifteen
twenty   thirty-two   forty-five   sixty
seventy-six   ninety-nine   one hundred eighty-seven
two hundred fifty
three hundred   one thousand   one million

3 **CD1 60** Make sure that students understand the different categories of number (fractions, decimals, and phone numbers). Students work in pairs and try to read the numbers. Monitor and check.

Play the recording and have students check their answers. Students practice the numbers again. If students have problems, play the recording or model the numbers yourself and have students repeat chorally and individually. If necessary, highlight the "rules" for saying numbers in *Possible problems* on page 44.

Answers and audio script
one and a half
two and a quarter
six point eight
seventeen point five
two one two, five five five, six four nine oh
nine one seven, five five five, six six seven eight

4 **CD1 61** This is a number dictation activity. Tell students they are going to hear four individual people talking, and a total of eight numbers of different types, including a decimal, a fraction, and a phone number.

Focus students' attention on the example and tell students they should write the numbers as numerals, not words. Play the recording. If necessary, pause after each number to give students time to write their answers. Check the answers with the class.

Answers and audio script
1 30, 17, 13   2 62, 860-555-9734   3 460, 16   4 280,000

CD1 61
1 There are thirty students in my class –seventeen boys and thirteen girls.
2 I live at number 62 Station Road. My cellphone number is 860-555-9734.
3 My father works in a big hotel. There are 460 rooms on sixteen floors.
4 The population of my town is 280,000.

EXTRA ACTIVITY

Have students do number dictations in pairs to reinforce the range of numbers covered in this section. Students prepare a list of random figures to dictate to their partner. They take turns dictating their list to each other. The student who is writing the dictated numbers writes the figures, not the words, and then reads the list back to their partner to check the answers.

Prices

5 Pre-teach/check students' understanding of *pound, dollar, cent,* and *euro* /'yʊroʊ/. Elicit the first price and then have students continue, working in pairs. Monitor and check.

If necessary, highlight the "rules" for saying prices in *Possible problems* on page 44.

Answers
1 seventy-five dollars
2 one dollar and fifty cents
3 forty-five cents
4 nineteen dollars ninety-nine cents/nineteen, ninety-nine
5 two hundred and seventy pounds
6 twelve euros

6 **CD1 62** This is another dictation activity. Tell students they are going to hear eight prices in different currencies, including dollars and euros.

Play the recording. If necessary, pause after each price to give students time to write their answers. Check the answers with the class.

You can have students do price dictations in pairs following the technique for numbers (see *Extra activity*).

Answers and audio script
1 $6.50   2 $24   3 $30,000   4 $9,500   5 79 ¢
6 $49   7 $250   8 1.4

Audio script
1 "How much is this book?"   "Six dollars and fifty cents."
2 "How much are these pictures?"   "Twenty-four dollars each."
3 I only earn $30,000 a year.
4 "How much is this car?"   "$9,500."
5 "Just this postcard, please."   "That's 79 cents, please."
6 "Can I have these jeans, please?"   "Sure, that's $49."
7 "How much is a round-trip ticket from New York to Chicago?"   "$250"
8 There are about 1.4 dollars to the euro.

7 This activity practices prices in a free-discussion activity. Briefly review the questions *How much is this (bag)?* for items in the singular and *How much are these (glasses)?* for items in the plural.

Ask two students to read the example conversation aloud. If students sound flat, focus on the stress and voice range of the lines. Remind students to start high and fall on the exclamations:

A *Excuse me! How much are these …?*

B *Oh, they're very original! They're two hundred dollars.*

A *What! That's crazy! That's much too expensive! No, thanks. Not today.*

With weaker students, elicit ways of continuing the conversation, e.g., *Well, what about this (bag)?/Well, we've also got these (glasses); It's only ($35)./It's on sale./There's a 20% discount today*, etc.

Divide the students into A/B pairs. Students practice the conversations, using the model in the Student Book. Monitor and help as necessary. If you have time, you can have students act out their conversations for the class.

8 Demonstrate the activity by talking about one or two numbers or prices that are significant to you, e.g., *$1,000 – My rent is $1,000 a month*. If necessary, provide useful vocabulary, e.g., *to cost, to pay (price) for something, bill, mortgage, ticket, bus/train pass*, etc.

Focus students' attention on the examples in the Student Book. Then have students continue in pairs or small groups. Elicit a few examples from the class.

SUGGESTION

You can give students extra practice with numbers and prices by bringing in advertisements, leaflets, and menus that show prices, and having students practice *How much is/are … ?*

Photocopiable Activity

UNIT 4 Numbers and prices TB p. 147

Note: For the discussion stage in exercise 2, it is useful to have students check the exchange rate with the currency in their country before you do this activity in class. US prices have been provided which are accurate at the time of publication, but you may need to adapt these depending on when you use the quiz.

Materials: One copy of the worksheet for each student.

Procedure: Explain that students are going to take a quiz to find out how much they know about numbers. This is followed by a group task to compare prices of everyday items/services in different countries. Pre-teach/check students' understanding of *piano keys, vote, coin,* and *speed limit*.

If appropriate, you can set up exercise 1 as a competition by keeping a record of students' answers on the board and then making the student/pair with the most correct answers the winner.

- Hand out a copy of the worksheet to each student. Ask question 1 as an example and elicit a range of answers. Don't confirm the correct answer at this stage.
- Give students time to answer the questions in the quiz, working individually. Students then check their answers in pairs.
- Check the answers with the class by eliciting a range of answers and encouraging discussion with the whole class. Then confirm the correct answers.

Answers							
1a	2b	3a	4c	5b	6c	7a	8a

- Check students know the exchange rate between the US dollar and their currency (see *Note* above). Ask students to read through the chart. Answer any questions about vocabulary. Give students time to

complete the chart for their country and for the US. Tell them it doesn't matter if they are unsure. The activity is for general discussion of prices, not a test of their knowledge.

- Provide useful language, e.g., *I think (a coffee) is about (price). Yes, I think so, too./No, I think it's more/less, maybe (price)*. Put the students in small groups to compare their ideas. Monitor and help as necessary. Check for accurate use of prices, noting any common errors. Don't interrupt or over-correct at this stage, as this is a fluency activity.

- Go over the possible answers for the US (accurate at the time of publication). If you have access to the most recent figures, then use those. Elicit students' reactions to the figures. Establish which countries in the world they think are expensive.

Possible answers	
	price in the US
a day train/subway pass in the capital city	$14.50 (to cover central zones)
a coffee and a daily newspaper	$5 (a large coffee); $1.25 (e.g., The Washington Post)
a movie ticket for an adult	$8 ($6 before 3:00pm)
a month's food shopping for two adults	$537
dinner for two in a 3-star restaurant	$150–$300
a top-20 CD	$11.99–$16.99
a gallon of gas	$2.59
a month's rent in a small apartment in the capital city	$1,692

ADDITIONAL MATERIAL

Workbook Unit 4

Ex. 8 Numbers
Ex. 9 Prices

Don't forget!

Workbook Unit 4

Ex. 10 Vocabulary
Ex. 11 *me/him/them*

Grammar Reference (SB p. 132)

Word list Unit 4 (SB p. 141)

Students can translate the words, learn them at home, or transfer some of them to their vocabulary notebook.

Tests (Online)

Unit 4 Test

Skills Test 1 (Units 1-4)

Stop and Check 1 (Units 1-4)

Video (iTools and Online)

Additional photocopiables and PPT™ presentations (iTools)

5 Super me!

can/can't • was/were/could • Words that go together • Polite requests
VIDEO A music school

Skills and ability are the themes of this unit. These are particularly suitable topics to introduce and practice *can/can't* (ability). However, the unit has two main goals in that we also introduce some past tenses for the first time: the past of *can* (ability) – *could*, and the Simple Past of the verb *to be* – *was/were*. The skills work includes a listening about the artist Picasso and a jigsaw reading about two talented members of the same family. These provide contexts for and practice of the grammar. **Note** The recordings for Units 5–8 are on CD2.

LANGUAGE INPUT

GRAMMAR
can/can't (SB p. 34)
Past – was/were, could (SB p. 36)

- Practicing *can/can't* to talk about ability.
- Practicing *was/were/could* to talk about the past.

VOCABULARY
Words that go together (SB p. 40)
Adjectives (SB p. 38)

- Understanding and practicing collocations: noun + noun, verb + noun, prepositions.
- Understanding adjectives in context.

EVERYDAY ENGLISH
Polite requests (SB p. 41)

- Understanding and practicing *can/could* to make polite requests.

SKILLS DEVELOPMENT

READING
A talented family (SB p. 38)

- A jigsaw reading about the life and success of two members of the same family.

LISTENING
Child prodigies (SB p. 37)
Pablo Picasso (SB p. 37)
Three conversations (SB p. 40)

- Listening for key words in a short monologue. **CD2 12** (SB p. 119)
- Listening for key words in a short conversation. **CD2 14** (SB p. 119)
- Listening for noun + noun combinations in three short conversations. **CD2 15** (SB p. 119)

SPEAKING
Talking about you (SB p. 36/37)
What do you think? (SB p. 38)

- Talking about the past and things you could do in the past.
- Talking about relationships.

WRITING
A formal email – Applying for a job (SB p. 104)

- Understanding key content points and more formal style, then writing an email to apply for a job.

MORE MATERIALS

Photocopiables – Words that go together (TB p. 148)   **Tests** (Online)   **Video** (iTools and Online)

Students have already practiced *can* in the *Everyday English* sections of Units 1, 2, and 3. In those units, it is used as a polite request in a range of useful expressions *Can I have … ?/ Can you tell me the time?/Can I open the window?/Can you help me?* and an offer *Can I help you?*

In Unit 5, the use of *can* is extended to cover ability, and all aspects of the form (statements, questions, negatives) are presented and practiced.

⚠ **POSSIBLE PROBLEMS**

- Sometimes after sustained practice of the Simple Present, students want to use *do/don't* and *does/doesn't* to form the question and negative of *can*.

  *Do you can swim?
  *I don't can swim.

- The pronunciation of *can* and *can't* can also create problems for students. They often find the different vowel sounds (/ə/ or /æ/ in *can* and /æ/ in *can't*) confusing. Because the final *t* in *can't* tends to get lost, it's difficult to recognize whether the sentence is affirmative or negative. Students also often have difficulty producing the correct sounds themselves.

I can swim.	/aɪ kən swɪm/
Can you swim?	/kən yu swɪm/
Yes, I can.	/yɛs aɪ kæn/
I can't come.	/aɪ kænt kʌm/

  For these reasons, we give special attention to the pronunciation in the unit by including exercises for recognition and production.

STARTER (SB p. 34)

This is intended to be a fun introduction to *can* for ability. Students talk about the comic book hero Superman and what he can do.

CD2 2 Focus students' attention on the photo of Superman and elicit any information that students know. Ask *What can he do?* and elicit a range of answers, but do not go into a full presentation of *can* at this stage.

Play the recording and have students compare the ideas in the recording with their ideas.

Audio script
Superman comes from the planet Krypton. He can fly at the speed of light; he can see through walls; he can jump over tall buildings; he can speak every language; he can turn back time. There's nothing Superman can't do!

SUPERMAN IS AMAZING! (SB p. 34)

can/can't

This presentation continues the theme of Superman and his skills. The speakers are two children, Alfie /ˈælfi/ and Ivy / ˈaɪvi/. They are cousins and the tone of the script is teasing but lighthearted, typical of the way children and teenagers often communicate. The recording is divided across three exercises, a first section presented as a fill-in-the-blanks exercise, and then the whole conversation as an unseen script with key information questions. Students then listen to the

whole conversation again and fill in the blanks with the target language.

1 **CD2 3** Focus students' attention on the photos and ask students to point to Alfie and Ivy. *Ask How old are they?* and have students estimate their ages. Ask *What does Alfie like doing?* (skateboarding).

Give students time to read the incomplete conversation. Play the recording and have students complete the missing words.

Check the answers with the class.

Answers and audio script
A = Alfie   I = Ivy
A Superman's amazing!
I Really? What can he do?
A He can do everything!
I No, he can't!
A Yes, he can. He **can fly** at the speed of light, he **can see** through buildings, and he **can speak** every language in the world!

2 **CD2 4** Tell students they are going to hear the rest of the conversation between Alfie and Ivy. Read the questions as a class, then play the recording through once without stopping.

Check the answers with the class.

Answers and audio script
They talk about Chinese and Spanish.
They talk about skateboarding and skiing.

CD2 4
A = Alfie   I = Ivy
A He can speak every language in the world!
I Really? I don't believe that.
A Well, he can! Can you speak any languages?
I Yes, I can. I can speak Spanish and a little Chinese. We learn them at school.
A Well, I can speak Spanish, too.
I Oh, yeah?!
A I can say *"Hola!"* and *"Gracias."*
I That's nothing! You can't speak Spanish at all!
A Well, I can skateboard. You can't!
I I don't want to skateboard. I like other things. What about skiing? Can you ski?
A Yeah, I can ski a little, but my mom and dad can ski really well!
I I love skiing. I can ski really well.
A OK, OK, we can do some things, but Superman can do everything. There's nothing Superman can't do.
I Oh, you and Superman! Remember he's not real, he's only a …

3 **CD2 5** The sentences in this exercise present the key forms of *can* and also provide exposure to adverbs that describe how well you can do something. These are further practiced and personalized in *Practice* exercises 4 and 5.

Check students' understanding of *ski*. Focus students' attention on the example. Then give students time to complete the sentences. Remind them to use the information from the conversation in exercise 2. With weaker students, go through the sentences orally with the class and then have them write their answers.

Allow students to check their answers in pairs before playing the recording as a final check.

If you think students will need help with pronunciation at this stage, focus on the *Grammar Spot* before students practice the conversation.

Answers and audio script
1 "Can you **speak** any languages?"
  "Yes, I can. I **can speak** Spanish and a little Chinese."
2 "You **can't speak** Spanish at all!"
3 "I **can** skateboard! You **can't**!"
4 "**Can** you **ski**?"
  "I **can ski** a little, but my mom and dad **can ski** really well."
5 "Superman **can do** everything. There's nothing Superman **can't do**!"

GRAMMAR AND PRONUNCIATION

1 Focus students' attention on the *Grammar and Pronunciation* box. Students work in pairs and say all the persons of *can/can't*. Ask them what they notice about the verb form for each person. Make sure that students are clear about the answer.

Answer
Can/can't are the same for all persons, so there is no -*s* added in the *he/she/it* forms. We do not use the auxiliary *don't/doesn't* to form the negative.

2 **CD2 6** This activity focuses on the pronunciation of *can/can't* in the affirmative, questions, and short answers.

Play the recording and have your students read and listen very carefully to the pronunciation of *can* and *can't*. First, ask the general question *Can you hear differences?* If necessary, repeat the sentences yourself, exaggerating the vowel sounds in *can* and *can't* and isolating them /ə/, /æ/, so that your students can fully appreciate the differences. Elicit the main stresses in each sentence. Ask *When is "can" pronounced* /kən/? (When it is unstressed.) Play the recording again and have students repeat chorally and individually.

3 Focus students' attention again on the sentence stress in the affirmative and negative sentences. Drill the sentences and then have students practice in pairs.

▶▶ Read Grammar Reference 5.1 on p. 133 together in class, and/or ask students to read it at home. Encourage them to ask you questions about it.

SUGGESTION
If your students need more practice with the pronunciation of *can/can't*, write out simple sentences in phonetic script and then have students practice saying the sentences in pairs, e.g.,
1 /ʃi; kən ski/
2 /wi; kən drɔ; bət wi; kænt raɪt/
3 /aɪ kən sɪŋ 'rɪli wɛl/
4 /kən yu pleɪ 'tɛnəs/ /noʊ aɪ kænt/
5 /kən ðeɪ dæns/ /yɛs ðeɪ kæn/

PRACTICE (SB p. 35)

Ivy can't cook. Can you?

1 **CD2 7** This is a recognition exercise that moves into production stages in exercises 2 and 4. This time the recording is a monologue with Ivy talking about her abilities.

Ask students what they can remember about Ivy and elicit a range of answers. Pre-teach/check students' understanding of *foreign*, including the pronunciation /'fɔrən/. Make sure students understand the convention of (**Y**) and (**N**). They need to put a (**Y**) next to the things that Ivy can do and an (**N**) next to the things she can't do.

Play the recording as far as *I can't cook at all* and focus students' attention on the examples. Then play the rest of the recording and have students complete the task.

Put students into pairs to compare their answers. Then check answers as a class. Let students listen again if necessary.

Answers and audio script

Can ...?	Ivy
speak a foreign language	Y
cook	N
skateboard	N
swim	Y
play tennis	Y
ski	Y
play any musical instruments	N

CD2 7

Ivy: So what can I do? Speak a foreign language ... Hmm. Well, yes, I can speak Spanish and a little Chinese. Cooking? No, I can't cook at all. My mom can, she's a great cook! Hmm. Sports – well, I think I'm pretty good at sports – my cousin Alfie says I'm not because I can't skateboard, but skateboarding's not a sport. I can swim, of course. Everyone can swim, can't they? I can swim very well. I like swimming and I like tennis. I can play tennis pretty well. But skiing is my best sport, I love it, and I can ski really well, really fast. Musical instruments? Uh ... well, no, I can't play any musical instruments. My dad can play the guitar really well and my mom can play the piano a little, but I can't play anything at all.

2 This exercise reinforces the question and answer forms. Practice the questions in the Student Book in open and closed pairs. Encourage students to distinguish between the strong and weak forms of *can*, and to use the correct intonation. Also make sure that they pronounce the *t* on the end of the negatives. The two consonants *nt* together are difficult for many speakers.

Students work in pairs and ask and answer questions about Ivy and each of the activities in the chart. Monitor and help as necessary, checking for accurate question formation and pronunciation.

3 **CD2 8** This exercise highlights adverbs for saying how well you can do things. Students may make mistakes with the word order due to interference from their own language, e.g., *I can speak very well German*. Be prepared to highlight and correct any problems in this area.

Focus students' attention on the photo of Ivy and elicit a few examples of things she can and can't do. Then focus their attention on words and phrases in the box. Explain that they are in order of meaning from "no talent" (*not at all*) to "enormous talent" (*really well*). Give several true examples to reinforce these two extremes, e.g., *I can't play tennis at all. Roger Federer can play tennis really well.*

Focus students' attention on the example. Then give students time to complete the sentences, working in pairs. With weaker students, go over the sentences orally with the class and then have them write their answers.

Play the recording and have students compare their answers.

Have individual students practice saying the sentences for the class. If they have problems with the sentence stress or any individual words, play the recording again and have students repeat chorally and individually.

Answers and audio script
1 She can speak Chinese a little.
2 She can't cook **at all**.
3 She can swim **very well**.
4 She can play tennis **pretty well**.
5 She can ski **really well**.
6 Her dad can play the guitar **really well**.
7 Her mom can play the piano **a little**.
8 She can't play anything **at all**.

4 The exercise is another personalized activity. Students complete column 3 of the chart in exercise 1 about their partner.

Practice the questions in the Student Book in open and closed pairs. Encourage students to distinguish between the strong and weak forms of *can*, and to use the correct sentence stress. Drill the questions and answers as necessary.

Students work in pairs and ask and answer questions about each of the activities in the chart. Go around and monitor and help as they do this. Check for accurate question formation, pronunciation, and use of the adverbs.

Discuss any common errors. If necessary, highlight the position of the adverbs in exercise 3 to reinforce that they come at the end of the sentence.

5 Focus students' attention on the examples and highlight the contrastive stress:

José can speak Spanish really well, but I can't.

Ask a few students to tell the others about their and their partner's abilities. In larger groups, students can do this stage in small groups and then share responses with the rest of the class.

6 **CD2 9** This is a discrimination activity to check that your students can recognize what they hear. Play the first sentence and elicit the answer as an example (*can*). Play the rest of the recording and have students choose the correct words.

Check the answers with the class, playing the recording again as reinforcement if necessary.

Answers and audio script
1 She **can** cook.
2 I **can't** hear you.
3 They **can't** come to the party.
4 **Can** you see my glasses anywhere?
5 You **can't** always get what you want.
6 **Can** you do the homework?

7 Demonstrate the activity by reading one of the sentences, changing the use of *can/can't* from the wording in exercise 6. Students choose the correct words.

Students continue in closed pairs. Encourage them to do the activity briskly to make it fun and to ensure that the pronunciation doesn't become too labored.

EXTRA ACTIVITY

Set up a short discussion activity with the class by asking *What can/can't computers do?* Elicit a few examples from the class, then ask students to continue in pairs/small groups. This is an opportunity to generate some freer speaking in English, so don't focus too closely on accuracy and don't worry if the activity is very short.

Sample answers

Computers can ...

do fast calculations, translate, check spellings, speak English (in a limited way), play music/DVDs, play chess, store a lot of information/images

Computers can't ...

write poetry, get sick, laugh, think (because they work completely in numbers), fall in love

ADDITIONAL MATERIAL

Workbook Unit 5
Ex. 1–3   *can/can't*

TODAY AND YESTERDAY (SB p. 36)

Past – *was/were/could*

These forms are the first introduction of a past tense in *American Headway 1*. They are presented by building on the present forms that students already know. The use of a set of parallel present and past sentences helps to make the form and meaning as clear as possible.

⚠ **POSSIBLE PROBLEMS**

- Students may have pronunciation problems with the past of *to be*. The vowel sound in *was* can be both weak (/ə/) and strong (/ʌ/):

  He was at home.   /hi wəz ət hoʊm/

  Was he at home?   /wəz hi ət hoʊm/

  Yes, he was./No, he wasn't.
  / yɛs hi wʌz/ /noʊ hi ˈwʌznt/

- The groups of consonants in the negatives *wasn't* /'wʌznt/, *weren't* /wɜrnt/ and *couldn't* /kʊdnt/ may be difficult for some students and may need extra choral and individual repetition.

1 **CD2 10** This is a very direct presentation of the past of the verbs *to be* and *can*. It reviews the present forms of the verbs and then moves straight to the past tense equivalents.

Focus students' attention on the photos to reinforce the concepts of present and past. Pre-teach/check students' understanding of *yesterday* and *last month/last year*. Play number 1 and elicit true answers to each question. Play the rest of the recording. Students listen and write in the answers.

When they have finished, go over the exercise with them, modeling the questions and answers for them to repeat, and focusing on the weak vowel sound of *was* (/wəz/) in statements and questions, and the strong vowel sound (/wʌz/, /wʌznt/) in short answers and negatives.

GRAMMAR AND PRONUNCIATION

1 Focus students' attention on the examples. Then put your students into pairs to complete the chart with the past of *to be*. Quickly check the answers with the whole class.

Answers

	Affirmative	Negative
I	was	wasn't
you	were	weren't
he/she/it	**was**	**wasn't**
we	were	**weren't**
they	**were**	**weren't**

2 Students complete the affirmative and negative forms of the past of *can*.

Answers
Affirmative   could (all persons)
Negative   couldn't (all persons)

3 **CD2 11** This is a repetition exercise to help reinforce the pronunciation. Play the recording through once and have students just listen. Play the recording again and have students repeat. Insist on accurate pronunciation of the strong and weak forms. Ask students *When is "was" pronounced* /wəz/? (When it is unstressed.)

Audio script
1 It was Monday.
2 We were at school.
3 "Was it sunny?" "Yes, it was."
4 "Was it cold?" "No, it wasn't."
5 "Were you at school?" "Yes, we were."
6 "Were they at school?" "No, they weren't."

▶▶ Read Grammar Reference 5.2 and 5.3 on p. 133 together in class, and/or ask students to read it at home. Encourage them to ask you questions about it.

2 Have students ask and answer the questions in open pairs. Use the opportunity to check and correct them carefully. Students then ask and answer the questions again in closed pairs.

3 This exercise practices the affirmative, negative, and, question forms.

Pre-teach/check student's understanding of *sick* and *on vacation*. Focus students' attention on the example and elicit the second verb (*was*). Give students time to complete the sentences, working individually. Then check answers with the class.

Answers
1 I wasn't at school yesterday because I **was** sick.
2 My parents **weren't** at work last week. They **were** on vacation in Mexico.
3 Where **were** you yesterday? You **weren't** at soccer practice.
4 I **could** read and write when I **was** just five.
5 My sister **couldn't** read until she **was** seven.

Talking about you

4 Drill the first question and possible answers in open pairs. Students continue asking and answering the questions in closed pairs. Monitor and help as necessary. Encourage students to ask about times other than those listed in the Student Book. Finish the activity by asking one or two students to tell the class about their partner.

EXTRA ACTIVITY

Extend the pairwork activity in exercise 4 by having students build a conversation about places/events they have been to recently. Put some skeleton dialogue prompts on the board and ask pairs of students to create conversations, e.g.,

… the soccer game last weekend?

… good?

… many people?

… the score?

Students can act out their conversation for the rest of the class.

Look at pics on screen

PRACTICE (SB p. 37)

Child prodigies

This section brings together the past of *can* and *to be*, and it also introduces *to be born*. It continues the theme of skills and talents, but this time focuses on some very talented children. Students are also given the opportunity to personalize the language.

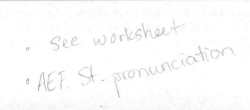

· See worksheet
· AEF. St. pronunciation

- *Was/Were born* is taught here as an expression, not as an example of the passive. Don't be tempted to go into the grammar of the passive at this stage. Some students translate directly from their own language and say *I am born*, so be prepared to highlight and correct this.

- There are Simple Past forms (*played*, *painted*) included in this section for recognition. There's no need to give a full grammar explanation of these forms at this stage. If students ask about them, just explain that they are a past form of the relevant verb. Students will cover Simple Past in Units 6 and 7.

1 Focus students' attention on the photos and ask them to guess how old they think the children are. Elicit information about what the children can do, and why they are "child prodigies".

Answers
Ryan Wang can play the piano.
Aelita Andre can paint pictures.
They are child prodigies because they are very young, but they have special talents.

2 **CD2 12** Pre-teach/check students' understanding of *prodigy* /ˈprɑdədʒi/ and *to be a success*. Give students time to read the incomplete sentences so they know what to listen for. If they ask about the use of *played*, just explain that it is a past form of *play*.

Play the first two lines of the recording and elicit the missing information in sentence 1. Play the rest of the recording and have students fill in the sentences.

Students take turns reading the sentences aloud. Monitor and check for correct pronunciation. If students have problems, play the recording again as a model and drill key lines chorally and individually. Students then repeat the pairwork.

Answers and audio script
Ryan Wang - Pianist.
1 He was born in 2008 in Vancouver, Canada.
2 He **can play** the piano really well.
3 He **could play** the piano when he **was four**.
4 He **could play** the piano very well after a year and a half.
5 When he was five, he played with the Shanghai Symphony. He was a big success.

3 **CD2 13** Pre-teach/check students' understanding of *exhibition*. Give students time to read the information about Aelita. If students ask about the use of *started*, just explain that it is the past form of *start*.

Elicit the information about where/when Aelita was born. Put students in pairs to continue the task. With weaker classes, elicit the information with the whole class first and then have students repeat the task in closed pairs. Monitor and check for correct use of *was born*, *could*, *was* and accurate pronunciation. Write down any common errors.

Play the recording and have students check their answers. Correct any major errors from the pairwork stage with the class.

Answers and audio script
Aelita Andre - Artist
Aelita Andre is an artist and a child prodigy.
1 She was born on January 9, 2007 in Melbourne, Australia.
2 She started to paint when she was just nine months old.
3 And she could paint beautifully when she was just one year old.
4 When she was two, some of her art was in an exhibition. Today, Aelita has fans around the world.

4 Elicit example questions and answers about Ryan (*When was he born? In 2008. Where was he born? In Vancouver. How old was he when he could play the piano? He was four.*) Drill the questions if necessary. Students continue working in pairs, asking and answering questions about the children. Monitor and check for correct use of *was born*, *could*, *was/were*, and accurate pronunciation. Write down any common errors and discuss them later as a class.

Listening

ABOUT THE LISTENING
The theme of talented youngsters is continued with a listening about one of the most influential artists of the 20th century. Born in Málaga in the south of Spain, Picasso was an accomplished and prolific artist from an early age. He trained as an artist in Madrid and Barcelona before moving to Paris, where he lived for many years. He helped to develop cubism and other forms of abstract art and his work is characterised by different periods such as the "Blue Period" and the "Rose Period." His works are held in prestigious museums all over the world, one of the largest collections being in the Museu Picasso in Barcelona.

In the listening script, there are three Spanish words: *Don* (= a title of respect used before a man's first name), *Doña* (= a title of respect used before a woman's first name), and *lápiz* (= pencil).

5 **CD2 14** Focus students' attention on the photo. Ask students what they know about Picasso's life and work. Give students time to read and complete the conversation individually. Then play the recording for students to check their answers.

Put students in pairs to practice the conversation. If students have problems with pronunciation, play key lines of the conversation again, having students repeat chorally and individually. Students then do the pairwork again.

Answers and audio script
Pablo Picasso, October 25th, 1881 to April 8th, 1973
A Hey, look at that painting! It's a Picasso!
B Oh, yes! It's wonderful!
A Where was Picasso born?
B In Málaga.
A Oh, so he **was** Spanish?
B Yes, he **was**.
A **Were** his parents rich?
B Well, they **weren't** rich and they **weren't** poor. His father, Don José, **was** a painter and a professor of art. His mother, Doña Maria, was a homemaker.
A So, **was** Picasso good at drawing when he **was** young?
B Oh, yes. He **was** a child prodigy. He **could** draw before he **could** speak. His first word **was** *lápiz*, which is Spanish for pencil.
A Wow! What a story!

Talking about you

6 Drill the questions in the *you* form, having students repeat chorally and individually. Make sure students can hear the difference between *where* and *were*, and insist on accurate intonation.

Students work in pairs and ask and answer the questions. At the end of the activity, ask a few students to tell you what they can remember, e.g., *Laura was born in Madrid in 1988. She could read when she was five.*

SUGGESTION

Students can think of some famous talented people, both children and adults, that they know and make similar sentences about where/when they were born and what skills they had at different ages.

If appropriate, you can extend this into a mini-project, having students research their chosen person and then give a short presentation to the class, using visuals if possible.

ADDITIONAL MATERIAL

Workbook Unit 5

Ex. 4 *was/were*
Ex. 5 *could/couldn't*
Ex. 6 Listening

WRITING (SB p. 104)

A formal email

Applying for a job

Unit 5 introduces a change of tone in the writing syllabus with a focus on more formal writing. Some of the key conventions of writing more formal emails, including greetings and endings, are shown in a model text. Students complete the model and then do a guided writing task, based on an advertisement for a job. This is the type of email students may need to write at some stage in their learning.

1 Focus students' attention on the photo of Carl. Ask *What does he do?* (He's a student.) *What does he want?* (a summer job). Briefly review the ways we read phone numbers and email addresses. Focus on the prompt *Last job* in the chart and check the verb form *Is or was?* (*was*).

Divide the class into pairs to ask and answer the questions. With weaker classes, go over the questions as a class first and then have students repeat the questions and answers in closed pairs. Monitor and help as necessary.

2 Give students time to read the ad. Answer any questions about vocabulary. Elicit the answers to the question.

Answers

Carl is interested in the job because:
he is over 18 (22).
he lives in Charleston and so probably knows it well.
he can speak Spanish and Portuguese.
he likes working with people.

3 Focus students' attention on the email headings. Ask *Who is the email from?* (Carl), *Who it is to?* (Linda Yates), *What is it for?* (to apply for the job of tour guide).

Elicit the answer for the first blank as an example. Then give students time to complete the email, using the information about Carl. Check the answers with the class.

Answers

1 tour guide	6 ski instructor
2 22	7 can
3 live	8 languages
4 student	9 like
5 free	10 was

Focus students' attention on the model email again and ask comprehension questions, e.g., *How many email addresses are there?* (two), *How do you begin the email? (Dear…)*, *Does the email use full or short forms, "I am" or "I'm"* (full forms), *What is a more formal way of saying "Please reply?" (I look forward to hearing from you.)*, *How do you end the email? (Sincerely).* Also ask *Why do you use "Ms." and not "Miss" or "Mrs?"* (because we don't know if Linda Yates is married or not). If necessary, establish the difference between *Miss* (for a single woman) and *Mrs.* (for a married woman).

4 Focus students' attention on the advertisement and elicit the job (*receptionist*). Check comprehension of the details, e.g., *Who do you email?* (Anne Watson), *Where?* (awatson@international.school.com), *What are the qualifications?* (like working with people, speak English and another language, have experience working in an office, use a computer, know your town well). Have students answer the questions in the advertisement about themselves.

Remind students to use Carl's email in exercise 3 as a model and to use the information provided in each paragraph as a guide. Give students time to write their email in class or assign it for homework.

5 Allow students to compare their emails, both for interest and to help each other with mistakes. When you collect students' emails, check for the correct use of greeting, ending, and full forms. Point out errors, but allow students to correct them themselves. Try to limit correction to major problems to avoid demoralizing the students.

READING AND SPEAKING (SB p. 38)

A talented family

ABOUT THE TEXT

This activity is another jigsaw reading task. This means it should result in not only reading practice, but also some freer speaking. The class divides into two groups and each group reads a different, but similar text about a talented member of the same family. It's important to remind students to read only their text and to get information about the other text via speaking. If necessary and possible, give the instructions for the jigsaw reading in L1.

The texts are based on real people and have been written to reinforce the grammar taught in this and previous units. There are also examples of Simple Past forms (*came, saw, started, wanted*) included in this section for recognition. There's no need to give a full grammar explanation of these forms at this stage. If students ask about them, just explain that they are a past form of the relevant verb.

Gio Benedetti /ˈdʒiʊʊ bɛnəˈdɛti/ is a successful businessman, originally from near Lucca /ˈlukə/ in Tuscany, central Italy. Despite humble beginnings, he has gone on to become a self-made millionaire and chairman of several companies.

Nicola Benedetti /ˈnɪkələ bɛnəˈdɛti/ is his daughter and a world-famous violinist. Born in Scotland, she started playing at the age of four and went on to attend the prestigious Yehudi Menuhin School for young musicians. She lives in London near her sister Stephanie /ˈstɛfəni/, also a violinist.

Encourage students to use the context to help them with new vocabulary and to pool knowledge with other students. With weaker classes or if you are short on time, ask students to look up some of the following vocabulary before the lesson:

Homework prior to the lesson

Introduction: *passion, businessman* /ˈbɪznəsˌmæn/

Nicola: *to be like someone, close* (adjective = connected by shared feelings and interests), *family occasions.*

Gio: *to afford something, dry cleaning, independent, concert, proud, country and western music, classical music, to cry, I can't help it* (= I can't stop myself), *sentimental.*

What kind of music do you like?

SUGGESTION

If possible, play a short section of music by Nicola Benedetti at some stage during the lesson. This will help to put the information in the text into a broader context.

1 Discuss the questions in exercise 1 with the whole class. Elicit a range of examples of talented people and what they can do.

2 Focus students' attention on the photos of Nicola and Gio. Elicit any information students know about them. Give students a short time to read the introduction to the article and answer the questions in pairs. Check the answers with the class.

Answers
1 She's a violinist.
2 She was BBC Young Musician of the Year.
3 She lives in London, near her sister.
4 She's a violoinst, too.
5 He's a businessman.

3 Put students into two groups, A and B. (With larger classes, you may need to have multiple sets of the two groups.) Assign a text to each group and remind students to read only their text:

Group A – Nicola

Group B – Gio

Get students to read their text quickly, asking others in their group for help with vocabulary if you didn't pre-teach the items listed in *About the text*. Monitor and help with any questions.

Give students time to read the questions and answer any questions. Have them work in their groups and answer the questions about their text, writing down the answers to each one. Monitor and help as necessary. The answers for each

group are provided below for reference, but don't check the answers with the whole class at this stage.

Answers
Nicola
1 No, it wasn't.
2 She was four.
3 Yes, he did.
4 They were poor.
5 Money is important to Gio, but for Nicola success isn't about money.
6 No, he doesn't.
7 She teaches him about music, he teaches her about business.
8 At family occasions, like weddings.

Gio
1 He was born near Lucca in Italy.
2 He couldn't afford it.
3 It was a dry cleaning business.
4 She was four.
5 No, he can't.
6 He likes country and western music. He doesn't like classical music.
7 Yes, she does.
8 He cries when he sees Nicola play. He's very sentimental.

4 Re-group the students, making sure there is an A and a B student in each pair. Demonstrate the activity by having a pair of students talk about the person in their text. Students continue talking about the answers to the questions in exercise 3 and exchanging the information about their person. Monitor and help. Also check for correct use of the present and past of *can* and *to be*. Write down any common errors, but discuss them with students at a later stage. Bring the whole class together to go over the answers. Encourage students to expand on their answers where possible.

Language work

5 This section focuses on the use of adjectives in the text. Focus students' attention on the example. Then give students time to complete the task, working in pairs.

Check the answers with the class, having students give full sentences to show the use of each adjective. Also check for correct use of the present and past of *to be*.

Answers
hardworking	Gio/Nicola's father was always hardworking.
poor	Gio's family were poor.
important	Money is important to Gio/Nicola's father.
classical	Gio doesn't like classical music much.
close	Nicola and her sister are very close.
difficult	It was difficult for Gio when he first came to Scotland.
expensive	The Jaguar was too expensive.
independent	Nicola was always independent.
proud	Gio is proud of Nicola and Scotland is proud of her.
passionate	Nicola is passionate when she plays the piano.
sentimental	Gio cries because he's very sentimental.

EXTRA ACTIVITY

Students personalize the adjectives in exercise 5 by writing true sentences about themselves/someone they know. They can write present or past tense examples and then compare with a partner.

What do you think?

This is an attempt to generate some personalized discussion and give further freer practice of the Simple Present. Don't worry if at this level it turns out to be a very short activity – even a little free speaking is still worthwhile. Don't correct students too much. The goal of this activity is fluency, not accuracy.

It can be helpful to ask students to discuss the topic in small groups, before you discuss students' responses with the whole class. It would also be a nice idea to encourage students to ask you questions about your family and who you are close to.

SUGGESTION

You can have students roleplay an interview between a journalist and Gio or Nicola. Assign roles of the journalist and Gio or Nicola, or allow students to choose the role they want. Have students prepare their interview, using the questions in exercise 3 to help them. Allow sufficient time for students to make notes, but discourage them from writing out the interview word for word. Have students practice the interview in pairs and then act it out in class.

ADDITIONAL MATERIAL

Workbook Unit 5
Ex. 9   Reading

VOCABULARY AND LISTENING (SB p. 40)

Words that go together

Collocation and word groupings are a key feature of English and it's important that students start to become familiar with them as early in their learning as possible. This vocabulary section focuses on verb + noun collocation, compound nouns (noun + noun combinations), and the use of prepositions in a range of high-frequency phrases/structures.

Noun + noun

1   Explain that this task focuses on noun + noun combinations. Focus students' attention on the examples. Point out that the first is written as two words and the second as one. Highlight the main stress on the words:

   post office   *businessperson*

   Ask *Where is the stress, on the first or second word?* (the first word). Drill the words as necessary.

   Have students write their answers to the task, so that they can focus on whether to write them as one or two words. Explain that *store* and *shop* have the same meaning although a *shop* is usually a smaller place than a *store*.

Check the answers, making sure students have written them correctly and that they stress the words accurately.

Answers
bookshop/store
motorcycle
sunglasses
living room
bus stop
handbag
train station
traffic lights
gas station

2   Focus students' attention on the examples in the book and have students say the exchanges in open pairs. Elicit one or two more example definitions and then have students test each other in pairs.

3   **CD2 15** Tell students they will hear three short conversations and that they should listen for noun + noun combinations from exercise 1. Focus their attention on the example and play conversation 1. Elicit the other nouns from exercise 1 (*bus stop, traffic lights*).

   Play the rest of the recording and have students complete their answers. Check the answers with the class.

   If you have time, ask students to turn to **CD2 15** on SB p. 119 and practice the conversations with a partner.

Answers and audio script
1   post office, bus stop, traffic lights
2   sunglasses, handbag, living room
3   gas station, train station, bookstore, traffic lights

CD2 15
1   A   Excuse me! Is there a post office near here?
    B   Yes. Can you see the bus stop over there?
    A   Yes, I can.
    B   Well, it's next to the bus stop. Near the traffic lights.
    A   Thanks.
2   A   I can't find my sunglasses.
    B   Not again! Look in your handbag!
    A   Where's my handbag?
    B   It's in the living room.
    A   Oh yes! There it is, and there they are!
3   A   Excuse me! Is there a gas station near here?
    B   A gas station? Yeah, go past the train station and the bookstore. It's just before the traffic lights.
    A   Great. Thank you.

4   With weaker classes, ask students what they can remember from the conversations in exercise 3, and elicit ideas for a new conversation with the whole class. Students then continue writing their own conversation in closed pairs. Monitor and help, and provide vocabulary as necessary.

   Ask some students to perform their conversations for the class.

Verb + noun

5   Students have learned most of these phrases as lexical items in earlier units. Point out that this task has verbs in list A and nouns in B. Focus students' attention on the example and then have them complete the task. Have students check answers in pairs before checking the answers with the whole class.

SUGGESTION

Ask students to brainstorm other nouns that go with the verbs, e.g., *play the piano/violin, drive a bus/taxi, ride a horse/bike*, etc. This can be done in class if you have time, or for homework. Remind students to write the verbs + nouns in their vocabulary notebook.

6 Focus students' attention on the example questions and answers in the Student Book. If necessary, drill the pronunciation, paying attention to the sentence stress. With weaker classes, elicit other possible questions before the pairwork stage, e.g., *Can you speak three languages? Do you watch television a lot?*

Students ask and answer questions in closed pairs. Monitor and help as necessary.

7 **CD2 16** Tell students they are going to hear ten short conversations and that they should listen for the verb + noun combinations from exercise 5.

Play number 1 as an example and elicit the verb + noun. Play the rest of the recording without stopping. Give students time to check their answers in pairs before checking the answers with the class.

Answers and audio script
1 send a lot of text messages
2 earn a lot of money
3 live on the third floor
4 wear a suit and tie
5 play the guitar
6 ride a motorcycle
7 drive a car
8 take care of children
9 watch TV a lot
10 speak foreign languages/Japanese/Spanish/Portuguese

CD2 16
1 A You send a lot of text messages!
  B I know. My cell phone is my best friend!
2 A Do you earn a lot of money?
  B What a question! Mind your own business!
3 A Do you live on the third floor?
  B Yes, I have a great view. I can see right over the town.
4 A Do you wear a suit and tie when you go to work?
  B No, no. Where I work is very casual. I wear jeans and a T-shirt.
5 A Can you play the guitar?
  B Yes, I can. And the piano. And the violin.
6 A Can you ride a motorcycle?
  B I can. Do you want to come for a ride? You can sit on the back.

7 A Can you drive a car?
  B Of course not! I'm only 14!
8 A You have a full-time job. Who takes care of your children?
  B They go to day care.
9 A Do you watch TV a lot?
  B No, not really, just in the morning, and in the evening, and sometimes in the afternoon.
10 A I can't speak any foreign languages.
  B I can. I can speak three languages. Japanese, Spanish, and Portuguese.

8 Refer students to **CD2 16** on SB p. 119. Have students memorize two conversations and practice them in closed pairs. Monitor and help as necessary. Ask some pairs to perform their conversations for the class.

Prepositions

9 **CD2 17** Pre-teach/check students' understanding of *What kind?* (= What type?), *phone/smartphone, be on the computer* (= using the computer). Focus students' attention on the example. Give students time to complete the task, working individually. Tell students that the lines are each part of a longer conversation. Play the recording and have students check their answers. Elicit as many replies as students can remember, then play the recording again.

Refer students to **CD2 17** on SB p. 120 and have them practice the conversations with a partner.

Answers and audio script
1 A Do you like listening to music?
  B Yes, of course. I have it all on my phone.
2 A What kind **of** music do you like?
  B All kinds, but especially jazz.
3 A Where's your girlfriend **from**? Is she Mexican?
  B No, she isn't. She's from Brazil. She speaks Portuguese.
4 A Is Paula married **to** Mike?
  B Yes, she is. Do you know her?
5 A Do you want to come shopping **with** me?
  B Oh, yes. Can you wait a minute? I'll get my coat.
6 A Were there any good shows **on** television last night?
  B I don't know. I was on my computer all evening.
7 A What do you want **for** your birthday?
  B Can I have a smartphone? Or is that too expensive?
8 A Can I speak to Dave? Is he **at** work today?
  B Sorry, he's on vacation all this week. He's back next week.

SUGGESTION

Ask students to personalize the language in the conversations in exercise 9. They can change the wording of the sentences but keep the language around the preposition the same, e.g., *I like listening to pop music.*

ADDITIONAL MATERIAL

Workbook Unit 5
Ex. 7 Verbs
Ex. 8 Noun + noun

Polite requests

> ⚠ **POSSIBLE PROBLEMS**
>
> Students already learned *can* for ability and its past form *could* earlier in this unit. This section focuses on *Can I … ?/Could I … ?* and *Can you … ?/Could you … ?* in polite requests. Students should recognize *Can I … ?* from earlier *Everyday English* sections, but may be confused at the use of *could* with present meaning. Although *Could you (do me a favor)?* has the same form as the past of *can*, the concept is in fact present. The *Caution box* covers the request and ability uses of *can/ could*, but be prepared to go over the time reference of key sentences with the class, e.g.,
>
> *Can/Could I use your phone?* (= present)
> *Can/Could you give me a lift?* (= present)
> *I can drive.* (= present)
> *I could drive when I was 17.* (= past)

1 **CD2 18** Start this section by making a couple of natural requests to students in the class, e.g., *Can you close the door, please? Could you switch on the lights, please?* etc. Focus students' attention on the photos. Give students time to read the conversations and guess the missing words. Play the recording and check the answers. Elicit where each conversation takes place (*1 in a café, 2 coming out of a building, 3 in a restaurant, 4 in the street*)

> **Answers and audio script**
> 1 **A** Can I have a **coffee**, please?
>   **B** Yes, of course.
> 2 **C** Can you open the **door** for me, please?
>   **D** Sure. No problem.
>   **C** Thanks.
> 3 **E** Could I have the **menu**, please?
>   **F** Certainly, ma'am.
> 4 **G** Could you **tell** me the **time**, please?
>   **H** It's 10:30.
>   **G** Thanks a lot.

2 Read the questions as a class. Give students time to discuss the answers in pairs before checking the answers with the class.

> **Answers**
> In conversations 1 and 2, the speaker uses *Can I/you …?*, in 3 and 4, he/she uses *Could I/you …?*
> *Could …?* is a little more polite than *Can …?*

Read the information about *can* and *could* as a class. Make sure that students understand the difference between *Can/Could I … ?* (to ask for things) and *Can/Could you … ?* (to ask other people to do things).

Review the ability use as a class.

If necessary, also go over the time references in the sentences (see *Possible problems* above).

3 **CD2 19** Focus students' attention on the intonation in the examples. The recording divides each sentence into three parts to make imitating the intonation easier. Play the recording. Students repeat each section of the sentences,

paying special attention to the intonation. If necessary, give students further practice with the conversations in exercise 1.

> **Audio script**
> | Can I …? | Can I have a …? | Can I have a coffee, please? |
> | Could you …? | Could you tell me …? | Could you tell me the time, please? |

4 **CD2 20** Focus students' attention on the example. Check students' understanding of *give me a hand* in number 6 (= help me) and then have students complete the task.

Play the recording and have students compare their answers. Elicit as many replies as students can remember, then play the recording again.

Refer students to **CD2 20** on SB p. 120 and have them practice the conversations with a partner. If students have problems with the request intonation, play key lines of the recording again and have them repeat.

> **Answers and audio script**
> 1 **A** Can I have a turkey and cheese sandwich, please?
>   **B** On white or wheat bread?
> 2 **A** **Could you** mail this letter for me, please?
>   **B** Yes, of course. No problem.
> 3 **A** **Can you** give me your email address?
>   **B** I think you have it already.
> 4 **A** **Can I** talk to you for a second?
>   **B** Can it wait? I'm a little busy.
> 5 **A** **Could you** lend me 20 dollars until tomorrow?
>   **B** I can lend you ten, but not 20.
> 6 **A** **Can you** give me a hand with this box?
>   **B** Of course. Do you want it upstairs?

5 Ask two students to read the example conversation aloud. Give students time to read the list of prompts. Answer any questions about vocabulary.

Put students in pairs to practice the conversations. Monitor and help as necessary.

> **SUGGESTION**
>
> Integrate the language of requests into your lessons in a natural way and encourage students to use the language themselves, e.g., asking students to open/close the window, hand out books/materials, sit in a particular place/work with a particular student, asking to borrow an object, asking for help with a word/exercise, asking someone to pass something to you.

> **Photocopiable Activity**
>
> **UNIT 5 Words that go together TB p. 148**
>
> **Materials:** One copy of the worksheet for each group of three/four students, cut up into dominoes. An uncut version of the game for you to use to check answers.
>
> **Procedure:** Explain that students are going to play a game to help them remember some of the language from the *Vocabulary* and *Everyday English* sections of the SB.
>
> • Divide students into groups of three or four and give each group a set of dominoes placed face down on the table.

- Pre-teach/check students' understanding of useful language for playing the game: *Whose turn is it? It's my/your turn. I can't go. Take another card. Do these cards match? I don't think that's right. Can you check with the teacher?*
- Students take three dominoes each and leave the rest in the pile face down.
- Explain the rules: the first student places a domino on the desk face up. The second student looks at his/her dominoes and tries to find a card that will match with the words on one of the sides. If he/she can't go, they have to take another card. He/She can put this card down if it matches, otherwise play passes to the next person. The game continues in the same way for each member of the group. The first player to get rid of all their dominoes is the winner.
- Students play the game in their groups. Remind students to think about the context of the words and to go for the most logical matches that might occur in everyday situations. Go around listening, helping, and correcting any incorrectly matched cards as necessary. (The answers appear on the uncut worksheet, reading from the bottom right up to top left and then across.)
- After playing the game, students take turns choosing a card and then trying to complete each sentence half orally. They can either try to remember what was on the dominoes, or they can come up with their own version.

ADDITIONAL MATERIAL

Workbook Unit 5
Ex. 10 Polite requests

Don't forget!

Workbook Unit 5
Ex. 11 Vocabulary
Ex. 12 *and/but/so/because*
Ex. 13 Prepositions of place
Ex. 14 Verb + noun
Grammar Reference (SB p. 133)
Word list Unit 5 (SB p. 141)
Students can translate the words, learn them at home, or transfer some of them to their vocabulary notebook.
Tests (Online)
Unit 5 Test
Video (iTools and Online)
Additional photocopiables and PPT™ presentations (iTools)

6 Life's ups and downs

Simple Past (1) – regular and irregular • **Describing feelings** • **What's the date?**

VIDEO ◄ Life events

The theme of "Life's ups and downs" provides the context for the presentation of both regular and irregular forms of the Simple Past. The formation of the question and negative is also introduced briefly as a lead-in to Unit 7, where it is one of the main grammatical goals. The skills work includes a *Reading and listening* section with a story about what matters in life, and a Writing section which focuses on linking words. These also provide further practice of the Simple Past.

LANGUAGE INPUT

GRAMMAR
Simple Past – regular verbs (SB p. 42)
Simple Past – irregular verbs (SB p. 44)

- Understanding and practicing the addition of -*ed* in Simple Past forms.
- Understanding and practicing irregular verb forms to talk about the past.

VOCABULARY
Describing feelings (SB p. 48)

- Understanding and practicing adjectives ending in -*ed* and -*ing* in the context of talking about feelings.

EVERYDAY ENGLISH
What's the date? (SB p. 49)

- Understanding and practicing ordinal numbers in the context of talking about dates (months and years).

SKILLS DEVELOPMENT

READING
The meaning of life (SB p. 46)

- A short fable about a fisherman and a businessman, and what is important in life.

LISTENING
A dotcom millionaire (SB p. 44)
The meaning of life (SB p. 46)
Four conversations (SB p. 48)

- Listening for key information in an interview. **CD2 28** (SB p. 120)
- Listening for key words in a short story. **CD2 31** (SB p. 121)
- Listening for adjectives ending in -*ed* and -*ing* in four short conversations. **CD2 33** (SB p. 121)

SPEAKING
Talking about you (SB p. 45)
What do you think? (SB p. 46)

- Talking about what you did yesterday and last week/month/year, etc.
- Discussing the moral of a story and what you think happened next.

WRITING
A biography – Combining sentences (SB p. 105)

- Reviewing and understanding linking words, then writing a biography of someone successful.

MORE MATERIALS

Photocopiables – Focus on feelings (TB p. 149)   **Tests** (Online)   **Video** (iTools and Online)

STARTER (SB p. 42)

Check comprehension of *great-grandparents*. Demonstrate the activity by telling the class about your own grandparents and great-grandparents, answering each question in turn and giving as much information as you can. Use photos you have brought to class if appropriate.

Focus students' attention on the examples. Then elicit information from the students about their grandparents and great-grandparents. In larger classes, students can work in pairs/small groups and then share their responses with the class.

CANADA'S CREATIVE GENIUS (SB p. 42)

Simple Past (1) – regular verbs

This presentation takes the form of a profile of the Canadian billionaire and creator of Cirque du Soleil, Guy Laliberté. When learning the Simple Past, students build on their knowledge of the Simple Present, in that both tenses use a form of *do* as an auxiliary in the question and negative. It is not such a big leap to learn that the same auxiliary is used in its past tense form, *did*, to make the Simple Past tense, especially as this form remains the same in all persons.

Many of the exercises in this unit provide opportunities to contrast the Simple Present and Simple Past tenses. There are examples of the superlative adjective *richest* just for recognition.

⚠ **POSSIBLE PROBLEMS**

- Although students should be helped by their knowledge of the Simple Present (see above), the use of *did* can still cause problems. Students often misuse the form or forget to use the auxiliary altogether:

  *Where you lived when you were young?

  *When she start school?

  *She no liked her job.

- The different ways of pronouncing the *-ed* at the end of regular verbs is a problem. Students often want to pronounce the *-ed* in its entirety – /ɛd/ – and not the /t/, /d/, /ɪd/ endings:

  cleaned * /ˈkliːnɛd/ instead of /kliːnd/

  worked * /ˈwərkɛd/ instead of /wərkt/

  visited * /ˈvɪzətɛd/ instead of /vɪzɪtɪd/

There is an exercise on SB p. 44 to help students distinguish the different endings, but we suggest not spending too much time having students produce the endings at this stage so as not to overload them.

1 Focus students' attention on the photos of Guy Laliberté /gi la libɛrteɪ/ and ask students if they recognize him. Elicit any information/guesses about him as a child and now as an adult.

Pre-teach/check students' understanding of *billionaire, to give money to charity, aluminum, circus, performance art show, accordion, harmonica, juggled, stilts, earn money, a huge hit, acrobats, have access to*.

2 **CD2 21** Text **A** is about Guy Laliberté's life now and so reviews the Simple Present before moving to the introduction of the Simple Past in texts **B** and **C**. Ask students to read and listen to text **A** and fill in the missing verbs. Play the recording and then check the answers. Make sure students have spelled their answers correctly.

Answers and audio script
A THE MAN
Guy Laliberté **is** the founder and owner of Cirque du Soleil, the famous international performance group. He **lives** in Montreal, Canada, but he **has** many homes around the world. He also has an island and a boat. Guy is one of the richest people in Canada. He **earns** millions of dollars every year. He **gives** a lot of money to charity.

Elicit the answers to the questions in exercise 2.

Answers
Yes, he is.
He lives in Montreal, Canada.
He earns millions of dollars every year.

Ask a few additional questions about Guy's life now, e.g., *What does he do?* (He's the founder and owner of Cirque du Soleil.) *Where are his homes?* (All around the world.) *What does he do with his money?* (He gives a lot of it to charity.)

3 **CD2 22** Tell your students that they are going to listen to and read about Guy's past in text **B**. Play the recording through once. Then check the answers to the questions in exercise 3.

Answers
He was born in Quebec City, Canada.
No, they weren't.
He produced several performance art shows. He learned to play the accordion and the harmonica.

GRAMMAR SPOT

Go over the exercises one by one, providing the answers after each exercise.

1 Students complete the sentences with the correct form of *live*. Check the answers.

Answers
Now he **lives** in Montreal.
When he was a child, he **lived** in Quebec City.

2 Refer students to text **B**. Have them find examples of the verbs. Check the answers.

Answers
...and his father **worked** at an aluminum company.
In high school, he **produced** several performance art shows.
He also **learned** to play the accordion and the harmonica really well.

Then have students figure out the rule for forming the Simple Past of regular verbs.

Answer
To form the Simple Past of regular verbs, add *-ed* or *-d* to the infinitive.

▶▶ Read Grammar Reference 6.1 on p. 134 together in class, and/ or ask students to read it at home. Encourage them to ask you questions about it.

4 **CD2 23** Check comprehension of *publish, join,* and *move.* Students work in pairs to decide on the Simple Past form of the verbs in the box. Have them try and practice the pronunciation.

Play the recording and have students check their answers. Play the recording again and have students repeat. Students spell the Simple Past forms. Pay particular attention to the additional *n* in *plan - planned*.

You can point out that the endings can be grouped according to pronunciation, but do not spend too long on this, as students will focus on pronunciation on p. 44.

Answers and audio script

played	traveled	joined	published
returned	planned	moved	earned

5 **CD2 24** Explain that text **C** gives more information about Guy's work and his more recent life. Explain that students need to use the verbs in exercise 4 in the Simple Past form.

Focus students' attention on the blank in the first sentence and play the first sentence on the recording. Play the rest of the recording without pausing and have students complete the text. Alternatively, students try to fill in the blanks with the verbs before they listen, and then listen and check their answers against the recording.

Go over the answers as a class, having students take turns reading aloud part of the text. Correct their pronunciation of past tense verbs in preparation for the exercise on pronunciation in the Practice section on p. 44.

Answers and audio script
C His success
When Guy was 18, he **moved** to Europe. He didn't have a lot of money, so on his first night in London he stayed on a park bench. Guy **earned** a little money by performing on the streets. He **played** instruments and juggled, and he learned to eat fire and walk on stilts! Soon he **joined** a group of performers. They **traveled** around Europe doing street shows. But he didn't earn much money. So did he give up? No!

Guy **returned** to Quebec. There, he **planned** some street parties and festivals. In 1984, his troupe received $1.2 million from the Quebec government to present a street show for a national celebration. The show, called Cirque du Soleil, was a success. Guy and his troupe organized more shows, and soon Cirque du Soleil was a huge hit. Now, it performs shows all over the world. Millions of people love the show's acrobats, its color, and its creativity. Laliberté is now a billionaire thanks to Cirque du Soleil.

His charity work
Laliberté started the One Drop Foundation in 2007. The foundation helps people all over the world have access to clean water. In 2009, Guy was the first Canadian private space explorer. From space, he took photos of the earth, especially of water. In June 2011, Laliberté published Gaia, a book that included these photos of the earth. Money from the sales of his book go to the One Drop Foundation. Laliberté is a man who makes a true difference in the world!

GRAMMAR SPOT

1 Refer students back to text **C** about Guy and have them find a question and two negatives. With weaker classes, review how to form Simple Present questions and negatives with *do/does* and *don't/doesn't*.

Answers
So did he give up?
He didn't have a lot of money,
But he didn't earn much money.

2 Go over the formation of questions with the whole class. Point out the use of the past auxiliary *did* in the *wh*-question. Point out that *did* is followed by the stem of the main verb: *did ... work* (NOT **did ... worked*).

3 Go over the formation of the negative with the whole class. Point out that *didn't* is followed by the stem of the main verb: *didn't have* (NOT **didn't had*). Having the main verb in the Simple Past form, although incorrect, may seem more logical to students.

▶▶ Read Grammar Reference 6.2 on p. 134 together in class, and/or ask students to read it at home. Encourage them to ask you questions about it.

6 **CD2 25** This exercise focuses on question formation in the Simple Past. Focus students' attention on the example and then have students work in pairs complete the questions.

Play the recording so that students can check their answers. Play the recording again, pausing after each question (or say them yourself) and have students repeat them both chorally and individually. Ask other students to provide the answers. Encourage natural falling intonation on each one.

Where did his father work?

Students continue practicing the questions and answers in pairs. Monitor and check for accurate formation of Simple Past questions and negatives. Be prepared to drill the forms again if students have problems.

Answers and audio script
1 Where did his father work?
  At an aluminum company.
2 What **did** his mother do?
  She was a nurse.
3 What instruments **did** Guy **play** in high school?
  Harmonica and accordion.
4 Where **did** he **move** when he was 18?
  Europe.

5 Who **did** he **travel** with around Europe?
A group of performers.
6 What **did** his troupe **present** in 1984?
Cirque du Soleil.
7 Where **did** he **travel** to in 2009?
To space.
8 When **did** he **publish** a book?
In 2011.

PRACTICE (SB p. 44)

Talking about you

1 This activity brings together the past of *to be*, *to be born*, and *did* in Simple Past questions, so that students become aware of the difference between the past of the verb *to be* and main verbs. Focus students' attention on the example and elicit the missing verb forms in number 2.

Have students complete the questions on their own first and then check their answers in pairs. Check the answers with the whole class, asking individuals to read their answers aloud. Drill the questions, encouraging natural falling intonation.

Answers
1 Where were your parents born?
2 Where **did** you live when you **were** a child?
3 **Did** you live in a house or an apartment?
4 When **did** you start school?
5 Who **was** your first teacher?
6 Who **was** your best friend?
7 When **did** you learn to read and write?
8 When **did** you get your first cell phone?

2 Put students in pairs or groups of three to ask and answer the questions. Monitor and check for correct Simple Past question formation and intonation. (Alternatively, you can do this activity by having the class mingle. Ask students to get up and walk around the class, asking each question to a different student.)

3 After a few minutes, bring the class back together to report what information they can remember. Focus students' attention on the examples in the Student Book and remind them of the third-person singular form *was born*.

Sample answer
Pablo's father was born in Mexico City and his mother was born in Belize City. He lived in an apartment in Mexico City when he was a child. He started school in 1987. His first teacher was Señor Garcia. His best friend was Diego Gonzalez. He learned to read and write when he was five. He got his first cell phone in 2010.

EXTRA ACTIVITY

As reinforcement of exercise 1, ask students to write a short paragraph about themselves for homework.

Pronunciation

4 **CD2 26** Play the recording. Students listen to and repeat the three different pronunciations of the *-ed* ending.

5 **CD2 27** Play the recording. Students write the verbs in the correct column. Have them check their answers with a partner before checking the answers with the class.

Play the recording again. Students practice saying the verbs.

Answers and audio script
/t/ talked watched
/d/ cleaned received studied moved interviewed
     opened
/ɪd/ wanted decided

CD2 27

cleaned received studied wanted moved talked
watched interviewed opened decided

ADDITIONAL MATERIAL

Workbook Unit 6
Ex. 1–2 Simple Past (1)

BEN'S UPS AND DOWNS (SB p. 44)

Irregular verbs

> ⚠ **POSSIBLE PROBLEMS**
> • See the notes on TB p. 61 on the use of *did*.
> • There are a large number of irregular verbs to learn. From now on students should be encouraged to consult the irregular verb list on SB p. 152 and learn the irregular verbs as and when needed. You can start assigning some to learn for homework and giving short tests on them at the beginning of some lessons!

The context for the introduction of irregular verbs is a profile of another real-life millionaire – Ben Way, who made his fortune in the computer boom of the 1990s. The term *dotcom* refers to a company or person that uses the Internet to sell products/services. Ben Way's company, Rainmakers, was created to exploit existing technologies on the Internet and develop new ones.

SUGGESTION

All of the irregular verbs in exercise 1 appear at some point later in this unit, so your students need to become familiar with them as quickly as possible. You can assign exercise 1 for homework prior to the lesson and then go over it quickly in class.

1 Refer students to the irregular verb list on SB p. 152. Make sure they understand that it is an important resource that they should refer to regularly.

Elicit one or two examples of the Simple Past forms. Ask students to work with a partner and check the other irregular forms. If appropriate, let students use dictionaries to look up new words.

Students read the correct answers aloud. Model pronunciation of the verbs and have students repeat chorally and individually. Check pronunciation of the more difficult forms, e.g., *caught* /kɔt/.

Read Grammar Reference 6.3 on p. 134 together in class, and/or ask students to read it at home. Encourage them to ask you questions about it.

2 Check students' understanding of the expression *ups and downs* (good and bad periods of life). Elicit a few examples of ups and downs that students have experienced.

Focus students' attention on the photos of Ben Way and check students' understanding of *dotcom millionaire* (a person who made a lot of money by selling products/services on the Internet). Give students time to read the introduction about Ben. Ask *What were Ben's ups and downs in life?* (He made his first million at 17. He was one of the first dotcom millionaires. Then he lost all his money, but now he's a millionaire again.)

3 Pre-teach/check students' understanding of *dyslexic*, *software program*, *company*, and *entrepreneur*. Read the first sentence of the profile on page 45 with the class and then elicit the missing verb for number 2 (*went*).

Give students time to complete the profile, working individually. Students check their answers in pairs before listening to the recording in exercise 4.

Listening

4 **CD2 28** Tell students that the recording is in the form of a conversation between Ben and an interviewer and that the profile in exercise 3 is a summary of what the speakers talk about. Students are required only to select key points to check the verbs in the profile.

Play the recording. Students listen and check their answers to exercise 3. Play the recording again if students have missed any of the key verbs. Check the answers with the class.

Play the recording again. Give students time to discuss in pairs any further information they understood. Elicit examples from the class.

Answers and audio script

1	was	7	began
2	went	8	left
3	couldn't	9	made
4	gave	10	had
5	took	11	won
6	wrote	12	lost

I = Interviewer   B = Ben Way

I Hi Ben. Nice to meet you. Can you tell us a bit about your life?

B Well, I was born on September 28th, 1980 in Devon in the southwest of England.

I Mm. And what did your parents do?

B My dad was an accountant and my mum was an artist.

I Did you go to school in Devon?

B Yes, I did. I went to a small village school.

I Did you enjoy school?

B No, I didn't enjoy it at all. I had problems because I was dyslexic, and couldn't read and write …

I Ah, that's difficult …

B Yes, but when I was nine my dad gave me a computer and it changed my life. I loved it, I took it everywhere with me. I helped my friends and my parents' friends with their computers.

I Very good – and then …?

B Then, I wrote my first software program when I was just 11, and when I was 15 I began my own computer company.

I Oh that's fantastic! Was it successful?

B Yes, very successful – so successful that I left school at 16 and …

I Yes, I know … you were a millionaire at 17!

B Yes, I made my first £1 million at 17 and at 19 I had £18.5 million.

I And at 20 you won "Young Entrepreneur of the Year."

B Yes, I did. I often went on TV and radio and talked about it. It was amazing!

I And then one year later …?

B Yes, and then just a year later, when I was 21, I lost everything. Disaster! The dotcom businesses everywhere went down.

I Yeah, but now you're up again! Another company, another £1 million!

B I know. I work hard but I'm also very lucky!

Note This interview with Ben Way is fictitious and is based on factual information from a number of sources.

5 Briefly review how to say 19– dates and if you think your students need to practice dates, ask the class to chant the years from 1990 to 2000.

Focus students' attention on the example question. Give students time to write the other questions in the exercise. Monitor and help as necessary. With weaker classes, go over the question formation as a class activity before students do the pairwork.

Focus students' attention on the example again and elicit the complete answer. Students work in pairs to ask and answer the rest of the questions. Insist on complete answers so that they get practice with the irregular past forms. Check for accurate question formation and falling intonation. If students have problems, drill the questions and answers in open pairs and then have students repeat the pairwork.

Check the answers with the whole class. Correct any mistakes in the question formation and use of irregular pasts carefully.

Answers

1 What did Ben's parents do? His father was an accountant and his mother was an artist.

2 Where did he do to school? He went to a small village school in Devon.

3 Why did he have problems at school? He was dyslexic.

4 What did his dad give him in 1989? He gave him a computer.

5 Who did he help with their computers? He helped his friends and his parents' friends with their computers.

6 Why did he leave school at 16? He left school at 16 because his first computer company was very successful.

7 When did he win "Young Entrepreneur of the Year"? He won "Young Entrepreneur of the Year" in 2000.

8 Why did he lose his money? He lost his money because dotcom businesses everywhere went down.

Regular and irregular verbs

1 **CD2 29** This exercise gives controlled practice of both regular and irregular past forms. Focus students' attention on the example. Give students time to complete the rest of the sentences. Remind them to look at the list of irregular verbs on p. 152 if they need help with any of the forms.

Play the recording and have students check their answers. With weaker students, go over each verb form and ask *Regular or irregular?* Also drill the pronunciation if students have problems.

> **Answers and audio script**
> 1 My granddad was born in 1932. He **died** in 2009.
> 2 My parents **met** in Los Angeles in 1983. They **got** married in 1985.
> 3 I **arrived** late for the lesson. It **began** at two o'clock.
> 4 I **caught** the bus to school today. It **took** just 40 minutes.
> 5 I **had** a very busy morning. I **sent** 30 emails before 10 o'clock.
> 6 Our soccer team **won** the game 3–0. Your team **lost** again.
> 7 My brother **earned** a lot of money at his last job, but he **left** because he **didn't like** it.
> 8 I **studied** Chinese for four years, but when I **went** to Shanghai, I **couldn't** understand a word.

Talking about you

2 Focus students' attention on the example. Give some true sentences about yourself, using a range of different prompts from the exercise. Give students time to make their own sentences. If you want to reinforce the formation of the past tense verbs, have students write the sentences out in their notebook. Monitor and help as necessary.

Demonstrate exchanges starting with both affirmative and negative forms. Highlight the use of extra information and follow-up questions to make the exchange more interesting, e.g.,

A *I watched TV yesterday.*
B *Oh, what did you watch?*
A *A show about a poor man who became a millionaire. What about you?*
B *I watched a soccer game, but my team lost.*
C *I didn't watch TV yesterday. I was out with friends. What about you?*
D *I watched the news and then I listened to music. Where did you go with your friends?*
C *We went to the movies. We saw the new Johnny Depp movie.*
D *Was it good?*
C *It was OK.*

Put the students in pairs to continue the pairwork. Alternatively, students can do the task as a whole-class mingle. Monitor and check for accurate use of Simple Past forms and question formation. Highlight and correct any common errors.

3 Focus students' attention on the time expressions, pointing out that we can't use *last* with parts of a day, except *night*. Check pronunciation and then have students give a few examples of the time expressions in context, e.g., *I went to the movies last night.*

Check pronunciation of the question form, highlighting the main stresses, e.g.,
When did you last have a vacation?
Drill the question form chorally and individually. Then put students in pairs to ask and answer the questions. You can suggest that they take notes about each other. Monitor and help as necessary.

4 With weaker classes, briefly check the past form of the verbs in the list in exercise 3. Bring the class together and elicit examples of what students learned about their partner.

> **SUGGESTION**
>
> You can provide further practice of the Simple Past by asking students to write a short description of the year they were born. Tell students where and when you were born and give examples of key people/events/trends in that year, e.g., world leaders, sports events, science, popular songs/artists/movies, trends in cars/fashion/design, famous people, etc. Write the above categories on the board and have students find out information about the year they were born for homework. If you have access to computers, students can do this during class time.
>
> With weaker classes, build a skeleton paragraph on the board with the students to help them with the writing task, e.g.,
>
> *I was born on … in … . In that year … was the leader of my country. Other important leaders were… . In sports … won … and … became world champion in … . In science … made … . Millions of people bought a … . In music, … sang … and … had hit records.*
>
> When students have written about the year they were born, put them into pairs or small groups to exchange information. Elicit any interesting examples from the class.

A biography
Combining sentences

*[handwritten: John likes running, and Mary likes it too.
(because) John likes running, so he bought a good pair of running shoes.
John likes running, but he hates biking.]*

The writing syllabus continues with the second focus on linking words. Students practiced *and*, *so*, *but*, and *because* in Unit 4. This section reviews those linking words and also includes *however*, *when*, and *until*. The theme of the biography is a successful person and the subject of exercise 1 is Ben Way, the dotcom millionaire students learned about on pp. 44–45. Students do a matching exercise and then a fill-in-the-blanks exercise to practice the use of the linking words, before writing a short text about a successful person that they know. The writing task also reinforces the use of Simple Present and Simple Past.

1 Focus students' attention on the photo of Ben Way and ask students what they can remember about him. Elicit a range of information.

Pre-teach/check students' understanding of *to continue*, *to run a company*, *to win a business award*, *to do well*. Check comprehension of *however* and *until* via translation or by having students look the words up in dictionaries.

Focus students' attention on the sentence halves in columns **A** and **C**. Explain that they are in the correct order and students have to choose the correct word in column **B** to connect them. They also need to pay attention to the punctuation at the end of column **A** to help them choose the correct answer. With weaker students, highlight the use of the capital letter in *However* to indicate the start of a new sentence.

As an example, elicit the correct word to connect the first sentence (*and*). Then give students time to complete the task in pairs.

CD2 30 Play the recording and have students compare their answers. Students then take turns reading the sentences aloud. Correct any pronunciation, drilling key lines as necessary.

> **Answers and audio script**
> Ben Way is 35 years old, **and** he runs a company called "Rainmakers."
> Ben's a computer millionaire. **However**, he wasn't always so successful.
> As a child he was dyslexic, **so** he didn't do well at school.
> He didn't read or write **until** he was nine and his father gave him a computer.
> He wrote his first software program **when** he was only 11.
> He didn't go to university **because** at 15 he started his own company.
> He first became a millionaire **when** he was just 17.
> He continued to be very successful **until** he was 21.
> He won a business award in 2000, **but** then in 2001 he lost it all.
> One year later he started "Rainmakers," **and** now he's a millionaire again.

2 Give an example by answering the questions in exercise 2 about someone you know who is successful. Then give students time to write notes about their chosen person, using the questions as prompts.

Divide the class into pairs and have students exchange information about their person, using the questions in the exercise and their notes. Check for correct use of Simple Present and Simple Past and, if necessary, briefly review the use of the tenses for present habits and past events.

3 Focus students' attention on the photo and pre-teach/ check students' understanding of *dress designer*, *artistic*, *fashion school*, and *stay in touch*. Give students time to read through the text quickly to get a general idea of what it is about. Elicit the first two missing linking words as examples and then have students complete the text. With weaker students, remind them to look carefully at the punctuation to help them choose their answers.

Give students time to check answers in pairs before checking answers with the class.

> **Answers**
> 1 and 2 when 3 because 4 until 5 However 6 so
> 7 because 8 but 9 when 10 so 11 However 12 because

4 Write a paragraph plan from the questions in exercise 2 for students to follow when they write their own text:

Paragraph 1: What is his/her name? How old is he/she? What does he/she do?

Paragraph 2: How do you know him/her?
Did he/she do well in school?
How did he/she become successful?
Did he/she have any ups and downs?

Paragraph 3: When and where do you see him/her?

With weaker students, elicit the key structures needed to write the biography, e.g., *My [person and name] is [age] … . He is a [job] … . We met in … [place] when we were … [age]*, etc.

Give students time to write their text in class or assign it for homework. If possible, display the texts on the classroom wall/noticeboard to allow students to read each other's work. You can ask them to vote for the most interesting biography. When you check the students' work, point out errors, but allow students to correct them themselves. Try to limit correction to major problems to avoid demoralizing students.

ADDITIONAL MATERIAL

Workbook Unit 6
Ex. 3–4 Simple Past (1)

LISTENING AND READING (SB p. 46)

The meaning of life

> **ABOUT THE TEXT**
>
> The reading section in this unit is in the form of a fable (a traditional story which teaches a moral lesson). It gives students the opportunity to enjoy a change of genre from the more factual texts of the earlier units.
>
> The story has narrative and dialogue sections and so provides recycling of Simple Present and Simple Past forms (regular and irregular). The conversation in **CD2 31** is a summary of the wording of the main story. Even though the wording in the recording isn't exactly the same as the main story, the key sections are close enough for students to be able to pick out the key words. There are examples of comparatives in the story, but these are for recognition only.
>
> *Harvard* /ˈhɑrvərd/ is a prestigious university in Cambridge, Massachusetts. It is the oldest institution of higher education in the USA. LA is short for *Los Angeles* /ˌlɔs ˈændʒələs/, the second largest city in the US, in California on the Pacific Coast. *Señor* is the Spanish for *sir*. The yellowfin tuna is one of the biggest species of tuna, found near the Hawaiian Islands, Indian Ocean, Caribbean, and Western Pacific.
>
> Encourage students to use the pictures in the Student Book and the context to help them with new vocabulary, and to pool knowledge with other students. With weaker classes or if you are short of time, ask students to look up the meanings of some of the following vocabulary before the lesson:
>
> **Homework prior to the lesson**
> *fishing village*, *boat*, *tuna fish*, *to take* (= need a particular amount of time), *to smile*, *to take a nap* (= have a short sleep in the afternoon), *fleet of boats*, *to export*, *to sell*, *gentleman*, *advice*.

1 Introduce the theme of the story by asking students *What does a businessman do? And a fisherman? How are their lives different?* Elicit a range of answers from the class.

Focus students' attention on the picture and ask students to point to the fisherman and the businessman. Elicit any other basic information about the situation.

Read the questions as a class and then give students time to read the first part of the story. Answer any questions about vocabulary if you didn't pre-teach the items listed in *About the text*. Check the answers with the class.

Answers
He was on vacation in a fishing village.
He met a young fisherman.
Yes, he did.
He said, "What beautiful tuna!"

---

2 **CD2 31** With weaker students, pre-teach/check understanding of some of the key vocabulary from the conversation (see *About the text*). Tell students they are going to hear a conversation between the two men. They don't need to understand every word, but should listen for key information about the fisherman's life and the suggestions that the businessman makes.

Play the recording through once. Elicit who the students think has a better life. Encourage them to give reasons for their answers.

Audio script
B = Businessman   F = fisherman
FC = Fisherman's children

B Good morning. What beautiful tuna! How long did it take to catch them?

F Oh, about two hours.

B Only two hours! Amazing! Why didn't you fish for longer and catch more?

F I didn't want to fish for longer. With this I have enough fish for my family.

B But what do you do with the rest of your day? Aren't you bored?

F I'm never bored. I get up late, play with my children, watch soccer, and take a nap. Sometimes in the evenings, I walk to the village to see my friends, play the guitar, and sing some songs.

B Really? That's all you do? Look, I am a very successful businessman. I went to an excellent college and I studied business. I can help you. Fish for four hours every day and sell the extra fish you catch …

F But …

B … Then, you can buy a bigger boat, catch more, and earn more money.

F But …

B … Then buy a second boat, a third, and so on, until you have a big fleet of fishing boats.

F But …

B … and you can export the fish, and leave this village, and move to the big city, and open a fishing business.

F OK, OK, but how long will all this take?

B Uh – let me think – uh, probably about 15 to 20 years.

F 15 to 20 years! And then what, sir?

B Why, that's the exciting part! You can sell your business and become very rich, a millionaire.

F A millionaire? Really? But what do I do with all the money?

B Well, let me think. Uh – I know, you can stop work and – uh, move to a beautiful, old fishing village where you can sleep late, play with your grandchildren, watch soccer, take a nap, and walk to the village in the evenings where you can play the guitar and sing with your friends all you want.

F Um – well …

FC Daddy, Daddy, did you catch many fish?

F I caught enough for us today and tomorrow and also some for this gentleman. Please, sir, have some of my beautiful fish. Goodbye, sir. Come on children, let's go home.

---

3 Put students in pairs to do the true/false task. Encourage them to do as many sentences as they can from memory. If students have problems, play the recording again and let them check/complete their answers.

Answers
1 True.
2 False. It took him two hours to catch the tuna.
3 True.
4 False. He is never bored.
5 True.
6 True.
7 True.
8 False. He went home with his family.

---

4 **CD2 31** Give students time to read and complete the story. Monitor and help as necessary.

Have students check their answers in pairs. Point out that the recording doesn't have exactly the same wording as the story in the Student Book, but the dialogue sections are the same and so students should be able to pick out the key words to check their answers.

Play **CD2 31** again. Check the answers with the class. Ask students to spell the Simple Past forms or to write their answers on the board.

Answers and audio script

1	two	5	some	9	about
2	didn't	6	went	10	stop
3	have	7	studied	11	did
4	late	8	earn	12	caught

CD2 31
See exercise 2 above.

---

5 This exercise gives students the opportunity to retell the story, using their own words where possible. If you have a large class, students can work in groups of about six to give everyone the opportunity to tell a part of the story. Read the opening of the story aloud: *An American businessman was on vacation in a fishing village in the south of Mexico. One morning … .* Then have the class continue the story, each student telling a small section before moving on to the next student. Encourage the class to help and prompt each other if they get any of the main events wrong or if they can't remember what happened next. With weaker students, write key words for each section on the board as prompts.

What do you think?

Check comprehension of *moral* (the main lesson of the story) and *what matters* (what is really important).

Put students into groups of three or four to discuss their answers. Monitor and help as necessary, but don't interrupt or over-correct as this is primarily a fluency task.

Allow the discussion to continue for as long as students' interest is held, and exchanges are taking place mainly in English! Elicit a range of opinions from the class and establish the moral of the story (*Understand what really matters in life.*)

EXTRA ACTIVITIES

- Ask students to imagine that the fisherman and the businessman meet again five years later. Students roleplay the conversation between the two men in pairs. They can then act out their conversations for the class and compare their ideas.
- If your students are interested in storytelling, have them research a fable or traditional short story from their own country for homework. They should take notes about the main characters and events, and not simply print out the complete story. Students then work in pairs/small groups to tell each other their story. This works particularly well in multilingual groups as students can exchange stories from a range of cultures.

ADDITIONAL MATERIAL

Workbook Unit 6
Ex. 5   Reading
Ex. 6   Listening

VOCABULARY AND LISTENING (SB p. 48)

Describing feelings

1   Demonstrate the activity by having students find the correct picture for *bored* (picture a). Students match the rest of the feelings to the pictures.

Check the answers with the whole class. Drill the pronunciation of the adjectives.

> **Answers**
> a bored   d interested
> b excited   e worried
> c tired   f annoyed

2   **CD2 32** Elicit the answer to number 1 as an example. Students continue the activity in pairs. Then play the recording and have students check their answers.

> **Answers and audio script**
> 1 I went to bed late last night, so I'm very **tired** today.
> 2 My soccer team lost again. I'm really **annoyed**!
> 3 I won $20,000 in the lottery! I'm so **excited**!
> 4 I can't find my house keys. I'm really **worried**.
> 5 I have nothing to do and nowhere to go. I am so **bored**.
> 6 The professor gave a great lecture. I was really **interested**.

-ed and -ing adjectives

Read the notes on *-ed* and *-ing* adjectives with the whole class. Using L1 if appropriate, explain that adjectives ending in *-ed* often describe a person's feeling or reactions, and that adjectives ending in *-ing* often describe the person or thing that causes those feelings or reactions.

3   Focus students' attention on the pair of sentences in number 1 as an example and elicit the missing adjectives (*exciting*, *excited*) Students complete the rest of the exercise.

Check the answers with the whole class. Drill the pronunciation of the pairs of adjectives, making sure students can clearly distinguish the *-ing* and *-ed* forms.

If students need further practice, drill the complete sentences in exercise 3 chorally and individually.

> **Answers**
> 1 Life in New York City is very **exciting**.
>   It's my birthday tomorrow. I'm really **excited**.
> 2 The marathon runners were very **tired**.
>   That game of tennis was very **tiring**.
> 3 The child's behavior was really **annoying**.
>   The teacher was **annoyed** because nobody did the homework.
> 4 We were very **worried** when we heard the news.
>   The news is very **worrying**.

SUGGESTION

You can give students further practice by asking a range of questions and having students respond with a suitable adjective in the correct form (sample questions and answers are given below). Elicit a range of answers by asking several students the same question.

Did you enjoy the last movie you saw? (Yes, it was interesting.)
Why don't you run six miles every morning? (Because it's tiring.)
How do you feel after the lesson? (A little tired.)
How do you feel before a test? (Very worried.)
How do you feel if your friend is late? (A little annoyed.)
Do you like soccer? (No, it's very boring.)
Do you like learning English? (Yes, it's interesting, but a little tiring.)

4   **CD2 33** Give students time to read the conversations. Answer any questions about vocabulary students may have and check the pronunciation of *laugh* /læf/. Students complete the conversations, working in pairs. With weaker students, write the missing adjectives on the board in random order to help them fill in the blanks.

Play the recording and have students check their answers. Students practice the conversations in their pairs. Monitor and check. If students have problems, play selected sections of the recording again and have students repeat. Students then practice the conversations again.

> **Answers and audio script**
> 1 A Did you enjoy the movie?
>   B No, I didn't. It was **boring**.
>   A Oh, I loved it. It was really **interesting** and very funny.
>   B I didn't laugh once!
> 2 A How was your exam?
>   B Awful. I'm very **worried**.
>   A But you worked really hard.
>   B I know, I studied until two in the morning, but then I was so **tired** today, I couldn't read the questions.
>   A Don't worry. I'm sure you'll be OK.
> 3 A That was a great game! Really **exciting**!
>   B Only because your team won. I was **bored**.
>   A But it wasn't **boring** at all! It was a terrific game!
>   B Well, I didn't enjoy it, and now I'm **annoyed** because I paid $45 for my ticket.
> 4 A When's Nina's birthday?
>   B You mean 'When *was* her birthday?' It was last Friday, March 24th.
>   A Oh no! Was she **annoyed** that I forgot?
>   B No, no, she was just **worried** that you didn't like her anymore.

5 Refer students back to the text on p. 47 to find examples of *-ed* and *-ing* adjectives.

> **Answers**
> Aren't you bored?
> Why, that's the exciting part!
> The young fisherman didn't look excited.

Photocopiable Activity

UNIT 6 Focus on feelings TB p. 149

Materials: One copy of the worksheet for each student.

Procedure: Explain that students are going to complete a worksheet to practice the language of feelings from the *Vocabulary and listening* section of the Student Book.

- Pre-teach/check students' understanding of the following *-ed/-ing* adjectives: *frightened/frightening, embarrassed/embarrassing, irritated/irritating, surprised/surprising*. There are examples of superlative adjectives in the sentences, but these are for recognition only.

- Hand out a copy of the worksheet to each student. Give the class time to read the statements in exercise 1. Answer any vocabulary questions. Students choose the correct adjectives in the statements 1–10. Check the answers with the class, addressing any pronunciation difficulties.

> **Answers**
> 1 tiring   6 interesting
> 2 frightened   7 bored
> 3 annoyed   8 worried
> 4 embarrassed   9 exciting
> 5 irritating   10 surprised

- Focus students' attention on the underlined sections of the sentences. Elicit different endings for sentence 1 from a range of students. With weaker students, go over all the sentences and make sure that students know which are present and which are past. Give students time to personalize each of the sentences, working individually. Monitor and help as necessary.

- Put students into pairs or small groups to compare their answers. Monitor and help as necessary, but do not interrupt or over-correct as this is the fluency stage of the activity. Write down any common errors, but discuss them at a later stage.

- As an extension, have students write three of their personalized sentences on strips of paper without writing their name. Collect the papers and redistribute them randomly to other students. Students take turns reading the paper aloud to the class and trying to guess who wrote it.

ADDITIONAL MATERIAL

Workbook Unit 6

Ex. 7 Describing feelings

EVERYDAY ENGLISH (SB p. 49)

What's the date?

> ⚠ **POSSIBLE PROBLEMS**
>
> Students will need regular review and practice to be able to say a range of dates fluently.
>
> * One of the main problems with ordinals is pronunciation. The sound /θ/ causes difficulty, and there are a lot of consonant clusters, e.g., *sixth* /sɪksθ/, *twelfth* /twɛlfθ/. In rapid speech, sounds are often dropped, for example /twɛlθ/ instead of /twɛlfθ/ and /fɪθ/ instead of /fɪfθ/.
>
> * Saying dates can also cause problems of form. We can begin with the month (April the third) or the date (the third of April), but in both cases we need to add *the*, which is usually not written, and in the latter case we need to add *of*, which is also usually not written. Years beginning 20– can also be read in two ways, e.g., 2012 = *two thousand twelve* or *twenty twelve*.
>
> * Some languages divide the date differently, e.g., 1999 – *one thousand nine hundred and ninety-nine*, so students need help with dividing the century and years correctly. Note that in American English, 3/8/12 means *the eighth of March 2012*, whereas in British English it means *the third of August 2012*.

1 **CD2 34** Focus students' attention on the example. Students work in pairs to match the words to the correct ordinals.

Check the answers by writing the ordinals on the board and eliciting the correct words.

Play the recording, pausing after each number and having students repeat chorally and individually. Drill the ordinals, correcting any mistakes.

> **Answers and audio script**
>
> | 1st | first | 6th | sixth | 17th | seventeenth |
> |-----|-------|------|-----------|------|---------------|
> | 2nd | second | 10th | tenth | 20th | twentieth |
> | 3rd | third | 12th | twelfth | 22nd | twenty-second |
> | 4th | fourth | 13th | thirteenth | 30th | thirtieth |
> | 5th | fifth | 16th | sixteenth | 31st | thirty-first |

2 Ask *What's the first month?* and elicit *January*. Students continue saying the months in order around the class. If necessary, review the pronunciation and word stress, drilling any difficult words chorally and individually. Check that students get the correct word stress in *January* /ˈdʒænyuˌɛri/ and *February* /ˈfɛbyuˌɛri/ and that they can distinguish *June* /dʒun/ and *July* /dʒuˈlaɪ/. Repeat until students can say all the months quickly and accurately, but don't let this stage go on too long.

3 Focus students' attention on the example and then have students ask and answer questions about the other months of the year. You don't need to let this go on for very long.

Focus on the notes about the different ways of writing and saying the dates. Highlight on the board how we divide dates beginning 18-, 19-, into two pairs of numbers and give practice of similar dates. Also have students practice a range of 20- dates.

4 **CD2 35** Elicit an example and then have students practice saying the dates. For the first five dates, they should practice saying them both ways. Students often have a lot of difficulty saying dates, so do the activity as a class and correct mistakes carefully.

Play the recording. Students listen and check.

> **Answers and audio script**
> 1 April first.
> 2 March second.
> 3 September seventeenth.
> 4 November ninth.
> 5 February 29th, 1976.
> 6 December nineteenth, 1983.
> 7 October third, 1999.
> 8 May 31st, 2005.
> 9 July 15th, 2015.

5 **CD2 36** Tell students they are going to hear six dates in total and they are given just as dates, not in a sentence or conversation context. Play number one as an example first.

Students listen and write down the dates they hear. Have them check answers in pairs before checking the answers with the class.

> **Answers and audio script**
> 1 October 31st
> 2 June 23rd
> 3 July 15th
> 4 March 4th, 2012
> 5 February 18th, 2020
> 6 September 17th, 1960

6 Students work in pairs to ask and answer the questions about dates. Monitor and discuss any common errors before checking the answers with the whole class.

> **Answers**
> (We can only give some of the answers.)
> 4 the 14th of February
> 7 the 21st century

7 Give a few examples of dates that are important to you, e.g., your birthday/wedding day, the start of your next vacation, the date of your next dentist's appointment, etc.

Students work in pairs to ask and answer the questions about dates. Monitor and help as necessary. Note any common errors and correct them after a short discussion with the whole class.

EXTRA ACTIVITY
You can give more practice of saying years by having students talk about key events in their country/around the world and having the rest of the class guess the year, e.g., *The Olympics were in Beijing* (2008). *Spain won the World Cup* (2010).

ADDITIONAL MATERIAL

Workbook Unit 6
Ex. 8   What's the date?

Don't forget!

Workbook Unit 6
Ex. 9   *do/does/did/didn't/was/were/had*
Ex. 10   *the* or no article
Grammar Reference (SB p. 134)
Word list Unit 6 (SB p. 142)
Students can translate the words, learn them at home, or transfer some of them to their vocabulary notebook.

Tests (Online)
Unit 6 Test
Skills Test 1 (Units 1–6)
Video (iTools and Online)
Additional photocopiables and PPT™ presentations (iTools)

7 Dates to remember

Simple Past (2) • Questions and negatives • Time expressions • Adverbs • Special occasions

VIDEO A special occasion

This is the second unit on the Simple Past tense, and it provides further practice and reinforcement of the grammar points in Unit 6, focusing particularly on question and negative forms. The title of this unit Is "Dates to remember" and the topics in the unit lend themselves to practice of the Simple Past and *ago*. The unifying theme of the unit is important moments in the past, with a quiz on important events in the 20th century, a *Speaking* section on "Talking about my life," and reading texts on progress in aviation.

LANGUAGE INPUT

GRAMMAR

Simple Past – questions and negatives   (SB p. 51)
- Understanding and practicing questions and negatives in the Simple Past.

Time expressions   (SB p. 52)
- Understanding and practicing *in/at/on* and *ago*.

VOCABULARY

Adverbs   (SB p. 56)
- Understanding and practicing regular and irregular adverbs in the context of telling a story.

EVERYDAY ENGLISH

Special occasions   (SB p. 57)
- Understanding and practicing the language of talking about special occasions; comparing special occasions in different countries.

SKILLS DEVELOPMENT

READING

Sixty years of flight   (SB p. 54)
- A jigsaw reading about the pioneers of air and space flight.

LISTENING

Angela's life story   (SB p. 53)
- Listening for key information in a conversation **CD2 42** (SB p. 122).

Noises in the night!   (SB p. 56)
- Listening and ordering adverbs in a short story **CD2 44** (SB p. 122).

SPEAKING

Bill's life   (SB p. 52)
- Information gap about a man's past.

Talking about my life   (SB p. 53)
- Telling your own life story.

Retelling a story   (SB p. 54)
- Retelling the story of the pioneers of air and space flight.

WRITING

Telling a story – Using time expressions   (SB pp. 106–7)
- Reviewing and understanding time expressions, then writing a description of a historical character.

MORE MATERIALS

Photocopiables – Adverb acting (TB p. 150)   **Tests** (Online)   **Video** (iTools and Online)

STARTER (SB p. 50)

> ⚠ **POSSIBLE PROBLEMS**
>
> The adverb *ago* is introduced in the multiple-choice answers in the *Starter* quiz. *Ago* is used when the point of reference is the present and it means "before now." It is used only with past tenses, not present or present perfect tenses. *Ago* can cause problems with word order, as it always comes after an expression of time, which may be different in the students' own language.
>
> Different languages express this concept in various ways.
>
> *two years ago* – *il y a deux ans* (French)
> – *vor zwei Jahren* (German)
> – *hace dos años* (Spanish)
> – *due anni fa* (Italian)
>
> **Common mistakes**
> - *I went there ago two weeks.*
> - *I went there before two weeks.*
> - *My cat died for two years.*

SUGGESTION

You can pre-teach *ago*, especially with weaker classes (see *Possible problems* above). Ask questions such as the following to help show the meaning of *ago*:
When was your last English lesson? (On Tuesday.)
How many days ago was that? (Two days ago.)
When did you last have a vacation? (In June.)
How many months ago was that? (Five months ago.)
When did you last go to the movies? (Last Friday.)
How many days ago was that? (Five days ago.)

1 Introduce the theme of the unit by asking *What was the most important event of the 20th century?* Elicit a range of answers from the class.

Briefly review the Simple Past irregular forms in the *Starter* quiz. Say the base form and elicit the past (*be – was/were, sell – sold, come – came, have – had*). Also review the way we say dates, e.g., *1903 – nineteen oh three, 1989 – nineteen eighty-nine*, etc.

Focus students' attention on the photos, ask *Who can you see?* and elicit any people/events that students recognize. Put students in groups of three to do the history quiz. Monitor and help as necessary.

2 **CD2 37** Play the recording and have students check their answers. Elicit any reactions to the answers and ask if students learned anything new.

If you didn't pre-teach *ago*, focus students' attention on questions 3 and 5 and explain its use now (see *Possible problems* and *Suggestion* above).

Answers and audio script
1 Henry Ford sold the first Model-T in 1908.
2 The first talking movie, *The Jazz Singer*, was in 1927.
3 Einstein published his theory of relativity about 100 years ago.
4 The Russian Revolution was in 1917.
5 The first nonstop flight around the world was about 60 years ago.
6 About 60 million people died in the Second World War.
7 The Berlin Wall came down in 1989.

8 People first landed on the moon on July 20, 1969.
9 The Beatles had 20 number 1 hits in the US.
10 The twentieth century ended at midnight on December 31, 2000.

THE GOOD OLD DAYS (SB p. 51)

Simple Past – questions and negatives

> ⚠ **POSSIBLE PROBLEMS**
>
> See the introduction to the Simple Past and problems associated with it on TB p. 60. There are a lot of opportunities to practice affirmative forms in this unit, but the main focus is on question forms and negatives. These present few problems of concept, but there can inevitably be mistakes of form.
>
> **Common mistakes**
> - *When you went home?*
> - *When did you went home?*
> - *Where did go Peter?*
> - *I no went out last night.*

Write the section heading *The Good Old Days* on the board. Explain that if you talk about *the good old days*, you mean a time in the past when you believe life was better. Ask students *How was life different when your grandparents were young?* Elicit a range of examples about everyday life from the class, e.g., work, school, transportation, vacations, etc.

1 **CD2 38** Focus students' attention on the photo of the people and ask students to identify Tommy and Bill. Also elicit what is shown in the other photos (*a beach vacation, an old car, an old black and white TV, an old-fashioned boys' comic*).

Check students' comprehension of the topics in exercise 1, making sure students don't confuse *housework* and *homework*. Tell students they are going to hear Tommy and Bill talking about the past, but that they don't need to understand every word to be able to do the task. Focus their attention on the example and play the recording through once. Check the answers with the class.

Answers and audio script
TV shows   allowance   housework   comic books   vacations

CD2 38
T = Tommy   B = Bill
T Grandpa, when you were a boy did you have television?
B Of course we had television! But it wasn't a color TV like we have now, it was black and white.
T And were there lots and lots of channels? How many TV channels were there?
B Only three. But that was enough! We loved it! And there weren't shows all day long. There was usually nothing on in the morning or in the afternoon!
T Oh, no! What time did TV shows start?
B At around 5:00 when children's TV started. There were some great shows for us children, I can tell you! We had real stories in those days!
T Did your mom and dad give you an allowance?

B Yes, but I worked for it! I cleaned the kitchen and did the dishes. We didn't have dishwashers in those days!

T That's terrible! How much allowance did you get?

B My dad gave me six cents a week. He didn't give me much, did he? But we bought comic books and candy.

T What kind of comic books did you buy?

B Well, I bought a comic book called *Pep Comics*, and it was full of adventure stories. And *Superman*! That was really exciting!

T Wow! Did you have vacations?

B Yes, but not like these days. People didn't go abroad. I never took a plane like people do now! It was too expensive!

T Where did you go on vacation?

B To the beach.

T How did you get there?

B My father drove. We had a Ford car, a Ford Coupe it was. We went to the same place every year.

T Why did you go to the same place? Why didn't you go somewhere different?

B Because we all liked it there!

T I'm glad I wasn't alive then! It sounds really boring!

B Oh, no! That's where you're wrong! It was the most fun ever!

2 **CD2 38** Pre-teach/check students' understanding of *TV channel, allowance, dishwasher, beach, go abroad, what kind?, adventure stories* and *drove* (past of *drive*). Focus students' attention on the example, then play the recording again and have students complete the questions. Ask them to write down the answer to each question.

CD2 39 Play the recording and have students check their answers. Check the answers with the class.

Answers and audio script
1 How many TV channels were there?
2 **What time** did TV shows start?
3 **How much** allowance **did** you get?
4 **What kind** of comic books **did** you **buy**?
5 **Where did** you **go** on vacation?
6 **How did** you **get** there?
7 **Why did** you go to the same place?

Students ask and answer question 1 in open pairs and then continue the task in closed pairs. With weaker classes, you can write the answers from the script in random order on the board (see *Answers* below). Monitor and help as necessary. If students have problems with the sentence stress and intonation, play the recording again and drill the questions. Check the questions and answers with the class.

Answers
1 How many TV channels were there?
Only three.
2 What time did TV shows start?
At around 5:00.
3 How much allowance did you get?
Six cents a week.
4 What kind of comic books did you buy?
A comic book called *Pep Comics* full of adventures stories, and *Superman*.
5 Where did you go on vacation?
To the beach.

6 How did you get there?
My father drove.
7 Why did you go to the same place?
Because we all liked it there.

3 Focus students' attention on the example. Point out that the answer is in the negative, and students should focus on the negative things that Bill says. Put students in pairs to try the task. If students can't remember all the information, play **CD2 38** again, or play it again for students to check their responses. With weaker students, write the sentences in fill-in-the-blank form on the board, e.g., *There ___ shows all day long,* etc.

Answers
It wasn't a color TV like we have now.
There weren't TV shows all day long.
I never took a plane like people do now!
He didn't give me much, did he?
We didn't have dishwashers in those days!
People didn't go abroad.

4 Check students' understanding of *theme parks* and *fast food*. Focus their attention on the example and then have students write sentences, using the other prompts. Check the answers, making sure students stress the sentences correctly.

We didn't have computers in those days.

Answers
We didn't have computers in those days.
We didn't have/use cell phones in those days.
We didn't have/eat fast food in those days.
We didn't have/go to theme parks in those days.

GRAMMAR SPOT

1 Focus students' attention on the Grammar Spot. Elicit the answers in the *Simple Past* column orally first. Then check the answers with the whole class again, writing the sentences on the board for students to copy.

Answers

Simple Present	Simple Past
I want to go.	I wanted to go.
He loves it.	**He loved it.**
Do you watch TV?	**Did you watch TV?**
Where does she work?	**Where did she work?**
I don't buy candy.	**I didn't buy candy.**
They don't go on vacation.	**They didn't go on vacation.**

Remind students that *he/she/it* has a different form in the Simple Present from the other persons, but that all forms in the Simple Past are the same. Highlight the use of *do/does* to form questions in the present and *did* in the past. Then highlight the use of *don't/doesn't* to form negatives in the present and *didn't* in the past.

2 This exercise covers *ago* and the prepositions of time *in/on/at*. Give students time to complete the sentences. Then check the answers. Highlight the

position of *ago* after the time expression, but don't spend too long on this section, as students will practice time expressions again on SB p. 52.

Answers
Henry Ford sold the first Ford-T **in** 1908.
I was born **on** April 17, 1991.
Our classes begin **at** nine o'clock.
Tommy saw Bill two days **ago**.

▶▶ Read Grammar Reference 7.1 and 7.2 on p. 135 together in class, and/or ask students to read it at home. Encourage them to ask you questions about it.

EXTRA ACTIVITY

You can give more practice on days, months, and years by having students create an "important year" quiz. Students do the research for world events of the 20th century for homework. Students then work in small groups and form questions to test the other groups.

Pre-teach expressions like *in the (1950s), in about (1995)* to enable students to give an answer even if they can't give an exact year. Have students ask their questions to another group. Have students share sentences about the most interesting/popular events with the rest of the class.

PRACTICE (SB p. 52)

1 **CD2 40** This task reinforces the formation of Simple Past questions with question words. Focus students' attention on the example, then give students time to complete the task.

Play the recording and have students check their answers. Put students in pairs to ask and answer the questions. Monitor and help as necessary. If students have problems with the stress and intonation, play the recording again and drill the questions. Students then repeat the pairwork.

Answers and audio script
1 Where did you go?
   To the mall.
2 When did you go?
   Yesterday.
3 Who did you go with?
   A friend from work.
4 How did you get there?
   By bus.
5 Why did you go?
   Because I wanted to.
6 What did you buy?
   A shirt.
7 How many did you buy?
   Only one.
8 How much did you pay?
   $29.

Bill's life

2 Focus students' attention on the photo and ask students what they can remember about Bill and his life.

Divide the class into pairs, having students work with a different partner than in exercise 1. Ask the A students to turn to p. 146 and the B students to p. 149. Demonstrate the activity by having students ask and answer the example questions in the Student Book in open pairs. Encourage a good, wide voice range. Remember that students may have difficulty in selecting the correct short response (*wasn't, didn't*), so you might want to go over them as a class first, especially with weaker groups.

Students work in closed pairs. Monitor and check for accurate question formation and irregular past forms. Correct any grammar and pronunciation errors carefully after the task. Students can check their answers by looking at their partner's text.

Time expressions

⚠ **POSSIBLE PROBLEMS**

Exercise 3 focuses on preposition + noun collocations, e.g., *on Saturday* and *in summer*. These prepositions can cause a lot of confusion and so will need a lot of practice and regular reviewing.

3 Focus students' attention on the prepositions and elicit one or two other prepositions for the time expressions. Monitor and check. If students have problems, give them these rules to help:

on + day/day of the week plus part of the day, e.g., *on Saturday morning*

in + part of the day (except *night*)/month/season/year/century

at + time

This leaves only *at night* that does not fit any of the categories.

Check the answers with the class.

Answers

at seven o'clock	**in** the morning
on Saturday	**on** Sunday morning
at night	**in** July
in 2009	**on** the weekend
in summer	**in** the twentieth century

4 Demonstrate the activity by having students practice the examples in the Student Book in open pairs. Students continue in closed pairs, asking questions with *When …?*, and answering the questions in the two different ways. Monitor and check that the questions are well formed, and that the voice starts high. Discuss any common errors in grammar or pronunciation after the pairwork.

5 Give an example by telling students about your day so far and then have students tell the class about their day. If you have a small group and sufficient time, you can ask each student to give their example. If you have a lot of students, you can have them work simultaneously in small groups, making sure the students who worked together in exercise 4 talk to different students.

Listening and pronunciation

6 **CD2 41** This is another discrimination activity. Play sentence 1 as an example. Then play the rest of the recording and ask students to choose the sentences they hear.

Answers and audio script
1 **a** Where do you want to go?
2 **b** I didn't go to college.
3 **b** Where was he?
4 **a** Do you like it?
5 **a** Why did he come?
6 **a** She doesn't work there.

You can make this receptive exercise productive by modelling each pair of sentences and having students repeat chorally and individually. Check for accurate pronunciation and differentiation between the sentences.

ADDITIONAL MATERIAL

Workbook Unit 7
Ex. 1–3 Simple Past (2)
Ex. 4–5 Time expressions

SPEAKING (SB p. 53)

Talking about my life

1 **CD2 42** Focus students' attention on the photo of Frank and Angela and ask students to identify them. Focus on the top photo and ask students where they think it is. Explain that it shows Angela when she was a young child.

Explain that Frank and Angela are meeting for the first time and Frank wants to find out more about Angela. Give students time to read Frank's questions. Check students' understanding of *grew up*. Give students time to read Angela's answers. Answer any questions about vocabulary. Check the pronunciation of *Córdoba* /ˈkɔrdoʊbɑ/, *psychology* /saɪˈkɑlədʒi/, *Buenos Aires* /ˈbwɛnoʊs ˈaɪreɪs/, and *junior* /ˈdʒunyər/. Ask students to read Frank's first two questions aloud and elicit Angela's answers from the notes. Students work in pairs to continue figuring out the wording for Angela's answers from the notes.

Play the recording and have students compare their wording. With weaker students, refer them to **CD2 42** on SB p. 122 to read the script after they have listened.

Audio script
A = Angela   F = Frank
F You aren't American, are you, Angela? Where are you from?
A No, I'm Argentinian. I was born in Córdoba.
F Is that where you grew up?
A Yes, I lived with my parents and two sisters in a house near the university. My father worked at the university.
F Oh, how interesting! What was his job? Was he a teacher?
A Yes, he was a professor of psychology.

F Really? And what did your mother do?
A She was a doctor. She worked in a hospital.
F So, where did you go to school?
A I went to a small private school. I was there for ten years, then, when I was 18, I went to college.
F What did you study?
A I studied philosophy and education at the college in Buenos Aires. I was there for four years.
F Wow! And did you start work after that?
A No, I traveled in the States for six months. I worked in a summer camp near Yellowstone National Park. It was amazing!
F That sounds great! And what's your job now?
A I work in a junior high school in Brazil. I teach Spanish and English.
F Your English is really good! Well, it was very nice to meet you, Angela!
A Nice to meet you too. Bye!

2 Demonstrate the activity with two students. Student A covers the questions and tries to ask them from memory, then Student B covers the answers and tries to answer from memory. Put students in pairs to practice the conversation. Monitor and help as necessary. Check for accurate question formation and use of Simple Past forms. Highlight and correct any Simple Past errors.

3 Write a few notes about your own life on the board, making sure students understand they don't need to give complete sentences, e.g., *born in New York City, lived with mom – a brother – house in suburbs; mother – worked in office.*

Give students time to write their notes. Monitor and help as necessary. With weaker students, you can write key words on the board as prompts, e.g., *born, family, school, college, first job,* etc.

4 Focus students' attention on the prompts and elicit possible questions, e.g., *Did you enjoy college? What did you study? How long did you stay there? Who did you meet?* Put students in small groups to compare their life stories. Monitor and help as necessary. Check for accurate question formation and use of Simple Past forms and note any common errors, but don't interrupt the groupwork. You can highlight and correct any errors at a later stage.

EXTRA ACTIVITY

Students give a short presentation of the life story of someone they admire. They can do the research for homework and make brief notes about the person's early life, family, education, career, and achievements. Make sure they don't just print out pages of information from Wikipedia or a similar source! Students then take turns giving their presentation to the class (or they can work in groups if you have a large class). The other students should be encouraged to ask questions about the speaker's chosen person. If you have access to video equipment, the talks can be recorded as an added incentive. They can be played in class and commented on, and can also be referred back to at a later date to show students how much progress they have made.

Sixty years of flight

ABOUT THE TEXT

This is another jigsaw reading task, which gives students an opportunity for not only reading practice, but also some freer speaking. The class divides into two groups and each group reads a different but similar text about a pioneer of aviation. It's important to remind students to read only their text and to get information about the other text via speaking. If necessary and possible, give the instructions for the jigsaw reading in L1.

The texts continue the theme of key dates in history, with a focus on groundbreaking developments in aviation. They have been chosen to reinforce Simple Past forms and time expressions. The use of a range of numbers in the texts provides for a number referencing task as part of the *Speaking* section.

Louis Blériot /ˈluwi ˈblɛrioʊ/ (1872–1936) was a French aviator, engineer, and inventor. He is best known for his flight over the English Channel, the first crossing of a large body of water in an aircraft, in 1909. The first text in this section is an account of the flight.

Neil Armstrong /nil ˈɑrmstrɔŋ/ (1930–2012) was one of the three astronauts who took part in the Apollo 11 moon mission in 1969. He is best known as the first man to walk on the moon and for his words, "That's one small step for man, one giant leap for mankind."

Encourage students to use the context to help them with new vocabulary and to pool knowledge with other students, or use a dictionary. With weaker classes or if you are short on time, ask students to look up some of the following vocabulary before the lesson:

Homework prior to the lesson

Introduction: *rocket, aviation, phenomenal.*

Louis Blériot: *flight, injury, compass, to take off* (leave the ground), *field, cliff, altitude, foot* (plural *feet*; 1 foot = approximately 30 cm), *fog, to wave a flag, to cut the engine, to crash, pioneer.*

Neil Armstrong: *to lift off, astronaut, to circle, landing, lunar module, to land, to rest, to take a step, leap, mankind, to collect samples, to set up scientific equipment, put up a flag, earth, inscription, peace, exploration.*

---

1 Focus students' attention on the photos. Make sure that students recognize the two men and can pronounce their names /ˈluwi ˈblɛrioʊ/ and /nil ˈɑrmstrɔŋ/. Elicit the answers to the questions in exercise 1 and any additional information students know about the two men.

Answers
Louis Blériot made the first long flight in 1909.
Neil Armstrong was the first person on the moon in 1969.

2 Students read the title and introduction. Check the answer to the question.

Answers
The progress in aviation in the 20th century was phenomenal.

3 Put students into two groups, A and B. (With larger classes, you may need to have multiple sets of the two groups.) Assign a text to each group and remind students to read only their text:

Group A – the first long flight

Group B – the first person on the moon

Have students read their text quickly, asking others in their group for help with vocabulary if you didn't pre-teach the items listed in *About the text* or assign them for homework. Monitor and help with any problems or questions.

Give students time to read the questions. Answer any questions. With weaker students, briefly review how to read numbers and years. Have them work in their groups and answer the questions about their text, writing down the answers to each one. Monitor and help as necessary. The answers for each group are provided below for reference, but don't check the answers with the whole class at this stage. Ask students to give full statements where possible in order to practice past forms.

Answers
The first long flight
1 The flight began in Calais in the north of France on July 25, 1909.
2 It took 37 minutes.
3 It was 22 miles.
4 He flew at 40 miles per hour.
5 The flight ended in Dover in the south of England.
6 It was the start of modern aviation.

The first person on the moon
1 The flight began at the Kennedy Space Center in Florida on July 16, 1969 at 9:30 in the morning.
2 It took three days.
3 It was 250,000 miles.
4 They flew at 21,600 miles per hour.
5 The flight ended on a part of the moon called the Sea of Tranquility.
6 It was the beginning of people's exploration of space.

4 Re-group the students, making sure there is an A and a B student in each pair. Demonstrate the activity by having a pair of students talk about the person in their text. Students continue talking about the answers to the questions in exercise 3 and exchanging the information about their person. Monitor and help. Also check for correct use of the present and past of *can* and *be*. Write down any common errors and discuss them at a later stage. Bring the whole class together to go over the answers. Encourage students to expand on their answers where applicable.

5 Students now look at both texts to get further information about each flight. Encourage students to help each other with vocabulary, or use a dictionary. With weaker students, you can pre-teach some of the items listed in *About the text* if you didn't assign them for homework.

Students work with the same partner to find the answers to the questions. Monitor and help as necessary.

Check the answers with the whole class, again having students give full statements where possible in order to practice past forms.

Answers
Blériot
1 He couldn't swim, he couldn't walk very well because of an injury to his leg, and he didn't have a compass.
2 No, it was foggy/there was fog.
3 He saw a French journalist waving a flag.
4 He won £1,000 (about $1,700).
Armstrong
5 They were too excited.
6 "That's one small step for man, one giant leap for mankind."
7 They spent two and a half hours walking on the moon.
8 They left a US flag on the moon.

Speaking

6 **CD2 43** Elicit the reference for the first two numbers, *37* and *4:30* (see *Answers.*) Then give students time to complete the task, working in pairs. Monitor and help as necessary.

Play the recording and have students check their answers.

Answers and audio script
In 1909 Blériot made the first long flight from Calais to Dover.
1 Blériot was just 37 years old when he flew across the English Channel. It took him just 37 minutes.
2 He took off from France at 4:30 in the morning.
3 He flew his plane at 40 miles per hour.
4 He flew at 250 feet above the sea.
5 He won a prize of £1,000.

In 1969 Neil Armstrong became the first person to walk on the moon.
6 Three astronauts flew in Apollo 11. The rocket took three days to get to the moon.
7 It circled the moon 30 times.
8 It landed at 8:17 p.m. on July 20, 1969.
9 Six hundred million people watched on TV.
10 Neil Armstrong said, "That's one small step for man, one giant leap for mankind."
11 The astronauts spent 22 hours on the moon.

SUGGESTION
Students can play a memory game based on the facts and figures in the story. Students take turns saying a number, and their partner guesses what it refers to. Encourage them to use different numbers from those in exercise 6, e.g.,
A 9:30 a.m.
B The time Apollo 11 lifted off.
A Yes, that's right.

7 Ask students to close their books. Elicit some information about the start of each of the flights from a few students.

Students continue retelling the stories in pairs. With weaker students, write key words and dates on the board as prompts. Monitor and help as necessary, but don't interrupt or over-correct. Write down any common errors for correction at a later stage.

ADDITIONAL MATERIAL

Workbook Unit 7
Ex. 6 Reading

VOCABULARY AND LISTENING (SB p. 56)

Adverbs

⚠ **POSSIBLE PROBLEMS**
The word order with adverbs can cause difficulties. We do not overtly give the rules for the order of adverbs (front position, mid-position, end position), because the rules are rather complicated. We do not suggest that you try to go into them at this stage. You can point out that adverbs usually follow the verb and object if there is one, whereas adjectives go before the noun (unlike many other languages). Otherwise, let students see how they do with exercise 4, and simply correct any mistakes.

1 Focus students' attention on the sentences and ask students to read them aloud. Explain that an adverb describes a verb. Elicit the adverb and verb in each example (*went well, flew beautifully, quickly went around, finally put up*).

GRAMMAR SPOT
1 Read the notes as a class. Ask students to identify the adjective that each adverb is formed from (*quick, slow, careful, quiet, bad, real*).
Highlight the spelling change in adjectives ending in *-y* to *-ily*, e.g., *happy – happily, noisy – noisily*.
2 Read the notes as a class. Explain that irregular adverbs are those that don't add *-ly* to the adjective.
▶▶ Read Grammar Reference 7.3 on p. 135 together in class, and/or ask students to read it at home. Encourage them to ask you questions about it.

2 Focus students' attention on the first pair of sentences as an example. Elicit the answers (*bad* – adjective, *badly* – adverb). Students then work in pairs. Check the answers with the whole class.

Answers
1 a *bad* – adjective
 b *badly* – adverb
2 a *carefully* – adverb
 b *careful* – adjective
3 a *hard* – adjective
 b *hard/hard* – adverb (*hard* is irregular)

3 This activity focuses on adverbs that collocate with common verbs and phrases. Elicit adverbs that can go with *work* as an example (*work carefully/fast/hard*).

Students work in pairs and continue the activity. Check the answers with the whole class. Elicit which adverbs in the chart are irregular (*fast, late, hard*).

4 Elicit the correct answer to number 1 as an example. Students put the word in parentheses in the correct place in the sentences. Tell them that sometimes more than one answer is possible. Students can work in pairs, or alone and then check with a partner.

Check the answers with the class and elicit if each word in parentheses is an adjective or adverb (see *Answers*).

Answers
1 We had a **terrible** vacation in Peru. (adjective)
2 **Unfortunately**, I lost my passport. (adverb)
3 I contacted the police **immediately**. (or I **immediately** contacted …) (adverb)
4 It was a **long** trip because the traffic was bad. (adjective)
5 Fortunately, Abby's a **good** driver. (adjective)
6 She speaks Spanish **well**. (adverb)

Telling a story

5 Point out that adverbs are often used in storytelling to make the actions sound more vivid. Focus students' attention on sentence 1 as an example. Elicit a range of other possible endings that will fit with the adverb *fortunately*, e.g., … *we were inside/the rain didn't last long*.

Check comprehension of *fast asleep* (in a deep sleep). Students continue working in pairs. Monitor and check if their answers fit with the adverbs given. Where possible, elicit a range of answers for each sentence that highlight the meaning of the adverb. If you want to double-check that students understand the adverbs, explain or translate them. You can also have students look up the definitions in dictionaries.

Possible answers
1 … fortunately, I had an umbrella/we were inside/the rain didn't last long.
2 … unfortunately, I couldn't go/I was sick/I was on vacation.
3 Fortunately, we had enough food/there was enough for everyone/they weren't very hungry.
4 Unfortunately, it was closed/I couldn't afford them/they didn't have them in my size.
5 … suddenly the phone rang/I heard a loud noise/the dog started to bark.
6 Immediately, I called an ambulance/went to help/ told a police officer.
7 I really liked her/thought she was beautiful/didn't want to see her again.
8 … went slowly across the room/to the window/down the stairs.

6 **CD2 44** Focus students' attention on the picture. Ask *How do you think the man feels? Why?* (scared/frightened/ nervous. He doesn't know who is downstairs.) Play the recording and elicit the answer to the question.

Answers and audio script
He heard a noise./He heard two men talking.

CD2 44
It was about two o'clock in the morning, and … suddenly I woke up. I heard a noise. I got out of bed and went slowly downstairs. There was a light on in the living room. I listened carefully. I could hear two men speaking very quietly. "Robbers!" I thought. Immediately I ran back upstairs and called the police. I was really frightened. Fortunately, the police arrived quickly. They opened the front door and went into the living room. Then they came upstairs to see me. "It's alright now, sir," they explained. "We turned the television off for you!"

7 **CD2 44** Play the first sentence of the recording again and elicit the first adverb as an example (*suddenly*). Students listen to the rest of the story again and number the adverbs in the correct order. Check the answers with the class.

Answers
8 quickly
4 quietly
2 slowly
1 suddenly
5 immediately
3 carefully
7 fortunately
6 really

8 Pre-teach/check students' understanding of *to wake up, robber, to come upstairs, to turn off the TV*. In pairs, students retell the story either one sentence at a time each, or one student first, then the other. Remind them to use the order of adverbs to help them. With weaker classes, you can write key words on the board as prompts.

ADDITIONAL MATERIAL

Workbook Unit 7
Ex. 7 Listening
Ex. 8 Adverbs

Photocopiable Activity
UNIT 7 Adverb acting TB p. 150
Materials: One copy of the worksheet cut up for each group of three to six students.

Procedure: Explain that students are going to play a miming game to practice adverbs. Demonstrate the activity by miming a simple activity and eliciting the verb + adverb, e.g., *run fast, breathe deeply*.

• Divide the class into teams of three to six students. Put a set of shuffled cards face down on the desk for each team. Explain how to play the game. Students need to give the exact wording on the card. If students suggest, for example, *drive slowly* and the wording required is *drive carefully*, the person miming needs to indicate that a similar word is needed. This helps students focus on suitable adverbs that collocate with the verbs. Students are not allowed to speak, but can make noises/give sound effects. They should also give

their answer in the form of verb + adverb rather than with *You … .* (This would require Present Continuous, which is covered later in Unit 10.)

- Ask the first student in each team to stand up, take the first card from the pile, and mime the action and adverb for the other students on his/her team to guess.
- When the team guesses the verb + adverb correctly, play passes to the next player. The team that guesses all the cards first wins the game.

WRITING (SB p. 106–7)

Telling a story

Using time expressions

The writing section is in the form of a historical narrative. This gives the opportunity to review and extend students' use of time expressions and also recycle Simple Past regular and irregular forms.

So use the pics to write their own answers. Then, use a–h sentences. (handwritten)

ABOUT THE TEXT

The theme of the narrative is the life of Christopher Columbus /kə'lʌmbəs/ (1451–1506), an Italian sailor and explorer, traditionally thought of as the first European to discover America. Current belief is that the Icelandic Leif /lif/ Ericson actually preceded Columbus by 500 years. He is referred to in the text as a *Norseman* (an ancient Scandinavian, specifically a Viking). Columbus was given money for his travels by the reigning monarchs of Spain at the time, Queen Isabella and King Ferdinand. His three ships were the Santa Maria, the Pinta, and the Niña /'ninyə/.

There are a number of places referred to in the text, so it would be helpful to bring in a map to help students plot Columbus's travels. You may need to go over the pronunciation of the following places: *Genoa* /'dʒɛnoʊə/, *Madeira* /mə'dɪrə/, *Cuba* /'kyubə/, and *Haiti* /'heɪti/.

Encourage students to use the context to help them with new vocabulary, to pool knowledge with other students, or to use dictionaries. With weaker classes or if you are short on time, ask students to look up some of following vocabulary before the lesson:

Homework prior to the lesson

explorer, to discover, sailor, to agree, voyage /'vɔɪɪdʒ/ *to sail, island* /'aɪlənd/, *to hit rocks, gold* (n), *wool, hero, to beg, pain, arthritis.*

The students' writing task is in the form of a project on a historical character from their own country. This will require students to do some research, so make sure you build in time for them to do this, probably for homework.

1 Write the name *Christopher Columbus* on the board and go over the pronunciation. Ask *What do you know about him?* and elicit one or two ideas from the class. Focus students' attention on the pictures on p. 106 and put students in pairs to share their ideas about Columbus's life.

Write key words for each pic on wb. (handwritten)

Elicit a range of ideas from the class, but don't confirm or reject them at this stage.

2 Give students time to read sentences a–h. Answer any vocabulary questions. If you didn't assign the vocabulary in the text for homework (see *About the Writing*), you can use the pictures to go over some of the key words now.

Elicit the answer for sentence a (3). Students continue matching the sentences and pictures, working in pairs. Check the answers with the class.

Answers
a 3 b 1 c 2 d 7 e 5 f 4 g 8 h 6

3 With weaker students, pre-teach/check students' understanding of the main vocabulary if you didn't assign it for homework (see *About the Writing*). Give students time to read the main story. Set a time limit for this of about three minutes so that students focus just on the main ideas. Elicit the missing sentence for the first blank (b).

Students continue completing the main story with the missing sentences, working in pairs. Remind them to use the linking words and punctuation to help them choose the correct sentences. Check the answers with the class.

Answers
1 b 2 c 3 a 4 f 5 e 6 h 7 d 8 g

4 Focus students' attention on the first two time expressions and elicit what they refer to (*for a long time* – the time that people believed that Columbus discovered America, *in 1451* – the year Columbus was born).

Students work in pairs to continue the referencing task. Monitor and help as necessary. Check the answers with the class.

Answers
For a long time – people believed that Columbus discovered America
in 1451 – Columbus was born
Between 1477 and 1485 – Columbus visited many countries
Finally – after a long time/number of events
On August 3, 1492 – Columbus left Spain
After three months – the number of months they were at sea
Two days later – after two days
Next – the next thing that happened
Then – the next thing that happened
Between 1492 and 1504 – Columbus traveled across the Atlantic
In the last years – at the end of his life
on May 20, 1506 – Columbus died

5 Put students in new pairs and ask them to cover the text of the story. Elicit some information about the start of Columbus's life from a few students.

Students continue retelling the story in pairs. With weaker students, write key words and dates on the board as prompts. Monitor and help as necessary.

Project

Read the task as a class and elicit a few examples of characters students would like to write about. If you have access to computers or encyclopedias, students can do their research and make notes during class time. If not, assign the research for homework.

Put students in pairs to talk about their chosen character. Encourage students to ask each other questions.

Give students time to write their story in class, or assign it for homework. Remind them to use the writing plan on SB p. 107.

If possible, display the texts on the classroom wall/ noticeboard to allow students to read each other's work. You can ask them to vote for the most interesting story. When you check students' work, point out errors, but allow students to correct them themselves. Try to limit correction to major problems to avoid demoralizing the students.

EVERYDAY ENGLISH (SB p. 57)

Special occasions

Common expressions for special occasions, such as *Happy birthday* and *Happy New Year* are introduced and practiced. This provides the opportunity for some very interesting discussion on cross-cultural traditions, especially if you have a multilingual class or if some of your students know foreign countries. What occasions different nationalities celebrate, and how they celebrate them, is a source of great interest to most students.

> **BACKGROUND NOTES**
>
> Here are some notes on how some American people celebrate the special days (though not all American people, of course).
>
> **Birthday**
> There is often a birthday cake, with candles to be blown out and everyone sings *Happy birthday*. People send birthday cards, and there may be a birthday party with family and friends.
>
> **Mother's Day**
> This is on the second Sunday in May. Children give cards and a present such as some flowers or chocolates.
>
> **Wedding day**
> People get married in a house of worship for a religious ceremony or a local government office for a civil ceremony. Rice or bird seed is thrown at the bride and groom to wish them luck, and the bride wears something old, something new, something borrowed, something blue, again, for luck. There is a party afterwards called a reception, and the bride and groom may go on a vacation called a honeymoon.
>
> **Halloween** /ˌhælə'win; ˌhɑlə'win/
> This is the evening of October 31, when it was believed that the spirits of dead people appeared. Customs associated with Halloween in the US and Britain are costume parties, where people dress up as famous people past and present, animals, etc. Children often celebrate by wearing masks or costumes and going "trick or treating" – going from house to house collecting candy.
>
> **Thanksgiving**
> This is a celebration of the harvest and other things that people have that make them thankful. There is a large meal of turkey and other traditional foods such as mashed potatoes, sweet potatoes, green beans, gravy, cranberry sauce, etc. It is always on the fourth Thursday of November.

New Year's Eve
People go to parties and wait for midnight to come, when they wish each other *Happy New Year*. In New York City many thousands of people celebrate New Year in Times Square where they can see a large crystal ball drop during the last minute of the year.

Valentine's /'væləntainz/ **Day**
People send Valentine cards to the person they love. Cards are sometimes sent anonymously! Men may give a gift of flowers or chocolates to the woman they love.

Graduation
When students graduate high school or college, they wear a special long gown and hat called a "mortar board" with a tassel hanging off of the right side. There is a special ceremony at the school, where each graduate walks onto a stage and receives a diploma from a school official. The graduate then moves the tassel to the left of the hat to symbolize their graduation. When all the graduates have received their diplomas, they throw their hats in the air.

1 Focus students' attention on the photos and the list of days in the box. Elicit the first special day (*birthday*) and then let the students continue in pairs. Students match the special days to the photos.

Check the answers with the class, dealing with any pronunciation difficulties as you go.

> **Answers**
> (in order from left to right)
> wedding day
> Mother's Day
> Valentine's Day
> Thanksgiving
> Halloween
> birthday
> New Year's Eve
> graduation

2 Check pronunciation of *special* /'spɛʃl/ and *fireworks* /'faɪərˌwɜrks/. Ask your students which special days they celebrate in their country. Elicit some examples of how they celebrate, using the ideas given and their own ideas. Students work in small groups to describe to each other how they celebrate. Monitor and help as necessary.

Have students briefly share their responses with the whole class. Write new vocabulary on the board for students to write in their vocabulary notebooks.

3 Students work in pairs to complete the conversations with the names of the days from exercise 1. Also give them time to name each of the occasions.

4 **CD2 45** Students listen and check their answers. Elicit the name of each occasion/day.

Using the recording as a model, drill the sentences in conversation 3, paying particular attention to stress and intonation. If students sound flat, exaggerate the voice range and have them repeat again. Ask three students to take a role each and act out the conversation for the class.

Put students in pairs and ask them to choose a different conversation (avoid 1, because it is a song). With weaker students, allocate conversations 2, 3, 4, 6, and 7. Students practice until they know their lines by heart, paying close attention to stress and intonation. Students take turns acting out their conversations for the class.

Answers and audio script

1 **birthday**
   Happy **birthday** to you.
   Happy **birthday** to you.
   Happy **birthday,** dear Grandma.
   Happy **birthday** to you.

2 **Valentine's Day**
   A Did you get any **Valentine** cards?
   B Yes, I did. Listen to this.
      Roses are red, violets are blue.
      You are my **Valentine***,*
      And I love you.
   A Wow! Do you know who it's from?
   B No idea!

3 **graduation**
   C You're in 11th grade, right, Laura?
   D Actually, I'm in 12th. I'm almost done with school.
   C Oh, really? Congratulations! When is your **graduation?**
   D It's next Sunday.

4 **wedding day**
   E Congratulations! That's great news!
   F Thank you very much. We're both very happy.
   E So, when's the big day?
   G Excuse me?
   E Your **wedding** day! When is it?
   F December 12th. You'll get an invitation!

5 **New Year's Eve**
   I   It's midnight! Happy **New Year**, everyone!
   I J K **Happy New Year!**

6 **Mother's Day**
   L Wake up, Mommy! Happy **Mother's Day!**
   M Thank you, honey. Oh, what beautiful flowers! And a cup of coffee! Well, aren't I lucky!
   L And we made you a card! Look!
   M It's beautiful! What creative children you are!

7 **weekend**
   N Thank goodness it's Friday!
   O Yeah! Have a good **weekend**!
   N You, too.

ADDITIONAL MATERIAL

Workbook Unit 7
Ex. 9 Special occasions

Don't forget!

Workbook Unit 7
Ex. 10 Word order
Ex. 11 Prepositions
Grammar Reference (SB p. 135 and iTools Online)
Word list Unit 7 (SB p. 142)
Students can translate the words, learn them at home, or transfer some of them to their vocabulary notebook.
Tests (Online)
Unit 7 Test
Video (iTools and Online)
Additional photocopiables and PPT™presentations (iTools)

8 Eat in or out?

Count and noncount nouns • *some/any* • *I like* and *I'd like* • *How much?* or *How many?* • **Food and drink** • **Shopping on Main Street**

VIDEO Food

The theme of this unit is food and drink, which lends itself to the presentation and practice of the target items – count and noncount nouns with a review of the determiners *some* and *any* (in Unit 4 they were introduced mainly with count nouns only), and a focus on *much/many*. The verb *like* is contrasted with *would like*, and the vocabulary and *Everyday English* focus is on shopping on Main Street. The skills material includes a reading text on the history of the sandwich, and a listening task on *World Sandwich Week!* There is also a project about students' favorite recipes.

LANGUAGE INPUT

GRAMMAR

Count and noncount nouns – *some, any, a lot of* … (SB p. 59)
- Understanding and practicing count and noncount nouns with determiners *some/any/a lot of*.

I like … and *I'd like* … (SB p. 59)
- Understanding and practicing the difference between *I like* … for general references and *I'd like* … in requests.

some/any, much/many (SB p. 60)
- Understanding and practicing *some/any* and *much/many* to talk about number and quantity.

VOCABULARY

Daily needs (SB p. 64)
- Understanding the vocabulary of, and practicing the pronunciation of, everyday objects.

EVERYDAY ENGLISH

Shopping on Main Street (SB p. 65)
- Understanding and practicing the language of shopping and ordering in a café; practicing sounding polite.

SKILLS DEVELOPMENT

READING

Everybody likes a sandwich! (SB p. 62)
- An article on the history of the sandwich.

LISTENING

What's your favorite sandwich? (SB p. 63)
- Listening for key information to complete a chart **CD2 54** SB p. 123

SPEAKING

How is it made? (SB p. 61)
- Guessing how to make a dish.

Project (SB p. 61)
- Researching and presenting your favorite recipe.

What do you think? (SB p. 63)
- Discussing favorite kinds of sandwiches.

WRITING

Two emails – Informal and more formal (SB pp. 108–9)
- Understanding the content and comparing the level of formality of two emails, then writing a thank-you email.

MORE MATERIALS

Photocopiables – *How much/many …?* (TB p. 151)   **Tests** (Online)   **Video** (iTools and Online)

STARTER (SB p. 58)

Count and noncount nouns Students often need help with the concept of count and noncount nouns, and need regular practice with the articles and determiners that can be used with them. Students also need to understand that a lot of nouns can be both countable and uncountable, depending on the context in which they are used, e.g.,

Two coffees, please. (countable and meaning "two cups of coffee")

Coffee is expensive. (uncountable and meaning "coffee in general")

Students can also have problems with interference from their own language, where some nouns which are noncount in English may be countable. This can lead to misuse, e.g.,

*They gave me advices.

*I'd like some informations.

some/any *Some* and *any* were first introduced in Unit 4, mainly with count nouns. This unit introduces and practices them with noncount nouns as well. The often-repeated rule that *some* is used in affirmative sentences and *any* in questions and negatives is not entirely true, but is still useful at this level.

Students may need ongoing help with the weak pronunciation of *some* /səm/.

1 Check students' understanding of *to be a picky eater*. Answer the questions in exercise 1 about yourself, writing examples of food you didn't like on the board. Ask students to write down their own examples. Then elicit a range of answers from the class, checking and drilling pronunciation as necessary. Review the alphabet by having students spell key words. Build up a vocabulary list on the board and have students copy it into their vocabulary notebooks. With weaker students, you can brainstorm food vocabulary with the class at the start of the activity and write key words on the board before looking at the questions.

2 **CD2 46** Elicit one or two examples with the class. Students match the food and drinks in columns **A** and **B** with the pictures.

Play the recording and have students listen and follow along in their books. Students then say the list aloud. Drill the pronunciation of any words students find difficult, highlighting the word stress as necessary.

Answers and tapescript

A		B	
l tea	w ice cream	i bananas	e onions
p coffee	k apple juice	a apples	c tomatoes
j soda	h bread	f strawberries	q eggs
v cheese	u milk	t potatoes	b cookies
n yogurt	o chocolate	r carrots	g chips
d pasta	s broccoli	x peas	m French fries

3 Ask students to identify which list (**A** or **B**) has plural nouns (list **B**). Put students into pairs to complete the sentences with *is* or *are*. Check the answers and elicit that we can't count *broccoli* or *apple juice*, but we can count *tomatoes* and *apples*.

Read Grammar Reference 8.1 on p. 135 together in class and/or ask students to read it at home. Encourage them to ask you questions about it.

Answers
Broccoli **is** good for you.
Tomatoes **are** good for you.
Apple juice **is** delicious.
Apples **are** delicious.

WHO'S A PICKY EATER? (SB p. 59)

Count and noncount nouns – *some, any, a lot of…*

The goal of this section is to review count and noncount nouns and provide practice of *some, any,* and *a lot of*.

1 **CD2 47** Focus students' attention on the photos. Explain that Evan and Nick are roommates and that they are talking about what they like and don't like to eat and drink, and what they liked and didn't like as children. Pre-teach/check students' understanding of *kid* (informal for *child*), *green vegetables*, and *fruit*. Play the recording as far as *Oh – you were a picky eater!* Elicit who was a picky eater (*Evan*). Play the whole recording and ask students to write down the foods that Evan did and didn't like when he was a child.

Give students time to check their answers in pairs before checking the answers with the class.

Elicit the answer to the question about where Evan and Nick go to eat.

Answers and audio script
Evan is the fussy eater.
He didn't like green vegetables, other vegetables (apart from potatoes), bananas, coffee, or tea.
He liked French fries, fruit juice, ice cream, chocolate, chips, cookies, and pasta.
They go to Romano's to eat.

CD2 47

E = Evan   N = Nick
N Oh, good, we have some tomatoes.
E Sorry, Nick. I don't like them.
N Come on, Evan! Tomatoes are good for you. I didn't like them much when I was a child, but I love them now.
E Hmm – I didn't like a lot of things when I was a kid.
N Oh – you were a picky eater! What didn't you like?
E I didn't like any green vegetables.
N Did you like any vegetables at all?
E Only potatoes. I loved French fries.
N What about fruit? Did you like fruit?
E I liked some fruit, but not all. I didn't like bananas. I liked fruit juice. I drank a lot of apple juice.
N And now you drink a lot of coffee!

E Yeah – and tea. But I didn't like coffee or tea when I was a kid.

N So what were your favorite foods?

E I liked ice cream, chocolate, chips, cookies, especially chocolate cookies – uh-, you know, I liked all the usual things kids like.

N All the unhealthy things!

E I liked pasta too. Pasta with tomato sauce. I love that!

N Tomato sauce!? But you don't like tomatoes.

E Tomato sauce is different. Hey, let's not eat in tonight. Let's go out to Romano's.

N Romano's – a great idea! It's my favorite Italian restaurant.

2　**CD2 47** With weaker classes, give students time to read the sentences with blanks and try to remember some of the answers before they listen. Focus students' attention on the example. Play the recording and have students complete the sentences. Check answers with the class.

Answers
1　Oh, good, we have some tomatoes.
2　I didn't like a **lot** of things when I was a kid.
3　I didn't like **any** green vegetables.
4　Did you like **any** vegetables at all?
5　I liked **some** fruit, but not all.
6　I drank a **lot** of apple juice.
7　I liked **all** the usual things kids like.

GRAMMAR SPOT

Look at the examples and question as a class. Allow students time to think about their answers before checking answers with the class.

Answer
We use *some* in affirmative sentences with both singular noncount nouns (*soda*) and plural count nouns (*tomatoes*). We use *any* in negative sentences and questions with both singular noncount nouns (*tea*, *coffee*) and plural count nouns (*bananas*, *apples*).

▶▶ Read Grammar Reference 8.2 on p. 135 together in class and/or ask students to read it at home. Encourage them to ask you questions about it.

EXTRA ACTIVITY

Give some examples of your own likes and dislikes, now and as a child. Students look at the lists of food and drinks on p. 58 and decide what they liked and didn't like as a child, and what they like and don't like now. They then work in pairs and talk about their likes and dislikes. Monitor and check. Have students briefly share some of their partner's answers with the class. e.g., *Ana likes fruit, but I don't.*

I like … and I'd like …

⚠ **POSSIBLE PROBLEMS**

like and *would like*　Would like is introduced for the first time, and this is the first time that students have seen the modal verb *would*. It is easy for students to confuse *like* and *would like*. Here are some common mistakes.

*Do you like a coffee?

*I like a cup of tea, please.

Are you hungry? *You like a sandwich?

It is relatively easy for students to perceive the difference between a general expression of liking and a specific request, but be prepared to deal with mistakes on an ongoing basis as students confuse *like* and *would like*, and especially the two auxiliary verbs *do* and *would*.

some **in requests and offers**　It is quite a subtle concept for students to grasp that *some* can be used in questions when there is no doubt about the existence of the thing requested or offered. The use of L1 might help to clarify this.

Students may hear *Would you like a tea or a coffee?* instead of *Would you like some tea or coffee?* The meaning here is *Would you like a (cup of) tea or a (cup of) coffee?* and that is why the article is used with the noncount noun. This form is a feature of spoken English, so encourage students to use *some* with plural and noncount nouns in offers and requests.

As in Unit 4, we do not suggest that you explore the use of *any* to mean "it doesn't matter which," as in *Take any drink you want.*

3　**CD2 48** Focus students' attention on the photo of Evan and Nick in the Italian restaurant. Pre-teach/check students' understanding of *starter, spaghetti with meat sauce* (spaghetti with a thick tomato sauce that has ground meat in it), *bottled/tap water.* Play the recording through once and have students follow along in their books.

4　Give students time to answer the true/false questions, working in pairs.

Answers
1　True
2　False. He really likes spaghetti.
3　True
4　False. He likes tomatoes and would like some in his salad.
5　False. They ask for some water.
6　False. He orders some tap water.

5　Students work in their pairs to practice the conversation in exercise 3. Monitor and check. If students have problems with pronunciation, play the recording again and drill difficult sentences as a class.

Students work with a new partner and practice the conversation again, changing the things they order.

GRAMMAR SPOT

1 Look at the *Grammar Spot* questions as a class. This section is intended to guide students to understand the difference between *I like* and *I'd like*. Do not attempt to go into a full presentation of the uses of *would* at this stage, just introduce it as a polite way of making requests and offers.

Answer

Would you like some coffee? and *I'd like some coffee* mean *Do you want …* and *I want …*

Point out that when we talk about things in general, we do not use an article/determiner with plural count nouns or with noncount nouns. You can write these examples on the board:

I like cookies. (NOT *I like some cookies.*)

I don't like tea very much. (NOT *I don't like any tea very much.*)

Do you like Chinese food? (NOT *Do you like any Chinese food?*)

2/3 These sections demonstrate the special use of *some* in requests and offers, and *any* in other questions and negatives. Read the notes as a class.

▶▶ Read Grammar Reference 8.2–8.3 on p. 135 together in class, and/or ask students to read it at home. Encourage them to ask you questions about it.

PRACTICE (SB p. 60)

Would/Do you like …?

1 **CD2 49** Elicit the answer to question 1 as an example with the whole class. Students work in pairs or small groups to choose the correct form.

Play the recording and have students listen and check their answers. Students practice the conversations in pairs. Monitor and check for accurate pronunciation. Drill any difficult sentences with the class if necessary.

Answers and audio script
1 A Excuse me, are you ready to order?
  B Yes. **I'd like** a steak, please.
2 A **Would** you like a sandwich?
  B No, thanks. I'm not hungry.
3 A **Do** you like Liz?
  B Yes. She's very nice.
4 A **Would** you like a cold drink?
  B Yes, please. Do you have any apple juice?

5 A Can I help you?
  B Yes. **I'd like** some stamps, please.
6 A What sports do you do?
  B Well, **I like** skiing very much.

2 **CD2 50** Play the first question and elicit the correct reply as an example. Students listen to the rest of the questions and complete the exercise. (See *Answers and audio script* below for the questions.)

CD2 51 Play the recording for students to listen and check their answers. Then have them practice the conversations in pairs.

Answers and audio script
1 A What kind of coffee do you like?
  B **I like dark roast coffee.**
2 A Would you like a turkey and cheese sandwich?
  B **Just turkey, please. I don't like cheese.**
3 A Who's your favorite author?
  B **I like books by Patricia Cornwell.**
4 A What do you want for your birthday?
  B **I'd like a new computer.**
5 A Do you have any pets?
  B **No, but I'd like a dog.**
6 A Do you want some ice cream for dessert?
  B **No, thanks. I don't like ice cream.**

a or *some*?

3 The goal of this exercise is to reinforce the concept of count and noncount nouns and practice the use of *a/an* and *some*. Use this exercise to check how well students have grasped the concept and be prepared to explain further, using L1 if possible.

Focus students' attention on the examples. Students then work in pairs to write *a*, *an*, or *some* before the nouns.

Answers
1 a banana
2 some fruit
3 an egg
4 some bread
5 some milk
6 some meat
7 an apple
8 some toast
9 some sandwiches
10 some cookies
11 a cup of coffee
12 some apple juice

ADDITIONAL MATERIAL

Workbook Unit 8
Ex. 1–2   Count and noncount nouns
Ex. 3–4   *I like…* and *I'd like…*
Ex. 5   *like* or *would like*?

EATING IN (SB p. 60)

some/any, much/many

> **NOTE**
>
> At the end of this section, there is a project activity on favorite recipes. You will need to build in time for students to do some research on their chosen recipe and take notes on the ingredients and method of preparation, probably for homework. Students can also bring in pictures of their chosen dish, if available.

The goal of this section is to practice *some/any* and introduce *(not) much/many* with both count and noncount nouns. The question forms *How much …?* and *How many …?* are also practiced.

1 Focus students' attention on the photo and ask students what they can remember about Evan and Nick (*They are students and roommates. They both like Italian food*, etc.). Ask *Who do they want to cook for?* (their friends).

Focus students' attention on the photo of the shepherd's pie. Explain that this is a traditional dish in the UK, and has also become popular in the US. It is often served as a family meal. Give students time to read the list of ingredients. Answer any questions about vocabulary, using the photos to help. Cheddar cheese is a type of hard yellow cheese, originally from the village of Cheddar in the county of Somerset, south-west England. Check pronunciation of *thyme* /taɪm/ and that students recognize the abbreviations *tbsp (tablespoon)*, *tsp (teaspoon)*, and *lb (pound)*.

Elicit the ingredients needed for the dish, as listed in the recipe.

2 Focus students' attention on the photo of the ingredients on the counter. Read the examples with the class. Drill the pronunciation if necessary, highlighting the weak pronunciation of *some* /səm/.

Put students in pairs to continue talking about the ingredients for the recipe. Monitor and check carefully for correct use of *many* with count nouns and *much* with noncount nouns. If students have problems, go through the *Grammar Spot* with the class, then have them repeat the pairwork.

Check the answers with the class. Correct any mistakes carefully. With weaker students, drill the sentences again by saying the ingredients in random order and having students say the sentences, e.g., *potatoes – there aren't many potatoes*.

> **Answers**
>
> These are given in the same order as the ingredients in the recipe.
> There are some onions.
> There isn't any ground beef.
> There isn't much oil.
> There aren't any carrots.
> There aren't many tomatoes.
> There isn't much thyme.
> There isn't any salt and pepper.
> There aren't many potatoes.
> There isn't much butter.
> There isn't much cheese.
> There's some milk.

3 **CD2 52** Explain that Evan and Nick are talking about the ingredients they have and don't have for the shepherd's pie. Pre-teach/check students' understanding of *herbs*, *to be left (in the bottle)*.

Read the first four lines as a class, including the example. Ask *Who can cook?* (Nick). Give students time to complete the conversation, working individually. Have students check their answers in pairs before playing the recording for a final check. If students ask about the use of *ones* in sentences 9 and 12 of the conversation, elicit the food items that it refers back to each time (*potatoes, tomatoes*).

Put students in pairs to practice the conversation. Monitor and check. If students have problems with pronunciation and intonation, play the recording again and have students repeat key sentences before practicing the conversation again.

> **Answers and audio script**
>
> N = Nick   E = Evan
>
> **N** This recipe for shepherd's pie looks easy.
> **E** But I can't cook at all.
> **N** Don't worry. I really like cooking. Now, vegetables – do we have any onions? Are there **any** carrots or potatoes?
> **E** Well, there are **some** onions, but there aren't **any** carrots, and we don't have **many** potatoes. How **many** do we need?
> **N** Four big ones.
> **E** OK, put potatoes on your list.
> **N** And how **many** tomatoes are there?
> **E** Only two small ones. Put them on the list too.
> **N** How **much** milk is there?
> **E** There's a lot, but there isn't **much** cheese or butter.
> **N** OK, cheese and butter. What about herbs? Do we have **any** thyme?
> **E** Yeah, we do. But don't forget the ground beef. How **much** do we need?
> **N** A pound and a half. Now, is that everything?
> **E** Uh- I think so. Do we have vegetable oil? Oh, yeah, there's **some** left in the bottle.
> **N** OK, first shopping, then I'll give you a cooking lesson!
> **E** Great! I hope Sarah and Lizzie like shepherd's pie.
> **N** Everyone likes shepherd's pie!

> **GRAMMAR SPOT**
>
> 1/2 Read the Grammar Spot as a class. Also point out to students the use of *many* with the plural verb *are* and *much* with the singular verb *is*.
>
> 3 Explain to students that *a lot of* is used with both count and noncount nouns. It describes a large quantity or amount of something.
>
> ▶▶ Read Grammar Reference 8.4 on p. 135 together in class, and/or ask students to read it at home. Encourage them to ask you questions about it.

PRACTICE (SB p. 61)

much or *many*?

1 Pre-teach/check students' understanding of *gas*. Focus students' attention on the example. Ask *Why "much," not "many?"* (*toast* is a noncount noun). Students work in pairs to complete the questions using *much* or *many*.

2 **CD2 53** Pre-teach/check students' understanding of *slice*. Focus students' attention on the example. Students choose an answer for each question in exercise 1.

Play the recording and have students check their answers. Put students in pairs to practice the questions and answers. If students have problems with pronunciation, drill some of the exchanges chorally and individually.

Check it

3 Students work in pairs to complete the task.

Elicit a range of answers from the class for each sentence. If there is disagreement, write the relevant sentences on the board and have students explain the reason for their choice. Encourage students to correct each other where possible.

Speaking   Cooking verbs gallery

4 Demonstrate the verbs in the box with simple mimes. Focus students' attention on the example and then elicit possible ways of continuing the recipe.

Put students into groups of three or four. Remind them to refer to the ingredients list to make sure they have included everything. Monitor and help, writing any additional cooking verbs on the board as necessary.

Refer students to the recipe on SB p. 151. Answer any questions about vocabulary and establish how well students predicted the recipe. Also ask if they would like to cook the recipe at home and elicit reasons why/why not.

Project

Make sure students have brought along their notes for their recipe. Put students into groups of three. In a multilingual class, ask students from different countries to work together to encourage an exchange of information.

Students take turns talking about their recipe. Make sure they use their notes just as a reference and don't read aloud the complete text of their recipe. Encourage the other students to ask questions. Monitor and help as necessary. Check for accurate use of *some/any*, *much/many*, food vocabulary, and cooking verbs. Write down any common errors, but don't discuss these until after the groupwork.

Ask students to choose their favorite recipe from their group and give reasons for their choice.

Photocopiable Activity

UNIT 8 How much/many …? TB p. 151

Materials: One copy of the worksheet cut up for each pair of students.

Procedure: Explain that students are going to practice talking about food in a recipe activity. Pre-teach/check students' understanding of the measurement *cup*, abbreviated *c* (1 *cup* = approximately 236 milliliters). Then continue with the new ingredients in the activity, drilling the pronunciation as necessary: *cloves of garlic, ginger* /'dʒɪndʒər/ *chicken stock, dried apricots* /'æprɪkɑt/, *almonds* /'ɑməndz/, *olive oil, vegetable stock, anchovies* /'æntʃoʊviz/, *couscous* /'kuskus/, and *crusty bread*. Also check students' understanding of the cooking verbs *heat, mash, peel, cover, sprinkle,* and *serve*.

- Write the following incomplete question on the board _____ oil and _____ tuna steaks do you need? Elicit the answers to review *How much* + noncount nouns (*oil*) and *How many* + count nouns (*tuna steaks*). Also review the abbreviations *tbsp* (tablespoon), *lb* (pound) and, *tsp* (teaspoon).

- Divide the class into A/B pairs. Ideally, ask students to sit face to face so that they can't see each other's recipe. Hand out the relevant half of the worksheet to each student. Demonstrate the activity by having a Student B ask a Student A the first question in the ingredients list *How much oil do you need? One tablespoon.* Also elicit the first question in numbered steps *What do you fry in the oil? The onion and garlic.* With weaker students, you can put all the A and B students into groups to prepare the questions before they do the information exchange. Students continue asking and answering to complete the *Aromatic chicken* recipe. Remind them not to show each other their recipe, but to exchange the information by asking and answering. Monitor and check for accurate question formation use of *How much/many …?* Write any common errors to discuss at the end of the activity.

- For exercise 2, students change roles and Student A asks Student B about the recipe for *Fresh tuna with tomatoes*. Continue monitoring and writing down common errors, but don't discuss them at this stage.

- Ask students to put their worksheets together to check their answers.

- For exercise 3, bring the class back together to discuss which recipe they would like to try. Elicit why they wouldn't like to try the other recipe. Also elicit examples of dishes students cooked at home and if they were successful.

- Highlight any common errors from the pairwork stage and have students self-correct where possible.

ADDITIONAL MATERIAL

Workbook Unit 8
Ex. 7 *some* and *any*
Ex. 8 *much* and *many*

WRITING (SB p. 108-109)

Two emails
Informal and more formal

This section of the writing syllabus allows students to look at aspects of tone and register by comparing two thank-you emails, one to a friend and the other to the friend's parents. Students focus on the choice of greeting and closing in the emails, as well as the overall tone of the language and use of emoticons (taken from *emotion* and *icon* – a symbol that shows how you feel, e.g., :-) means happy or friendly).

1 Focus students' attention on the photo of Evan on p. 108 and ask students what they can remember about him, e.g., *He's a student. He shares an apartment with Nick. They prepared shepherd's pie for their friends.* Now focus their attention on the photo of Sarah and read the instructions for exercise 1 with the class. Ask *Where is Sarah?* (Washington, DC) *And Evan?* (New York). Focus students' attention on the email and ask *Why is Sarah writing to Evan?* (To say "thank you" for her visit to New York.) With weaker students or if you are short of time, pre-teach/check students' understanding of *Just kidding* (= (I'm) only joking), *starving, disgusting, to be a real friend* (=someone who does something kind and helpful), *to miss someone*. Give students time to read Sarah's email to Evan. Set a time limit of one to two minutes so that students don't spend too long on it.

Put students in pairs to discuss their answers. Monitor and help as necessary. Check the answers with the class.

Answers
1 Yes, she did.
2 She says the meal is fantastic, but we know from p. 61 that Evan says he can't cook.
3 She wants to cook shepherd's pie for her friends in Washington, DC.
4 She traveled by bus.
5 She danced all night and went to bed at 4 a.m.
6 He got up early to take Sarah to the bus station.
7 She would like to see him soon.
8 It's informal.
9 She visited him before exams.

2 Focus students' attention on Sarah's second email and read the instructions for exercise 2 with the class. Ask *Who is the email to?* (Evan's parents), *When did Sarah write it?* (April 21st), *Was that before or after the email to Evan* (before).

Give students time to read Sarah's email to Evan's parents. Again, set a time limit of one to two minutes so that students don't spend too long on it.

Put students in pairs to discuss their answers. Monitor and help as necessary. Check the answers with the class. If appropriate, ask students to refer to relevant parts of the email to support their answers (see text in parentheses in *Answers*).

3 Elicit the difference in tone in the beginnings and endings of each email as an example (to Evan: *Hi/S*; to Mr. and Mrs. Owen: *Dear Mr. and Mrs. Owen/Best wishes*). Sarah also uses her full name in the more formal email to his parents.

Put students in pairs to compare the main paragraphs of the two emails. With weaker students, you can write prompts on the board to help, e.g., information included/ omitted, full sentences, direct language, informal language, adjectives, linking words, expressive language/ emoticons, etc. Monitor and help as necessary.

Elicit the main differences, having students refer to the two emails to give examples.

4 Give students time to write their email in class, or assign it for homework. Remind students to use a fairly informal style, as they are writing to a friend. Allow students to exchange their email with a partner and recommend ways to make it more formal.

If possible, display the emails on the classroom wall or noticeboard to allow students to read each other's work. If appropriate, you can have students send the emails to each other over a computer network. When you check the students' emails, point out errors, but allow students to correct them themselves. Try to limit correction to major problems to avoid demoralizing the students.

READING AND SPEAKING (SB p. 62)

Everybody likes a sandwich!

ABOUT THE TEXT

The theme of food is carried through in this section with an article on the history of the sandwich. The text plots the development of the sandwich from the 1st–21st century. Students get to brainstorm different types of sandwiches, listen to people talking about their favorite sandwich, and then exchange ideas in a *What do you think?* section.

The following people/characters mentioned in the text:

Hillel /ˈhɪlel/ **the Elder** was an important Jewish religious leader during the 1st Century BC. Hillel and his descendants established academies of learning and were the leaders of the Jewish community in the Land of Israel for several centuries. The *matzohs* /ˈmɑtsəz/ referred to in the text are crisp biscuits of unleavened bread, traditionally eaten by Jews during Passover.

John Montague /ˈmɑntəgyu/ (1718–1792) was a British nobleman of high rank, with the title Fourth Earl of Sandwich. Now the title of "Sandwich" has become synonymous with the food sandwich.

Eliza Leslie /ˈlɛzli/ (1787–1858), frequently referred to as *Miss Leslie*, was an American author of popular cookbooks during the nineteenth century. She also gained popularity for her books on etiquette.

Dagwood Bumstead /ˈdægwʊd ˈbʌmstɛd/ is a character in the long-running comic strip *Blondie*. He first appeared in 1933 and became famous for inventing tall, multi-layered sandwiches held together with an olive on a toothpick. The term *Dagwood sandwich* has entered American English.

Encourage students to use the context to help them with new vocabulary and to pool knowledge with other students, or use a dictionary. With weaker classes or if you are short on time, ask students to check some of the following vocabulary before the lesson:

Homework prior to the lesson

rabbi, recorded, nuts, spices, chef, ham, mustard, supper, portable, cartoon character, layer.

Students can also look up the food items in the listening task in exercise 5.

1 Introduce the topic by asking *What's good about sandwiches?* Elicit possible answers (e.g., They are quick to make. You can take them to school/work. You can eat them anywhere. You can use different fillings, etc.) Read the questions in exercise 1 as a class and elicit a range of answers. If appropriate, ask where students think they get the best sandwiches – at home or in a café/sandwich shop.

2 Have students read the text through quickly and find the information about the four people/characters. Encourage students to focus on finding just the key information and tell them not to worry about new vocabulary at this stage. You might want to set a time limit of one or two minutes to encourage students to scan the text for the correct information.

Answers
Hillel the Elder was a rabbi who made the first recorded sandwich.
John Montague, the fourth Earl of Sandwich, liked playing cards. He was hungry, but he didn't want to stop playing, so the chefs at his club put some beef between two pieces of bread and he ate while he played. This became popular with other men in the club and they called it the "sandwich" after the Earl.
Eliza Leslie introduced sandwiches to America in her 1837 cookbook with a recipe for meat sandwiches.
Dagwood Bumstead, an American cartoon character, gave his name to the "Dagwood" sandwich. It is very big and is made with many layers of meat, cheese, tomatoes, eggs, and vegetables.

3 Elicit the answer to question 1 as an example (*he put it between two matzohs or pieces of flat bread*). Put students in pairs. They read the text again more slowly and find the missing information from the text. Monitor and help as necessary. Check the answers with the class.

Answers
1 he put it between two matzohs or pieces of flat bread
2 open sandwiches
3 play cards and eat
4 some beef between
5 meat sandwiches
6 they were easy to make and they were a wonderful, cheap, portable meal for workers and school children.
7 an American cartoon character
8 many layers

4 Focus students' attention on the photos on p. 63 and elicit the types of sandwich/ingredients shown. Students work in pairs and write down as many types of sandwich as they can think of. If appropriate, set this up as a competition with the students working in small teams to a limit of two–three minutes.

Elicit possible answers, checking pronunciation as you go.

Possible answers
Types: toasted sandwich/toastie, white bread/brown bread sandwich, pita bread, wrap, baguette/French bread, melt, roll, ciabatta, croque monsieur (a hot ham and cheese grilled sandwich, originally from France), open sandwich, club sandwich, submarine (or *sub*, an oblong roll of crusty bread filled with various meats, cheeses, vegetables, and sauces), and possibly hamburger and hotdog.

Typical fillings: BLT (bacon, lettuce, and tomato), peanut butter and jelly, cold meats (ham, beef, chicken, turkey, salami, chorizo, pastrami, bacon, sausage), fish/seafood (tuna, shrimp, smoked salmon, crab), eggs, cheese, salad/vegetables (lettuce, cucumber, tomatoes), onions, peppers, avocado, asparagus, pickles, mayonnaise, chutney, dressing.

LISTENING (SB p. 63)

5 **CD2 54** Read the instructions as a class. Check comprehension and pronunciation of the items in the box. (If students have done the above homework task in *About the text*, they should not have too many difficulties.) Also pre-teach/check students' understanding of *national sandwich, baguette, melted, grilled, mayonnaise, mackerel, bread roll, raw.*

Play the recording of Linh as an example and elicit the answers to complete the first section of the chart.

Play the rest of the recording without stopping and have students write their answers. With weaker students, play a paused version of the recording, stopping after each speaker. Play the recording again and have students check/complete their answers.

Check the answers, then elicit any additional information that students understood about each speaker.

Answers and audio script

	favorite sandwich
Linh	vegetables and chicken
Larissa	mozzarella, roast beef, and tomatoes
Dylan	steak, cheese, and onions
Kumiko	fried noodles, egg, mayonnaise
John	mackerel and onions

CD2 54
Linh
I come from Vietnam. Our national sandwich is Bánh Mi. It's a baguette filled with meat and vegetables. My favorite kind of Bánh Mi is made with grilled chicken. Mmmm, delicious. Would you like to try one?

Larissa
I'm from Brazil, so for me it's the Bauru. It's named after the Brazilian city of Bauru, and it's really popular here in Brazil. It has melted cheese — usually mozzarella — and slices of roast beef and tomatoes. I love it!

Dylan
I live in Philadelphia, here in the US. Philadelphia is famous for the cheese steak sandwich. It's the best sandwich in the world! It's made with thin slices of steak with melted cheese and grilled onions on top. I love it!

Kumiko
Oh, the best sandwich in the world is definitely Yakisoba-pan. It's a hot dog bun filled with fried Japanese noodles. I usually have an egg and some mayonnaise on top. And it's delicious with a little salt and pepper — mm, I'd like one right now!

John
I was in Turkey by the sea, and a fisherman called to me, "Come, try a 'Balik Ekmek'." I think this means "fish in bread." He gave me a sandwich — it was fresh grilled mackerel in a bread roll with raw onions. Amazing!

6 Give an example of your own favorite sandwich including the type of bread/roll, filling(s), sauces, and seasonings. Give students a few moments to think of their own favorite sandwich. Provide vocabulary as necessary. Then elicit a range of examples from the class and students' reactions to the sandwiches described.

What do you think?

Read the questions as a class. Students work in small groups and discuss the questions. This will obviously be a very productive activity in a multilingual group, but students in a monolingual group can also discuss their own habits and preferences.

Have several students share their responses with the whole class, encouraging students to compare what is popular in different countries.

SUGGESTION

Students can do a survey with their classmates to find out the most popular sandwich from a list. Put students in groups to invent eight different sandwiches. Remind them to use their imagination and include the type of bread/roll, filling(s), sauces, and seasonings for each sandwich. Students write their lists and then survey other students to find out what they like/dislike, recording the numbers of votes for each "recipe." The results from each group are then checked by the whole class and the three most popular sandwiches are chosen.

EXTRA ACTIVITY

Students do a mini-project on their favorite national/regional dishes. Give examples of your own favorite national dishes and describe them in a natural way. Elicit examples of famous national or regional dishes, e.g., goulash from Hungary, paella from Spain, etc. Elicit one or two other examples from the class.

Then give students time to research their favorite dishes, probably for homework, making notes about ingredients, cooking methods, and a little of the history of the dish if appropriate.

Students can then give a short presentation about their chosen dish to the class or discuss their national/regional foods in small groups.

ADDITIONAL MATERIAL

Workbook Unit 8
Ex. 6 Listening
Ex. 9 Reading

Daily needs

Having practiced a large lexical set of food and drinks, students now focus on the vocabulary of everyday items such as *aspirin*, *envelopes*, and *shampoo*. The pronunciation focus is on stress, with students categorizing key words according to word stress patterns.

1 Ask students *Apart from food and drinks, what everyday items do you regularly buy? Where do you buy them?* Focus students' attention on the shopping list and the pictures. Elicit the correct picture for *aspirin*. Then have students complete the task, working in pairs.

Check the answers with the class.

Answers

n	aspirin	e	phone case
b	chocolate	m	toothpaste
c	light bulb	i	shampoo
k	flowers	d	batteries
l	adaptor	a	screwdriver
f	envelopes	g	magazine
j	Band-Aids	h	newspaper

2 **CD2 55** Focus students' attention on the example and remind students of the convention of stress patterns in the Student Book – the circles indicate the number of syllables and the larger circle indicates the main stress.

Say *aspirin* and ask *How many syllables?* (two). With weaker students, go through the list of words in the same way, establishing the number of syllables.

Play the recording, pausing after each word, if necessary, to give students time to write their answers. Allow students to check their answers in pairs before checking answers with the class.

Play the recording again and have students repeat chorally and individually. Make sure they can reproduce *aspirin* and *chocolate* correctly, both of which are pronounced with only two syllables.

Answers and audio script

●•	•●	●••	•●•	••●
aspirin chocolate light bulb flowers Band-Aids toothpaste phone case	shampoo	envelopes screwdriver newspaper batteries	adaptor	magazine

CD2 55

aspirin	phone case
chocolate	toothpaste
light bulb	shampoo
flowers	batteries
adaptor	screwdriver
envelopes	magazine
Band-Aids	newspaper

3 Focus students' attention on the picture of Main Street and check pronunciation of the names of the stores in the box. Make sure students understand that a card shop sells paper and writing materials. Focus students' attention on the example. Students then work in pairs and continue categorizing the items in exercise 1.

Check the answers with the class. You can extend the activity by having students brainstorm other items that can be bought at the stores in exercise 3. Have them check the spelling and pronunciation, recording both in their vocabulary notebooks.

NOTE

The words *shop* and *store* are both used, for example hardware *shop* and hardware *store*. A *shop* is usually a smaller place selling fewer items. The word *shop* can also be used to convey that the place is smaller and cozier than a store.

Answers
bookstore: magazine, newspaper (batteries, notebook, envelopes, phone case might be sold here, too)
hardware shop: adaptor, light bulb, batteries, screwdriver
drugstore: aspirin, Band-Aids, toothpaste, shampoo , flowers, phone case, chocolate
card shop: notebook, envelopes, phone cases (flowers might be sold here, too)

EXTRA ACTIVITY

Students do a discussion activity on the pros and cons of shopping in a supermarket and on Main Street. Draw a simple table on the board and elicit some examples, e.g.:

	Pros	Cons
Supermarket	do all your shopping in one place	no local/individual products
Main Street	personal service	can be expensive

Give students time to think about further arguments for and against each way of shopping. Put students in small groups to discuss their ideas. Discuss the main arguments as a class and establish which way of shopping the class prefers and why.

ADDITIONAL MATERIAL

Workbook Unit 8
Ex. 10 Food
Ex. 11 Daily needs

Shopping on Main Street

This section focuses on the language of asking for things in stores and cafés, and how to sound polite. It recycles the language of polite requests from Unit 5 *Can/Could I …?* and also reinforces *would like* from this unit. The conversations in exercise 1 include examples of *too* and *enough*.

NOTE

This is not intended to be a full presentation of the uses of *too* and *enough*, but the opportunity to use the items in context. *Much* and *many* are recycled with *too,* and students also learn *too* + adjective. *Enough* is used in the context of *not enough people*, so there is no need to go into the adjectival use, e.g., *not big enough,* at this stage.

An example of the Present Continuous *I'm looking for …* is also provided in context. There's no need to go into a full presentation of Present Continuous at this stage. This is covered in Unit 10.

SUGGESTION

You can help to add authenticity to the role plays in this section by bringing in some props for exercises 2, 3, and 6. If it is difficult to supply real objects, you can bring in empty containers of aspirin, toothpaste, etc. for exercise 2, and empty (paper or plastic) plates, cups, etc. for exercise 6. Having objects to handle can help students remember their lines, encourage them to interact with their partner more fully, and also build confidence, especially in weaker students.

1 **CD2 56** Tell students they are going to hear three conversations in Main Street stores. Give students time to read the conversations quickly. Ask *Where are the people in each conversation?* (1 a flower shop, 2 a hardware shop, 3 a card shop).

Focus students' attention on the example and play conversation 1. Give students time to complete the missing words. Play the rest of the recording and have students complete the task.

Check the answers with the class.

Answers and audio script
1 **A** I'd like some flowers, please. How much are the roses?
 B They're $36 a dozen.
 A Oh, that's **too much**. I can't spend that much.
 B Well, how about some tulips? They're **only** $15 a dozen.
 A That's much **better**. I'll take a dozen.
2 **C** Can I help you find something?
 D Yes, I need a light bulb.
 C What **kind** do you need?
 D A 13 watt mini bulb.
 C OK. Let's see … here's a pack of six.
 D Thanks. But that's **too many** … I just need one.
 C Oh, sorry, we don't sell them individually. Not **enough** people want to buy only one.

3 E	Do you have any cases for this phone?
F	Let me see … yes, here's one. It's very popular.
E	Thanks. Uh, actually it's **too big**.
F	Oh, sorry. I can order a small one for you.
E	Uh, no thanks.
F	OK. Anything **else**?
E	That's **all**, thanks.

2 Check pronunciation of *enough* /ɪˈnʌf/. Then put students into pairs to learn two of the conversations. If possible, pair weaker students with a stronger classmate. Ask students to change roles after the first conversation so that they both play the customer and the clerk. Monitor and check pronunciation. If students have problems, play the recording again and drill key lines chorally and individually.

Hand out appropriate props if you are using them (see *Note* above). Students act out their conversations for the class. Encourage the class to prompt if students forget their lines.

3 Refer students back to the shopping list in exercise 1 on p. 64. Give students time to choose which stores (bookstore, hardware shop, drugstore, card shop) they want to set their conversations in, and which objects they are going to ask for. With larger classes, you may need to allocate stores and objects to ensure there is a variety of content.

Hand out appropriate props if you are using them (see *Note* above). Students roleplay their conversations in closed pairs. Monitor and help, providing vocabulary as necessary. Remind students to change roles after each conversation. Write down any common errors, but don't discuss these until after the activity.

If you have time and your students enjoy doing role plays, you can have them act out some of their conversations for the class.

Sounding polite

This section gives students the opportunity to analyse structures they know in terms of politeness and also focus on their pronunciation in order to sound polite.

4 **CD2 57** Pre-teach/check students' understanding of *smoothie* (a thick, smooth drink of fresh fruit puréed with milk, yogurt, or ice cream) and *latte* (a shot of espresso coffee with frothy steamed milk). Give students time to read the sentences. Then play the recording and ask students to choose the sentences that sound more polite.

Check with the class. Ask students *What is the problem with the other sentences?* (they are too direct to use with someone you don't know).

> **Answers**
> I'd like a coffee, please.
> Can I have a sandwich?
> Could you bring me a smoothie?

5 **CD2 58** Pre-teach/check students' understanding of *croissant* /krəˈsɑnt; kwaˈsɑnt/ and *bagel*. Give students time to read through the incomplete conversation. Check that students understand that *For here* means to eat in the cafe or restaurant and *to go* means the same as to take the food out of the restaurant and eat it elsewhere.

Give students time to complete the conversation. Remind them of the need to sound polite.

Play the recording and let students check their answers. Put students in pairs to practice the conversation. Monitor and check for accurate pronunciation and intonation. If students sound flat, focus on the main stress and voice range on the lines. Exaggerate the voice range if necessary, drilling key lines chorally and individually.

> **Answers and audio script**
> **A** Hi! What can I get you?
> **B** I'd like a latte, please.
> **A** Sure. For here or to go?
> **B** For here.
> **A** And what size do you want? Small, medium, or large?
> **B** **Large**, please.
> **A** Would you like anything to eat? A croissant? A bagel?
> **B** **I'd like** a bagel, please. Toasted.
> **A** No problem.
> **B** **Can I have** some butter with the bagel?
> **A** Sure. Have a seat and I'll bring it over.

6 Briefly review food and drinks that you can buy in a café. Put students in new pairs to practice the conversations. With weaker students, elicit an example conversation first with the whole class, having students say a sentence each.

Hand out appropriate props if you are using them (see *Note* above). Students roleplay their conversations in closed pairs. Monitor and help, providing vocabulary as necessary. Remind students to change roles after each conversation so that they both play the customer and the clerk. Write down any common errors, but don't discuss these until after the activity.

If you have time and your students enjoy doing role plays, you could have them act out some of their conversations for the class.

ADDITIONAL MATERIAL

Workbook Unit 8
Ex. 12 Shopping on Main Street

Don't forget!

Workbook Unit 8
Ex. 13 Articles – *a/an*, *some* or nothing?
Ex. 14 Adverbs
Grammar Reference (SB p. 135)
Word list Unit 8 (SB p. 143)
Students can translate the words, learn them at home, or transfer some of them to their vocabulary notebook.
Tests (Online)
Unit 8 Test
Skills Test 2 (Units 5–6)
Stop and Check 2 (Units 5–8)
Video (iTools and Online)
Additional photocopiables and PPT™ presentations (iTools)

9 City living

Comparative and superlative adjectives • City and small town • Directions
VIDEO City living

This unit has three presentation sections. The theme is describing places: cities and small towns, New York's biggest indoor food market, and megacities. These are useful contexts to practice comparatives and superlatives. The skills section includes a jigsaw reading and listening about three megacities. **Note** The recordings for Units 9–12 are on CD3.

LANGUAGE INPUT

GRAMMAR
Comparative adjectives (SB p. 66)
Superlative adjectives (SB p. 68)

- Understanding and practicing comparative adjectives.
- Understanding and practicing superlative adjectives.

VOCABULARY
City and small town (SB p. 72)

- Understanding and practicing adjectives, nouns and compound nouns related to life in cities and small towns.

EVERYDAY ENGLISH
Directions (SB p. 73)

- Understanding and practicing prepositions of movement and the language of asking for and giving directions.

SKILLS DEVELOPMENT

READING
Megacities (SB p. 70)

- A jigsaw reading about the cities of Tokyo, Mumbai, and Mexico City.

LISTENING
People talking about where they live (SB p. 67/p. 70)

- Listening for comparative adjectives in a description of life in Paris **CD3** **5** (SB p. 124).
- Listening for key information in a description of life in Tokyo, Mumbai, and Mexico City **CD3** **11** (SB p. 125).

SPEAKING
Comparing cities (SB p. 67)
Project (SB p. 70)
Your town (SB p. 72)

- Making comparisons about two capital cities.
- Giving a presentation on a megacity.
- Talking about where you go in your town for different activities.

WRITING
Describing a place – Relative pronouns *that, who, where* (SB p. 110)

- Understanding relative pronouns for things, people, and places, then writing a description of your favorite city.

MORE MATERIALS

Photocopiables – The best place to live (TB p. 152)   **Tests** (Online)   **Video** (iTools and Online)

STARTER (SB p. 66)

The *Starter* introduces the topic of city life and gets students thinking about cities they know. Students are not asked to generate comparative forms at this stage – there will be plenty of opportunities to practice these in the activities that follow.

1 **CD3 2** Focus students' attention on the prompts. Briefly review *north* /nɔrθ/, *south* /saʊθ/, *east* /ist/, and *west* /wɛst/ by drawing a simple compass on the board. Elicit more precise locations, e.g., south-east by asking about towns and cities where your students are studying. Check the pronunciation of *mountains* /ˈmaʊntnz/. Give students time to think of a town or city in their country and describe its location. If appropriate, you can ask the rest of the class to guess the name of each place.

2 Play the recording and elicit the name of each city.

> **Answers and audio script**
> 1 This city is in the northeastern part of the country. It's very big, and very old. It's very near the ocean, and it's also on the Hudson River. (New York City)
> 2 This city is in the northern central part of the country. It's about 400 kilometers from the ocean and it's on the River Seine. It's one of the most popular tourist destinations in the world. (Paris)

NEW YORK AND PARIS (SB p. 66)

Comparative adjectives

> ⚠ **POSSIBLE PROBLEMS**
>
> The concept of comparing two things is usually not difficult for students. They may, however, experience difficulty in producing and pronouncing the comparative forms because of all the different parts involved, and sometimes because of interference from their own language. Some languages use the equivalent of *more* + adjective for all comparatives and so students forget to apply the *-er* ending for short adjectives. Students may also include *more* and the *-er* ending in the same sentence.
>
> **Common mistakes**
> - *She's more tall than me.*
> - *She's more taller than me.*
> - *She's taller that me.*
>
> Pronunciation can also present problems if equal stress is given to each word and syllable. In natural speech, the *-er* ending and *than* is usually pronounced with /ər/, e.g.,
>
> /ər/
> *New York's bigger than Paris.*
>
> Be prepared to highlight and drill natural-sounding connected speech if students have problems with pronunciation in the early stages.

1 **CD3 3** Focus students' attention on the photos and check the pronunciation of *Empire* /ˈɛmpaɪər/ and *Eiffel Tower* /ˈaɪfl ˈtaʊər/. Ask students what they know about New York and Paris. Elicit their opinions of the cities if they have been to them.

Pre-teach/check students' understanding of *romantic*. Then play the recording and have students follow in their book. Focus students' attention on the example comparison between New York and Paris. Then ask students to find the other differences given in the conversation.

Elicit the key sentences, checking the pronunciation carefully. Drill the sentences chorally and individually, focusing particularly on the /ər/ sounds (see *Answers* below). Ask students whether /ər/ is used on stressed or unstressed words/parts of words (*unstressed*). Tell students that the /ər/ sound is always present at the end of the *-er* comparative. Isolate *bigger* and *than* and then drill them together as connected speech: *bigger than* / ˈbɪgərðən/.

> **Answers**
> /ər/
> New York's bigger than Paris.
> /ər/
> Paris is much smaller, but it's more romantic.
> /ər/
> The food is better.

GRAMMAR SPOT

1 Read the notes as a class. Students work individually to write the comparative forms and try to formulate any rules they can. They may have a clear idea from doing exercise 1 or they may need prompting and guiding, but try not to just give them the rules. You can write the rules on the board as you go along. Make sure students understand the doubling of consonants in examples like *big – bigger*.

> **Answers**
> big **bigger**
> romantic **more romantic**
> small **smaller**
>
> *-er* is used with short adjectives such as *small – smaller*. Short adjectives ending in one vowel and one consonant double the consonant such as *big – bigger*.
> *more …* is used with longer adjectives such as *romantic – more romantic*.

2 Make sure students understand that some comparatives are irregular and so don't follow the *-er* rule – we don't say *gooder or *badder. Focus students' attention on the example *good – better* and elicit/teach *bad – worse*, checking the pronunciation /wərs/ carefully.

> **Answers**
> good better   bad **worse**

▶▶ Read Grammar Reference 9.1 on p. 136 together in class, and/or ask students to read it at home. Encourage them to ask you questions about it.

2 This exercise gives students the opportunity to practice the formation of comparative adjectives without having to worry about forming a whole sentence.

Pre-teach/check students' understanding of *tall, rainy,* and *polite*. Focus students' attention on the examples *taller* and *more expensive*. Ask why "-er" and why "more?" (*-er* with short adjectives, *more* with longer adjectives). Students work individually to write the comparative forms, using their dictionaries if appropriate. Some of the comparative forms were given in exercise 1 and the *Grammar Spot*. Monitor and help as necessary. Then check the answers with the whole class. Point out that adjectives ending in *-e*, add just *-r*, e.g., *nice – nicer*. With weaker classes, you can put the examples into groups according to their pattern: *+ -er, y* changes to *i +-er*, doubling of consonant, *more + adjective*, and irregular.

Briefly review the alphabet. Demonstrate the pairwork with two students:

A *hot*

B *hotter – H - O - T - T - E - R*

Then put students in pairs to test each other. Remind them to spell the comparative forms. Monitor and check. Discuss any form, spelling, or pronunciation errors with the whole class.

<table>
<tr><td colspan="2">Answers</td></tr>
<tr><td>tall – taller</td><td>warm – warmer</td></tr>
<tr><td>expensive – more expensive</td><td>cold – colder</td></tr>
<tr><td>hot – hotter</td><td>polite – more polite</td></tr>
<tr><td>cheap – cheaper</td><td>beautiful – more beautiful</td></tr>
<tr><td>nice – nicer</td><td>bad – worse</td></tr>
<tr><td>rainy – rainier</td><td>good – better</td></tr>
</table>

3 Focus students' attention on the photos and ask students to identify which show Paris and which show New York. Focus students' attention on the example. Check which other adjective in exercise 2 could be used to describe the Eiffel Tower and the Empire State Building (*beautiful*) and elicit a comparison, e.g., *I think the Eiffel Tower is more beautiful than the Empire State Building*. With weaker students, elicit the adjectives they can use in the rest of the sentences (*Metro/Subway – expensive, weather – hot/rainy, buildings – beautiful, parks – nice/beautiful*).

Put students in pairs to compare their ideas. Monitor and help as necessary. Check for accurate formation of comparatives and a natural delivery in the pronunciation. Correct any errors with the class, highlighting the use of /ər/ on the unstressed syllables if necessary.

CD3 4 Tell students they are going to hear six sentences, using the same prompts as in exercise 3. Play the recording and have students compare the sentences with their own versions. (If students ask about the height of the Eiffel Tower and the Empire State Building, confirm that the Eiffel Tower is 300m (986 feet) and the Empire State Building is 381m (1,250 feet).

Refer students to **CD3 4** on SB p. 124. Have them practice the sentences. Monitor and check pronunciation. If students have problems, drill the sentences from the recording or model them yourself. If necessary, break up the sentences into sections, isolating the comparative forms + *than*. Try to get a natural flow in the repetition of the sentences.

Audio script
1 The Empire State Building is taller than the Eiffel Tower.
2 The Métro is more expensive than the New York City Subway.
3 Paris has warmer winters than New York.
4 Paris is rainier than New York.
5 I think the buildings in Paris are more beautiful.
6 I think the parks in Paris are nicer.

4 **CD3 5** Pre-teach/check students' understanding of *public transportation, architecture, Londoner, modern,* and *have a good time*. Focus students' attention on the examples. If students ask about the spelling of *rainier*, point out that adjectives ending in *-y* form the comparative with *-ier*, e.g., *noisy – noisier*.

Give students time to read the sentences with blanks. Explain that the recording is in the form of a short monologue, but students should be able to pick out the key words to complete the sentences. Play the recording and have students complete Rob's opinions. Give them time to check their answers in pairs. Play the recording again if necessary and have students check/complete their answers. Check the answers with the class.

Answers and audio script
1 The New York City Subway is **cheaper** than the Métro.
2 New York has **colder** winters than Paris.
3 Paris is **rainier** than New York, but New York has **bigger** storms.
4 The architecture in Paris is **more beautiful**, but the buildings in New York are **more modern**.
5 Life is **faster** in New York.
6 People in New York work **harder**, and they make **more** money.
7 In Paris, having a good time is **more important** than making a lot of money.

CD3 5
Well, I like both New York and Paris. But they're very different cities. Take public transportation for example. The New York City Subway is cheaper than the Métro, but they're both easy to use. And the weather ... well, New York has colder winters than Paris. Paris is rainier than New York, but New York has bigger storms. What about the buildings? Well, ... the architecture in Paris is definitely more beautiful, but the buildings in New York are more modern. And living in the two cities? Well ... life is faster in New York. And the people? ... Mmm, people in New York work harder, and they make more money. In Paris, having a good time is more important.

5 Ask students to close their books and elicit one or two examples of what Rob said about New York and Paris. With weaker classes, you can write key words on the board as prompts, e.g., *public transportation, weather, buildings,* etc.

Students work in pairs to continue the task. Monitor and check. Discuss any form or pronunciation errors with the whole class.

Finish the activity by asking if students agree with Rob's opinions and eliciting their reasons.

Comparing cities

1 **CD3 6** In this exercise the use of *much* to emphasize comparatives is introduced. Students are only asked to recognize it at first, and not produce it until the following exercise.

Put the conversations in a context and tell your students that two people are discussing different cities they know.

Focus students' attention on the example. Point out that the students have to fill in the opposite adjectives in B's comments to those that A uses. Then ask students to work in pairs to complete the conversations.

Play the recording and have students check their answers.

> **Answers and audio script**
> 1 **A** Dubai is older than Rio de Janeiro.
>   **B** No, it isn't! Dubai is much **more modern**!
> 2 **A** Tokyo is **cheaper than** Bangkok.
>   **B** No, it isn't! Tokyo's much **more expensive**!
> 3 **A** Seoul is **bigger than** Beijing.
>   **B** No, it isn't! Seoul is much **smaller**!
> 4 **A** Miami is **safer than** Los Angeles.
>   **B** No, it isn't! It's is much **more dangerous**!
> 5 **A** Taxi drivers in New York are **better than** taxi drivers in London.
>   **B** No, they aren't! They're much **worse**!

2 Focus students' attention on the example and highlight the main stress and intonation arrow. Drill the pronunciation chorally and individually. Also check the pronunciation of these cities: *Tokyo* /ˈtoʊkioʊ/, *Seoul* /soʊl/, *Beijing* /beɪˈdʒɪŋ/, and *Johannesburg* /dʒoʊˈhænɛsbərg/.

Have students practice the conversations in open pairs. Encourage the Bs to sound really indignant when they disagree with A. If students have problems, give them exaggerated models yourself or play the recording again to make it clear that you want them to produce good stress and intonation and connected speech. You can give further support by writing these models on the board:

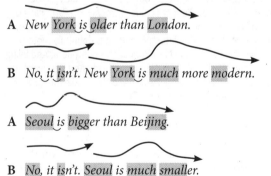

A *New York is older than London.*

B *No, it isn't. New York is much more modern.*

A *Seoul is bigger than Beijing.*

B *No, it isn't. Seoul is much smaller.*

Students practice the conversations in closed pairs. Remind them to focus on pronunciation, particularly stress and intonation.

3 This is the personalization stage. Decide on two cities that you and all, or most, of the students know and demonstrate the activity.

Students continue in pairs. Monitor and check for accurate use of comparative forms and pronunciation.

Have a few students share their responses with the rest of the class. Discuss any common mistakes in grammar or pronunciation after the pair and classwork stages.

> **SUGGESTION**
> You can give further practice of comparatives by asking students to write a series of true/false statements comparing towns/cities/countries. Students exchange their statements with a partner and test their knowledge.

ADDITIONAL MATERIAL *The Odd Couple*

Workbook Unit 9
Ex. 1–3   Comparative adjectives

NEW YORK'S BEST FOOD MARKET (SB p. 68)

Superlative adjectives

> ⚠ **POSSIBLE PROBLEMS**
> As with comparatives, students usually experience little difficulty with the concept of comparing three or more things but experience more difficulty in producing and pronouncing the forms. This is because of all the different parts involved and sometimes because of interference from their own language. Some languages use the equivalent of *(the) most* + adjective for all comparatives and so students forget to apply the *-est* ending to short adjectives. Students may also include *most* and the *-est* ending in the same sentence. One further problem is the tendency to omit *the* in superlative forms.
>
> **Common mistakes**
> • *He's the most tall student in the class.*
> • *He's the most tallest student in the class.*
> • *He's tallest student in the class.*
>
> Pronunciation can also present problems if equal stress is given to each word and syllable. Be prepared to highlight and drill natural-sounding connected speech if students have problems with pronunciation in the early stages.

1 Focus students' attention on the photo of Chelsea Market and elicit any information students know about it. Ask any students who have visited Chelsea Market to give a brief description of their experience.

Read the introduction to the text with the class. Focus students' attention on the example and then give students time to complete the chart. Check the answers with the whole class.

> **Answers**
>
> | Adjectives | Superlatives |
> | --- | --- |
> | 1 good | best |
> | 2 big | **biggest** |
> | 3 popular | **most popular** |
> | 4 busy | **busiest** |

2 Pre-teach/check students' understanding of *indoor, elevated, unique, locals*. Give students time to read the rest of the text to get a general idea of the content.

Check the answers with the class, having students spell the superlative forms. Students should be able to identify the *-est* endings in the short adjectives and the *most* form with longer adjectives, but be prepared to prompt them if necessary. (Do not go into a full explanation of the rules, as this is the focus of the Grammar Spot.)

Answers

1 oldest	4 newest
2 cheapest	5 most unique
3 most delicious	6 best

3 **CD3 7** Focus students' attention on the example. Put students in pairs to make the other sentences, using the prompts and referring back to the text as necessary. Monitor and check. If students have a lot of problems, do the activity on the board with the whole class.

Play the recording as a check. Have students read the sentences aloud. If necessary, drill the pronunciation chorally and individually, using the recording as a model.

Possible answers and audio script
It's the best place in the city to have lunch.
It's New York's biggest and most popular food market.
The market is busiest on weekends.
The food is amazing.
It's New York's newest and most unique park.
It's one of TV's best cooking shows.

GRAMMAR SPOT

1 Students look back at the superlatives in exercise 1 and try to figure out the rules. Prompt and guide them if necessary. Write the rules on the board as students figure them out, taking the opportunity to remind them of the comparative forms. Make sure students understand the doubling of consonants in examples like *big – biggest*.

Answers
– *(the) … -est* is used with short adjectives. Short adjectives ending in one vowel and one consonant double the consonant such as *big – biggest*. Short adjectives ending in *-y* drop the *-y* and add *-iest* such as *busy – busiest*.
– *(the) most* is used with longer adjectives such as *popular*, *(more popular)*, *the most popular*.
– some superlatives are irregular such as *good – best*.

American Speak Out Grammar page

---

2 Elicit the forms for *small* as an example. Students write the other comparative and superlative forms, using their dictionaries if appropriate.

Answers
small, smaller, (the) smallest
expensive, more expensive, (the) most expensive
hot, hotter, (the) hottest
easy, easier, (the) easiest
beautiful, more beautiful, (the) most beautiful

▶▶ Read Grammar Reference 9.1 on p. 136 together in class, and/or ask students to read it at home. Encourage them to ask you questions about it.

A PARISIAN IN NEW YORK (SB p. 69)

This exercise continues the focus on Paris and New York, this time with an interview with a Parisian woman in New York.

4 **CD3 8** Focus students' attention on the photo of Chantal. Ask *What nationality is she?* and elicit *She's French.*

Tell students to close their books and listen to the interview with Chantal. Play the recording through once. Elicit the answers to the questions. Allow students to share any other information about Chantal that they understood.

Answers and audio script
Chantal lives in New York. She works in a bank.
Yes, she is.

CD3 8
I = Interviewer   C = Chantal
I Hello, Chantal!
C Hi!
I Now, you're French, but you live in New York. Is that right?
C Yes, that's right.
I And are you … on your own here in New York?
C No, no! I'm here with my husband, André.
I Oh, I see. Do you work in New York?
C Yes, I do. I work in a bank. I really like my job.
I Oh that's good. And … Where do you live in New York?
C Well, we're renting an apartment in Chelsea. It's probably the smallest apartment in the city! But we love the neighborhood.
I Yes, Chelsea's a fun neighborhood. So, what does your husband do?
C He has a cheese shop in Chelsea Market … he sells French cheese. I think it's the most delicious food at the market!
I Wow, that's great! And tell me, do you have a car here?
C No, I don't. The subway is the easiest way to get around New York.
I OK! Thank you very much! I hope you enjoy your time here!

5 Give students time to read the questions and answers. Ask *Who's André?* (Chantal's husband.) *What's Chelsea?* (A neighborhood in New York)

Play the recording through without stopping. With weaker classes, play the recording again for students to add any answers they missed. Check the answers with the whole class.

Have students practice the questions and answers in pairs. If necessary, play the recording again, drilling the questions and answers that students have problems with.

Answers and audio script
It's probably the **smallest** apartment in the city!
I think it's the **most delicious** food at the market!
The subway is the **easiest** way to get around New York.

CD3 8 See Exercise 1.

ADDITIONAL MATERIAL

Workbook Unit 9
Ex. 4   Comparing two people

PRACTICE (SB p. 69)

It's the biggest!

1 **CD3 9** This activity reinforces superlative forms in a set of sentences about places in New York. Pre-teach/check students' understanding of *spotting celebrities*. Focus their attention on the example and explain that they should look at the second sentence in each pair to help them decide on which adjective to choose. With weaker classes, elicit the base form of the missing adjectives before students complete the sentences.

Give students time to complete the task. Play the recording and have students check their answers.

If you think your students need more pronunciation practice, play the recording again and have them repeat. Encourage them to imitate the stress and rhythm of the sentences, with the main stress falling on the superlative adjective.

Elicit a few examples about the town/city where your students are studying. Then put students in pairs/groups of three to continue the task. If possible, try to put students from different places together to encourage an exchange of information. Monitor and check for accurate formation of superlative adjectives. Discuss any common errors and have students correct them.

Answers and audio script
1 The tallest building in New York is One World Trade Center. It's 1,776 feet (541 meters).
2 The **most expensive** hotel is the St. Regis. It costs more than $800 a night!
3 The **biggest** park in New York is Central Park. It's 843 acres.
4 The **most popular** tourist attraction is Times Square. It has 39,000,000 visitors a year.
5 The **most famous** building is the Empire State Building. Everyone knows it.
6 The **best** restaurant for spotting celebrities is *Nobu*. They all go there.

Making comparisons

2 This activity reinforces comparative forms and pairs of opposite adjectives. Focus students' attention on the examples and explain that students need the opposite of the adjective in bold in each pair to complete the sentences. With weaker classes, elicit the base form of the missing adjectives before students complete the sentences.

Give students time to complete the task. Have students check their answers in pairs before checking answers with the class.

Answers
1 The music here is too loud. Can we go somewhere quieter?
2 The 10:00 train is too **slow**. Is the 11:30 train a **faster** one?
3 You're **late**. Why weren't you here **earlier**?
4 This apartment is too **far** from the center of town. I need somewhere **nearer**.
5 Five minutes is too **short** for a break. We need a **longer** one.
6 This exercise is too **easy**. Can I do something **harder/more difficult**?

Check it

3 Elicit the correct sentence in the first pair. Ask students to work in pairs to choose the correct sentence in each pair. Ask them to work quickly, then check the answers with the class.

Answers
1 Yesterday was hotter than today.
2 She's taller than her brother.
3 I am the youngest in the class.
4 This exercise is the most difficult in the book.
5 This is the coldest day of the winter.
6 What is the most beautiful park in the city?
7 That's the most expensive restaurant in town.

SUGGESTIONS

- You can give freer speaking practice in a personalized activity by asking the class to compare different students. This should be fun, provided you warn students to be careful not to offend other people! Briefly check/review the irregular comparatives *good/better/best, bad/worst/worst, far/farther/farthest*. Write a few short and long adjectives on the board as prompts, e.g., *tall, good at English, talkative, funny,* etc. Elicit a few examples from the class, then have students continue in small groups. Give them enough time to describe a few other people, but do not let the activity go on too long.

- Students write the name of their favorite movie or sports star and then compare their favorites in pairs/small groups, e.g., *(Johnny Depp) is more popular than (Ben Stiller)*. With weaker students you can write possible adjectives on the board, e.g., *talented, successful, good, interesting, rich, famous, old,* etc.

Workbook Unit 9

Ex. 5–7 Comparatives and superlatives

Photocopiable Activity

UNIT 9 The best place to live TB p. 152

Materials: One copy of the worksheet each student.

Procedure: Explain that students are going to complete and discuss a questionnaire to practice superlatives and talking about cities/regions.

- Hand out a worksheet to each student. Focus students' attention on the example. Check students' understanding of *reputation*. Give students enough time to complete the questions. Check the answers.

Answers

1	the biggest	6	the busiest
2	the worst	7	the most expensive
3	the most beautiful	8	the friendliest
4	the best	9	the most dangerous
5	the most interesting	10	the most modern

- Students write their answers to the questions. Remind them that when they are giving an opinion, they should not always choose their own city/region.

- For exercise 2, divide the class into groups of three. Pre-teach/check students' understanding of useful language for the discussion stage, e.g., *What did you put for question (1)?, I think …, I agree/don't agree with …, I prefer …*, etc. Have students discuss their answers. Monitor and check for accurate use of superlatives.

- For exercise 3, bring the class back together. Elicit a number of examples promoting different cities/regions. Encourage students to persuade their classmates to accept their choice. This should lead to natural use of comparatives and superlatives, and to some lively debate! Don't interrupt or over-correct students, as this is the fluency stage of the activity.

  With monolingual classes, you can extend the activity by having students decide on the best/worst place to live in their country.

READING AND LISTENING (SB p. 70)

Megacities

NOTE

At the end of this section, there is a project activity on megacities. You will need to build in time for students to do some research and take notes on a megacity, probably for homework. Students then give a short presentation about their chosen city to the class. In larger groups, you may need to schedule the presentations across a series of lessons, or have students give their presentations in groups.

Pre-reading: compare & contrast - city living vs.
rural living → better/worse (partners)
city
more diverse   rural
*   cheaper*

ABOUT THE TEXT

This is another jigsaw reading task, which gives students an opportunity for not only reading practice, but also some freer speaking. The class divides into three groups and each group reads a different, but similar, text about a megacity (a city with more than 10 million people). It's important to remind students to read only their text and to get information about the other texts via speaking.

The texts continue the theme of city living with a focus on three of the largest cities in the world. They have been chosen to review superlative forms and the language of describing a city. They also reinforce present and past tenses.

Tokyo The capital of modern Japan has developed into a megacity from a small fishing village. Prior to 1868, Tokyo was known as Edo. It became Japan's political center in 1603 when the Emperor Tokugawa Ieyasu established his feudal government there. A few decades later, Edo had grown into one of the world's most populous cities. In 1868, the emperor and capital were moved from Kyoto to Edo, which was renamed Tokyo. Large parts of Tokyo were destroyed in the Great Kanto Earthquake of 1923 and in the air raids of 1945.

Shinto is the main religion of Japan, characterized by devotion to invisible spiritual beings and powers called *kami*. A shrine is a sacred place where *kami* live. Every village and town or district in Japan will have its own Shinto shrine, dedicated to the local *kami*.

Mumbai The capital of the Indian state of Maharashtra, Mumbai was formerly known as Bombay until it was renamed in 1995 for political reasons. The Hindu nationalist party Shiv Sena won elections in the state of Maharashtra and presided over a coalition that took control of the state assembly. After the election, the party announced that the port city had been renamed after the Hindu goddess Mumba Devi, the city's patron deity. They argued that *Bombay* was a corrupted English version of *Mumbai* and an unwanted legacy of British colonial rule.

Bollywood is the hugely successful Hindi film industry, located mainly in Mumbai. The name is said to derive from *Hollywood* and *Bombay*.

Mexico City The city now known as Mexico City was founded by the Amerindians Mexica, also called the Aztecs, in 1325. The city was originally built on an island of Lake Texcoco and called Tenochtitlan.

The Historic Center has been declared a World Heritage Site by UNESCO. Famous landmarks in the Historic Center include the Plaza de la Constitución (Zócalo), the main central square, where Spanish-era buildings and an ancient Aztec temple are within a few steps of each other.

Encourage students to use the context to help them with new vocabulary and to pool knowledge with other students, or use a dictionary. With weaker classes or if you are short on time, ask students to look up some of following vocabulary before the lesson:

Homework prior to the lesson

Tokyo: *to move fast, commuter, up-to-date, emperor, earthquake, Shinto shrine, humid, cherry blossom, huge.*

> **Mumbai:** *commercial center, independence, snacks, headquarters, skyscraper, shopping mall, slums, running water, electricity, sanitation, sunrise/sunset, stone, crowded, poverty unique.*
>
> **Mexico City:** *indigenous, to invade, colonial, handicrafts, high-end goods, valley, air quality.*

1 **CD3 10** The goal of this exercise is to generate some interest in the topic of megacities, and hopefully provide some motivation to read the texts.

Give students time to read the exercise and number the cities, working individually. Students then compare their answers in pairs and briefly justify their order.

Give students time to read the questions in exercise 1. Pre-teach/check students' understanding of *inhabitants* and *rural*. Then play the recording through once and check the answers to the order of the cities. If necessary, play the recording again and check the answers to the questions.

2 Focus students' attention on the photos and elicit a brief description of each city. Use this opportunity to provide key words from the texts if your students didn't learn the vocabulary for homework (see *About the text* above), e.g., *Tokyo: to move fast, commuters, the latest fashions, Shinto shrine, cherry blossom; Mumbai: skyscraper, slums, running water, sanitation, sunrise/sunset, poverty; Mexico City: skyscraper, colonial, air quality.*

Focus students' attention on the headings and elicit the answers to the questions in exercise 2.

3 Put students into three groups, A, B, and C. (With larger classes, you may need to have multiple sets of the three groups.) Assign a text to each group and remind students to read only their text:

Group A – Tokyo

Group B – Mumbai

Group C – Mexico City

Have students read their text very quickly, asking others in their group for help with vocabulary if you didn't

pre-teach the items listed in *About the text* or assign them for homework. Monitor and help with any questions.

Check students' understanding of the headings. Give students time to write down the headings to make recording their answers easier. You can ask students to choose one person to record their answers. Remind students to write their answers in note form. With weaker classes, demonstrate which words can be left out by eliciting the notes for one of the headings (see *Answers*).

Have students work in their groups and make notes. Monitor and help as necessary.

The answers for each group are provided below for reference, but don't check the answers with the whole class at this stage.

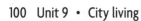

Mexico City

The city and its people

largest city in North and South America; offers variety of experiences; in valley in south central area, surrounded by mountains; air quality not good; visitors need to be careful, but city offers rich cultural mix; 20.5 million people; busy markets selling Mexican food + indigenous handicrafts

Money and business

richest city in Latin America; elegant shops selling high-end goods, expensive restaurants, really cool cafes; also a lot of poverty

Buildings and history

in main square, the National Palace, historic buildings, modern skyscraper; a lot of museums and theaters; European squares + colonial houses; Aztecs called it Tenochtitlán; already important city when Spanish invaded in 1521; became independent in 1821

Climate

rainy season June to October; warmest months April and May

Transportation

largest and cheapest subway system in Latin America; traffic slow – often faster to walk

4 Re-group the students, making sure there is an A, a B, and a C student in each group. Demonstrate the activity by having a group of students talk about their city. Encourage students to discuss the cities using comparative and superlative forms where possible, e.g.,

Tokyo has the biggest population.

Mexico City is more multicultural than the other cities.

Mumbai has a film industry, but the other cities don't.

All three cities have skyscrapers.

Students continue exchanging the information about their city. Remind them to use their notes, rather than read sections directly from their text. Monitor and help as necessary. Check for correct use of the present and past tenses, and for comparative and superlative forms. Write down any common errors, but discuss them at a later stage.

Bring the whole class together for students to share their ideas. Get information about all three cities, encouraging your students to compare and contrast. This way, you may get some freer use of comparatives and superlatives, but don't force this; just be happy if it happens! The goal of this discussion is to encourage some fluency practice. Finally, ask students which city they would/wouldn't like to live in and why.

Listening

5 **CD3 11** Tell students they are going to hear three people talking about their city, first Makiko from Tokyo, then Vimahl from Mumbai, and finally Lourdes from Mexico City. Pre-teach/check students' understanding of *auto rickshaw, vendor, enthusiastic, smell* (n). Play the first paragraph of Makiko's description and elicit what she says. With weaker students, you can write prompts on the board to help students focus on the key information, e.g.,

> *advantages of Tokyo – safe, _____, _____*
>
> *favorite time of year?*
>
> *exciting city – why?*

Play the recording through without stopping. Students may tell you they didn't understand anything, but have them pool their ideas in pairs or small groups before sharing their ideas with the class, as this will help build their confidence. Play the recording again if necessary to allow students to listen for any information they missed, but don't be tempted to keep repeating the recording. Students need to get used to picking out key information the first or second time they listen.

Audio script

Makiko from Tokyo

The first thing to say about Tokyo is that it is very safe. Women can walk everywhere anytime day or night. Little children walk to school. You can leave something on the table in a restaurant while you go out for a minute and nobody will take it.
Tokyo is also very clean, and it is very easy to travel around.
All the trains and buses run on time.
Personally, my favorite time of year is spring, when it's dry and the cherry blossoms are on the trees.
Tokyo is a very exciting city, because there are always new things to do, new places to go, new things to eat. It changes very quickly!

Vimahl from Mumbai

I have two strong impressions of Mumbai. First, it is a city that is so full of activity! It is busy, busy, busy all day long and all night long! It's a city that doesn't sleep much. The day begins early because it is so hot. It's a noisy place. There are cars going beep, beep, auto rickshaws by the thousands, fast trains rushing past, vendors shouting and trying to get you to buy their food, their drinks, their clothes. And people, people everywhere trying to get to work.

The second thing to say is that the people are very, very enthusiastic. Life isn't easy in Mumbai for a lot of people, but we really work hard and we really want to do our best. Every new day brings new possibilities! The future is exciting for us!

Lourdes from Mexico City

There are three things I like about living in Mexico City. First, the weather. It is warm and sunny most of the year. The second is the fresh fruit and vegetables – the markets are wonderful, the colors and smells are great! And the third is that I'm never bored because there is so much to see and do! We have museums, theaters, art exhibitions, parks, restaurants, … everything!
My favorite time of year in Mexico City is the end of December, from the 16th to the 31st. The city is full of lights, there are parties everywhere, and we eat and drink and give presents. Everyone's really happy! I love it!

EXTRA ACTIVITY

Students use the descriptions in **CD3 11** as a model for a description of their own town or city. Ask students to underline useful expressions from the script, e.g., *The first thing to say about … is …, My favorite time of year in … is …, I have (two) strong impressions of …, It's a city that …,* etc. Students work in small groups to describe their city. Encourage them to ask questions about each place.

Project

SUGGESTION

You can help students structure their presentation by preparing a handout with some key expressions:

Introduction

Good morning/afternoon/evening, everyone. Thank you for coming.

Starting the talk

I would like to start by …
Then, … Next, … After that, …
And finally, …

Main part of talk

So, let's begin with …
Moving on to …/Let's move on to …
My next point deals with …

Ending the talk

To sum up, …
In conclusion, you can see that …
Thank you for listening. Does anyone have any questions?

See *Note* at the start of this section. Ask students to use their notes from exercise 3 to help them do the research and organize their notes. If appropriate, encourage them to bring some visuals to support their presentation, e.g., a map and photos. If you have access to computers, students can give their talk with the support of a presentation program.

When students give their presentation, ask them to come to the front of the class (or stand up in front of their group in larger classes) and make sure the rest of the class is quiet and pays attention. Allow students to refer to their notes, but don't let them read the information from a script. Encourage the class/groups to ask questions to the presenter. Be generous with praise after students have presented their talk, as it can be rather nerve-wracking, especially for weaker students.

ADDITIONAL MATERIAL

Workbook Unit 9

Ex. 8   Reading
Ex. 9   Listening

VOCABULARY AND SPEAKING (SB p. 72)

City and small town

This section focuses on the objects and facilities typically found in urban and rural areas. Students match vocabulary to pictures and then use the key words in context. This also gives an opportunity to recycle comparative forms. Students then discuss how different places and facilities are used, and where they go in their town when they have free time.

SUGGESTION

You can introduce the topic by asking students to brainstorm the objects and places related to city life and small town life. Write the headings CITY and SMALL TOWN on the board and elicit suggestions as to which words belong where. Write the words in the correct category or ask individual students to come up to the board to write the answers. Take the opportunity to review the alphabet by having students spell the words.

1   Focus students' attention on the pictures. Check the answer to the questions (*the picture at the top shows the city and the one at the bottom shows the small town*).

2   Focus students' attention on the examples and ask students to point to the square in the relevant picture. Students work in pairs and continue matching. They can use their dictionaries or they can ask you about words they don't know.

Check the answers with the class, dealing with any pronunciation difficulties as you go. Make sure students understand the difference between a library (where you borrow books) and a bookstore (where you buy books).

Answers

7	square /skwɛr/	14	field
2	mall	13	farm
8	statue /ˈstætʃu/	16	woods
6	farmer's market	19	bridge
9	city hall	17	path
4	street	20	river
12	library /ˈlaɪbrɛri/	22	cottage /ˈkɑtɪdʒ/
10	parking lot	21	hill
3	traffic light	23	mountain /ˈmaʊntn̩/
5	sidewalk	15	ice-cream parlor
1	office building	18	lake
11	gas station		

As an extension, you can elicit examples of what you usually find only in a small town. Students may disagree here based on their own experience, so be prepared to accept a range of reasonable answers, e.g., *woods, farm, field, lake, mountain, cottage.*

3   The goal of this exercise is to reinforce the city and small town vocabulary and review comparative forms. Pre-teach/check students' understanding of *mayor* /ˈmeɪər; ˈmɛr/ and *pedestrian*. Focus students' attention on the example and then give students time to complete the sentences. Check the answers with the class.

Answers

1   A mall is bigger than a farmer's market.
2   A mountain is higher than a **hill**.
3   A **cottage** is smaller than a house.
4   A city is bigger than a **town**.
5   In my city, there's a **statue** of George Washington sitting on his horse. It's in the main **square**.
6   The mayor has an office in **city hall**.
7   Cars drive on the **street**. Pedestrians walk on the **sidewalk**.

4   Focus students' attention on the example and put students in pairs/groups of three to discuss the other places. In

multilingual classes, put students of different nationalities together so they can compare the function of the places listed.

Elicit a range of answers from the class

Your town

5   Check students' understanding of *tourist sights* and elicit some examples of popular sights in the students' own countries. Give examples of where you go to do the things listed.

Students then work in small groups to discuss their answers. Monitor and help as necessary.

Elicit a range of answers from the class. If appropriate, establish which places are the most popular with your class.

EXTRA ACTIVITY

If you would like to give more fluency practice on the topic of this section and review comparative adjectives, you can set up a debate on city vs. small town. Divide the students into two main groups *CITY* and *SMALL TOWN*. Have students from each category work together in pairs/groups of three to brainstorm the benefits of living in their area, e.g., *city – good public transportation, small town – clean air.*

Then put students into groups of four, with two "City" students and two "Small Town" students. Provide useful language for the discussion stage, e.g., *Life in the (city) is better because … / Don't forget that (small towns) have … / In the (city) you can … / You can't say that life in the (city) is … / That's true, but … / I know, but … .* Each pair gives arguments as to why their area is better and tries to persuade the other students that they are right.

Monitor and help as necessary. Check for accurate use of comparatives and acceptable pronunciation, especially of the /ər/ sound in comparatives.

ADDITIONAL MATERIAL

Workbook Unit 9
Ex. 10 City and small town

Describing a place

Relative pronouns *that, who, where*

This section continues the focus on cities with a short descriptive writing task on the students' favorite city. The language focus is the relative pronouns *that*, *who*, and *where*. Students will be familiar with *who* and *where* as question words and so should not have too much difficulty with the controlled practice. Exercise 2 reinforces the use of the relative pronouns in clauses and also serves as a model for students' own description of their favorite city.

Exercise 3 contains examples of non-defining relative clauses, as well as defining relative clauses. The punctuation needed for students to do the task is already in place, so do not go into an explanation of the difference between the two types of clause at this stage.

> **NOTE**
>
> The places mentioned in the description of London are:
>
> *Buckingham Palace*, the official home of the British Royal Family
>
> *the Houses of Parliament*, the buildings in which the members of the British parliament meet. *Big Ben* is actually the large bell in the clock tower of the Houses of Parliament, but the name is often used to refer to the clock itself.
>
> *Harrods,* a large department store in the Knightsbridge area of London. It has the reputation of being able to provide anything a customer wants.
>
> *the London Eye*, the world's tallest observation wheel, located on the banks of the River Thames. It offers spectacular views of London and its famous landmarks such as Big Ben, Buckingham Palace, and St. Paul's Cathedral.
>
> *Hamleys*, whose store in Regent Street is one of the biggest toy shops in the world and a very big tourist attraction.
>
> The text also refers to the *Congestion Charge*, a fee for drivers traveling within areas of central London.

1   Go over the *Grammar Spot* with the class.

GRAMMAR SPOT

1   Read the examples with the whole class and elicit the answers.

Answers
1 things   2 places   3 people

Ask students which words are replaced by the relative pronoun in sentences 1 and 3 (1 *it*, 3 *she*). Point out that the reference to place in sentence 2 *in it* is replaced by *where* and so is not repeated.

2   Elicit the answer to number 1 and then have students complete the task, working individually. Check the answers with the class.

3 Have students read the text about London, ignoring the blanks, just to get an idea of the content. Check students' understanding of *to land, to ride, traffic, pollution, air,* and *toy shop.*

Elicit the answer to number 1, pointing out the use of *ago* to help students choose the past tense to answer where the Romans landed. Give students time to complete the exercise, working in pairs. Encourage them to pool their knowledge of London. Check the answers with the class.

SUGGESTION

If you think your students will need additional help in preparing for the writing task, build in a content planning stage. Brainstorm things to say about a favorite city, e.g., population, history, buildings, tourist attractions, problems, etc. Elicit a few example statements from students about their favorite city or give some examples about yours. Give students time to make notes about their city. Divide the class into pairs and have them talk about their city. Elicit any interesting facts/opinions in a short class discussion.

4 Read the instructions as a class. Focus students' attention on the paragraph plan and elicit possible answers to each of the questions. With weaker classes, draft a sample first paragraph on the board with the whole class.

Give students time to write their description in class or assign it for homework. Point out that students should try to write four paragraphs of roughly equal length. If possible, display the descriptions on the classroom wall or noticeboard to allow students to read one another's work. When you check the students' descriptions, point out errors, but allow students to correct them themselves. Try to limit correction to major problems to avoid demoralizing the students.

EVERYDAY ENGLISH (SB p. 73)

Directions

The theme of city and small town living provides an ideal context for the language of giving directions, including prepositions of movement.

1 Focus students' attention on the map and ask students to give a brief description of Fairview, e.g., *There's a river in the middle. The town has a library, a modern hotel and a railway station,* etc.

Check pronunciation of the words in the box. Then have students locate them on the map.

2 **CD3 12** Briefly review *left* and *right*. Have students locate *YOU ARE HERE* and Route 312 to Westfield at the top of the map. Focus their attention on the example and give students time to read the directions and predict their answers.

Play the recording and have students fill in the blanks. With weaker students, have them mark the route across the map with a pencil when they first listen. Then play the recording again for them to write in their answers.

Check the answers with the class. Deal with any pronunciation difficulties as you go.

3 **CD3 13** Tell students they are going to hear three sets of directions, all starting from the *YOU ARE HERE* spot on the map. Pre-teach/check students' understanding of *crosswalk* /ˈkrɔswɔk/. With weaker students, give them time to look carefully at the map and name each of the places/features shown.

Play number 1 as an example and elicit the answer (*the farmer's market*). Play the rest of the recording, pausing at the end of each set of directions. Allow students to check their answers in pairs. If there is any disagreement, play the recording again and have students follow the route a second time.

4 Drill the pronunciation of the places in the list – *Appleton* /ˈæpltʌn/ and *Milltown* /ˈmɪltaʊn/. Point out that we say *the train station* and *the Town Hall* (not *a …*) because there is usually only one in each town.

Remind students of the fall/rise intonation used in polite requests (see exercise 3 on SB p. 41). Focus students' attention on the speech bubbles. Elicit complete examples, encouraging students to use the appropriate stress and intonation. Drill questions and answers in open pairs.

Students continue to work in closed pairs. Monitor and check that students are using the key language correctly and attempting the polite intonation.

If appropriate, ask some of the pairs to act out their conversations for the rest of the class.

5 Demonstrate the activity by giving some directions to a few places near your school and having students call out when they think they know the answer.

Students continue working in pairs. Monitor and help as necessary.

ADDITIONAL MATERIAL

Workbook Unit 9
Ex. 11 Directions

Don't forget!

Workbook Unit 9
Ex. 12 Prepositions
Grammar Reference (SB p. 136)
Word list Unit 9 (SB p. 143)
Students can translate the words, learn them at home, or transfer some of them to their vocabulary notebook.
Tests (Online)
Unit 9 Test
Video (iTools and Online)
Additional photocopiables and PPT™ presentations (iTools)

10 Where on earth are you?

Present Continuous • *something/nothing* … • Describing people • Social expressions (2)

VIDEO What are you doing?

This is the first unit where students are introduced to the Present Continuous in the context of "Where are you and what are you doing?". Students are already familiar with the Simple Present now and should be ready to compare and contrast the two present tenses. Further practice is provided in the context of describing people and what they are wearing. The unit also practices *something/nothing*, etc. The skills section includes reading and listening tasks about the International Space Station, and this provides further practice of the grammatical goals.

LANGUAGE INPUT

GRAMMAR
Present Continuous (SB p. 74)

Simple Present or Present Continuous? (SB p. 76)
something/nothing … (SB p. 77)

- Understanding and practicing the Present Continuous to talk about activities happening now and around now.
- Understanding and practicing the difference between present tenses.
- Understanding and practicing compounds with *some*, *any*, *every*, and *no*.

VOCABULARY
Describing people (SB p. 80)

- Understanding and practicing adjectives and nouns to describe people.

EVERYDAY ENGLISH
Social expressions (2) (SB p. 81)

- Understanding and practicing expressions in everyday situations.

SKILLS DEVELOPMENT

READING
The International Space Station (SB p. 78)

- An article about living in space.

LISTENING
Who's who? (SB p. 76)
An interview with an astronaut (SB p. 78)
Descriptions of people (SB p. 80)

- Listening and identifying people **CD3 19** (SB p. 126).
- Listening for key information in an interview **CD3 21** (SB p. 126).
- Listening and matching a description to a photo **CD3 22** (SB p. 126).

SPEAKING
What can you see? (SB p. 75)
Project (SB p. 78)
Describing someone in the room/in the news (SB p. 80)

- Describing a scene through the classroom window.
- Giving a presentation about an astronaut.
- Giving descriptions of people.

WRITING
Comparing and contrasting – Linking words *but, however, although* (SB p. 111)

- Understanding linking words for expressing contrast, then writing a comparison of two people you know.

MORE MATERIALS

Photocopiables – Something's happening (TB p. 153)   **Tests** (Online)   **Video** (iTools and Online)

STARTER (SB p. 74)

This section reviews and extends the use of the prepositions *in/at/on* + place.

Focus students' attention on the example and highlight the use of *on, at,* and *in* + the different places. Ask *Where are you?* to the class and elicit one or two more examples. Put students in pairs to continue the task. Monitor and help as necessary.

Then check the answers with the class. Encourage students to record the answers in categories according to the preposition as in the *Answers* below.

	Answers
in	my car/a meeting/bed/a café/my office/town/the store/the kitchen
at	a party/work/home/the airport/the bus stop/school/college/Jenny's house
on	my way home/the train/vacation/the bus

Give a few examples of where your friends and family are now. Then let students continue sharing examples in pairs or small groups.

I'M SITTING ON THE TRAIN (SB p. 74)

Present Continuous

> ⚠️ **POSSIBLE PROBLEMS**
>
> The Present Continuous has no equivalent form in many other languages, which use the present tense to convey the two concepts of "action which relates to all time" and "activities happening now." For example, in French, *il mange deux oeufs par jour (he eats two eggs a day)* and *il mange maintenant (he is eating now)*, the present tense *mange* expresses both ideas.
>
> Students not only confuse the two concepts of the Simple Present and the Present Continuous, they also confuse the forms. When they have seen the *am/is/are* in the Present Continuous, they tend to try to use it in the Simple Present.
>
> **Common mistakes**
> *She's come from Spain.
> *She's coming from Spain.
> *I'm come to school by bus.
> *What does he doing?
> *Does he coming to the party?
>
> The Present Continuous can also be used for activities happening in the near future. Examples of this use are included for recognition, but there's no need to go into a detailed explanation at this stage, as it is covered more fully in Unit 11.

This presentation is carefully staged to help students get used to the form of the Present Continuous and understand its use. Students first identify where the key characters are, then focus on just the *I* form of the Present Continuous in simple sentences before moving on to a wider range of forms in short conversations. The use of the photos helps to support the context of "activities happening now."

1 **CD3 14** Focus students' attention on the photo of Alice and Tony and then on Kate and Tim. Tell students they are going to hear each character saying a line and they simply have to identify who is speaking. Pre-teach/check students' understanding of *laptop*. Play number 1 as an example and point to the photo of Kate.

Play the rest of the recording and elicit the name of the character speaking. Play the recording again and have students repeat chorally and individually. Make sure students can reproduce the /m/ of *I'm* /aɪm/.

Answers and audio script
1 Kate	3 Tim
2 Tony	4 Alice

CD3 14
1 "I'm cooking."
2 "I'm reading the paper."
3 "I'm watching the soccer game."
4 "I'm working on my laptop."

2 **CD3 15** Focus students' attention on the photos again. Ask *Who is on the phone?* (Tony and Kate). Give students a few moments to read the incomplete conversations. Ask *Who is calling Tony?* (Nina) and *Who is calling Kate?* (Pete). Ask *Who are Nina and Pete, do you think?* (a friend or relative).

Focus students' attention on the example and play the recording as far as *for the weekend.* Play the recording through to the end and have students fill in their answers. Play the recording again if necessary and have students check/complete their answers.

Put students in pairs to practice the conversations. If students have problems with pronunciation/intonation, play the recording again as a model and drill key lines chorally and individually.

Answers and audio script
1 **Tony** Hello?
  Nina Hi, Tony! It's Nina. Where are you?
  Tony We're on the train. We're going to Washington, DC for the weekend.
  Nina Oh, great! How's the trip going?
  Tony Fine. I'm **reading** the paper, and Alice **is doing** something on her laptop.
2 **Kate** Hello?
  Pete Kate, hi! It's Pete. How are you? What **are** you **doing**?
  Kate Fine. We're at home. I'm just **cooking** some dinner.
  Pete What's Tim **doing**?
  Kate He's **watching** the soccer game. Can't you hear?
  Pete **Oh**, right!

3 **CD3 16** Focus students' attention on the example. Students ask and answer the question in open pairs. Students continue in closed pairs. Monitor and check for accurate formation of the questions and answers, and that students are including the correct contracted form of *to be* each time. With weaker students, drill some of the questions and answers chorally and individually and then let students continue in closed pairs.

Play the recording and have students check the questions and answers. If students need further practice, put them in new pairs to practice the conversations again.

Negatives

This section continues the theme of "Where are you?" and gives students the opportunity to practice the negative forms alongside the affirmative.

4 **CD3 17** Pre-teach/check students' understanding of *to tell the truth*. Focus students' attention on the photo and read the instructions as a class. Ask students to identify Beth (*the girl with the phone*) and Ellie. Ask *Where are they?* (at the mall/in town).

Pre-teach/check students' understanding of *to shout* and *to take care of*. Play the recording once and elicit the answer to the gist question *Is she telling the truth?* (No, she isn't.). Focus students' attention on the negative example and elicit as many other negative sentences as the students can remember. Play the recording again if necessary. With weaker students, you can write prompts on the board, e.g., *Internet, homework, Ellie's sister*.

Check the answers with the class, drilling the pronunciation chorally and individually. Make sure students can reproduce the negative forms accurately.

5 **CD3 18** Refer students back to the people on p. 74. Ask them to identify Tony, Kate, Alice, Tim, Beth, and Ellie. Play sentence 1 and focus students' attention on the example. Ask students to identify the negative form (*isn't sleeping*) and the positive form (*'s working*).

Play the rest of the sentences, pausing after each one and having students correct the information. With weaker students, you can write the key words on the board as support, e.g., *Atlanta/Washington DC, lunch/dinner*, etc.

Repeat the pairs of sentences until students can say them fluently, drilling chorally and individually. If necessary, highlight the contrastive stress in sentences with singular and plural forms:

Alice isn't sleeping! She's working on her laptop!

Alice and Tony aren't going to Atlanta. They're going to Washington DC.

GRAMMAR SPOT

1 Read the notes with the whole class. Elicit other examples by pointing to people in the class, e.g., *Yuko is sitting next to Adam, the teacher is standing at the front of the class*, etc.

2 Have students complete the chart, using contracted and full forms. Check the answers with the whole class.

Answers

I	'm (am)	
You	're (are)	learning English.
He/She	's (is)	sitting in a classroom.
We	're (are)	listening to the teacher.
They	're (are)	

Name the tense and then have students figure out the negative and question forms. Have students do this in pairs and then write the answers on the board, or refer students to Grammar Reference 10.1 and 10.2 on p. 137.

Answers
Questions

Am	I	
Are	you	learning English?
Is	he/she	sitting in a classroom?
Are	we	listening to the teacher?
Are	they	

Negatives

I	'm not	
You	aren't	learning English.
He/She	isn't	sitting in a classroom.
We	aren't	listening to the teacher.
They	aren't	

3 Focus students' attention on the sentences. Have students figure out the difference between the two tenses. Make sure they understand that the Simple Present describes things that are always true, or true for a long time, and that the Present Continuous describes activities happening now and temporary activities. (At this stage, do not overload students by focusing on the use of the Present Continuous with future meaning. There are examples of this use included for recognition later in this unit and it is covered more fully in Unit 11.)

If students need more help, you can write more sentences on the board to discuss with the whole class, e.g.,

Simple Present	**Present Continuous**
She usually wears jeans.	*She's wearing a dress today.*
He works in a bank.	*He's working in the garden today.*
They speak French.	*They're speaking English right now.*
I like music.	*Not usually possible: *I'm liking music.*

▶▶ Read Grammar Reference 10.1 and 10.2 on p. 137 together in class, and/or ask students to read them at home. Encourage students to ask you questions about them.

PRACTICE (SB p. 75)

Questions and negatives

Exercises 1 and 2 give controlled practice in the question and negative forms, using a series of picture prompts.

1 Pre-teach/check students' understanding of *a romance novel* (= a romantic story). Ask two students to read aloud the example question and answer. Give students time to write the other five questions, using the base verb each time. With weaker students, focus on the answers in the speech bubbles and elicit the question words students need before they form the questions.

Check the answers by having several pairs of students ask and answer questions aloud in front of the class. Check that students stress the questions correctly, with the auxiliary *are* unstressed and pronounced /ər/:

/ər/
What are you reading?

Answers

1 What are you reading? A romance novel.
2 What are you watching? The news.
3 Where are you going? To my bedroom.
4 Who are you talking to? My friend.
5 What are you wearing? Jeans and a T-shirt.
6 Why are you crying? Because it's a sad movie.

EXTRA ACTIVITY

If you want to give further practice of the Present Continuous *wh-* and *yes/no* question forms, you can write prompts on the board for questions about the pictures in exercise 1, e.g.,

1 Where/she/sit? (by the fire); she/listen to music? (no)
2 Where/he/sit? (on the sofa); he/watch the news? (yes)
3 What/he/carry? (a backpack); he/go upstairs? (yes)
4 Where/he/stand? (on the beach); he/use his cell phone? (yes)
5 Where/she/wait? (at the station); she/sit/in a car? (no)
6 What/she/do? (watching a movie); she/feel/happy? (no)

2 Pre-teach/check students' understanding of *romantic comedy*. Then focus students' attention on the example. Give students time to write their sentences, working individually. With weaker students, you can elicit the verb students will need in each negative sentence.

Check the answers with the class. You can have students give an affirmative sentence to say what each person is doing as in the sentences in parentheses in the *Answers* below.

Answers

1 She isn't reading a detective story. (She's reading a romance novel.)
2 He isn't watching a movie. (He's watching the news.)
3 He isn't going out with his friends. (He's going to his bedroom.)
4 He isn't talking to his mother. (He's talking to his friend.)
5 She isn't wearing a dress. (She's wearing jeans and a T-shirt.)
6 She isn't watching a romantic comedy. (She's watching a sad movie.)

Talking about you

3 This activity provides practice with the Present Continuous in a personalized way. Demonstrate the activity by giving two or three examples about yourself. Have students work individually and write their answers.

Have students work in pairs and exchange their answers. Monitor and check for correct use of the Present Continuous. If necessary, drill pronunciation before eliciting a range of answers from students.

Answers

1 I'm learning English.
2 We aren't learning Chinese.
3 I'm sitting next to the window./I'm not sitting next to the window.
4 It's raining./It isn't raining.
5 The teacher is talking to us./The teacher isn't talking to us.
6 The students are listening to the teacher./The students aren't listening to the teacher.

4 This exercise gives students the opportunity to practice the Present Continuous in a spontaneous way by describing a scene. Focus students' attention on the examples. Then look out of the window and give a brief description of the scenery and any actions people are doing, e.g., *I can see the street and a small park. Some people are talking and two children are eating ice cream.*

Pre-teach the expression *I can see …* and have two confident students look out of different windows if possible and give a description of the scene. Encourage them to be as detailed as possible (people/buildings/ animals/traffic, etc.) and include colors and other adjectives in their description.

Monitor and check for accurate use of the Present Continuous. Point out any common errors and drill the corrections and pronunciation as necessary.

SIMPLE PRESENT OR PRESENT CONTINUOUS?
(SB p. 76)

Who's who?

This section contrasts the two present tenses and helps reinforce the different uses that students focused on in the Grammar Spot on p. 75. Exercises 1 and 2 are based on identifying and describing people in a listening task. Exercise 3 brings together the two present tenses in questions and exercise 4 challenges students to complete sentences using the correct present tense.

1 **CD3 19** This serves as a gist listening task in which students simply have to identify the people in the picture. Ask *Where are the people?* (in an art gallery). Read the instructions with the whole class. Explain that students don't need to understand every word to be able to do the task.

Play the whole recording once. Students listen and write the names next to the correct people.

Check the answers, allowing students to share any additional information they understood.

Answers and audio script
From left to right: Helena, Roger, Annie, Sam, Paul, Sophie

CD3 19
A Oh, no! I don't know anybody. Who are they all?
B Don't worry. They're all very nice, I'll tell you who everybody is. Can you see that man over there?
A The man near the window?
B Yes. That's Paul. He's talking to Sophie. He's a banker. Very rich. And very funny. He works in New York City.

A Wow! So he's Paul. OK. And that's Sophie next to him?
B Yes. She's laughing at Paul's jokes. She's really nice. She's a professor at New York University. She teaches business studies.
A And who's that woman on the left?
B That's Helena. She's drinking orange juice. She's a writer. She writes stories for children. They're excellent. A very nice woman.
A And who's that man she's talking to?
B Helena's talking to Roger. Roger's eating chips. He's an interesting man. He's an art dealer. He works for the Museum of Modern Art.
A Really? Wow! What a job! So that's Paul and Sophie … Helena and Roger … Now there are two more. Who are they?
B They're Sam and Annie. They're looking at photos on Sam's phone.
A And what do they do?
B They're designers. They make clothes for children.
A OK. So that's everybody. Thanks.
B No problem.

2 **CD3 19** This activity focuses on the detail in the recording and helps reinforce the difference between the two present tenses.

Pre-teach/check students' understanding of *banker, to laugh at, joke, professor, business studies, art dealer, designer* (n). Focus students' attention on the chart and read aloud the questions at the top of each column. Remind students that *What's he/she doing?* refers to the activities in the gallery and that *What does he/she do?* refers to information about his/her job. Read aloud the names of the people in the chart. Play the recording again as far as *He works in New York City* and focus students' attention on the example for Paul.

Remind students to look at the picture in exercise 1 as they listen to help them understand who is talking to whom. Play the recording again and have students complete the chart. Have students check their answers in pairs before checking answers with the whole class.

Answers

	What's he/she doing?	What does he/she do?
Paul	He's talking to Sophie.	He's a banker. He works in New York.
Sophie	She's laughing at Paul's jokes.	She's a professor at New York University. She teaches business studies.
Helena	She's drinking orange juice.	She's a writer. She writes stories for children.
Roger	He's eating crisps.	He's an art dealer. He works for the Museum of Modern Art.
Sam and Annie	They're looking at photos on Sam's phone.	They're designers. They make clothes for children.

See exercise 1 for **CD3 19**

3 This exercise gives further practice of question forms in the two present tenses. Focus students' attention on the first pair of sentences. Ask *Which question refers to the activity in the gallery?* (Who's he talking to?) *Which talks about work and means "for a long time?"* (Where does Paul work?).

Put students in pairs to continue asking and answering about the other people. Monitor and check for correct choice of tense and formation of the questions. Highlight

and correct any errors carefully during the checking stage. If students have problems with the choice of tense, use the concept question again: *Happening in the gallery or true for a long time?*

Answers
1 Where does Paul work?
  Who's he talking to?
2 Why **is** Sophie **laughing**?
  Where **does** she **teach/work**?
3 What **is** Helena **drinking**?
  What **does** she **write**?
4 Who **does** Roger **work** for?
  What **is** he **eating**?
5 What **do** Sam and Annie **make**?
  What **are** they **looking** at?

4 This final exercise of the section brings together all the elements students have learned by asking them to complete sentences with the verbs in the correct tense. Focus students' attention on the first pair of sentences and elicit the answer (*works*). Ask *Why Simple Present?* (because it's always true). Now focus their attention on the second sentence and elicit the answer (*'m working*). Ask *Why Present Continuous?* (because it's happening now – a temporary situation). Put students into pairs to complete the task. Check the answers with the class.

Answers
1 My father **works** in a bank.
2 I**'m working** very hard right now. I need the money.
3 Hi, Dave! Are you on the train? Where **are** you **going**?
4 I always **go** to the movies on Fridays.
5 Let's have lunch tomorrow. I usually **have** lunch at 1:00.
6 I'm sorry! **Are** you **having** lunch? I'll call you back later.
7 Sh! I**'m doing** my homework. You**'re making** too much noise!
8 In my house, my mom usually **makes** the dinner, and my dad usually **does** the dishes.

SUGGESTION

Students can get further practice by roleplaying the situation in exercise 1. Put students into groups of four and ask them to imagine they are at the art gallery. Allocate the roles of the people in exercise 1 to two of the students and let the other two play themselves. Briefly review the language of greeting and introducing people, *This is … . Hello, nice to meet you. Nice to meet you, too.* Provide other possible questions to practice the Present Continuous, e.g.,

Are you traveling a lot right now?

What are you writing now?

Are you enjoying it?

What are you designing at the moment?

What's happening in the world of art?

Students introduce each other and then ask "getting to know you" questions, using Simple Present and Present Continuous. Ask students to change roles and repeat, so that they all have the opportunity to play themselves. Monitor and check for correct use of Simple Present and Present Continuous, but wait until after the roleplay to discuss any common errors.

ADDITIONAL MATERIAL

Workbook Unit 10
Ex. 1   Prepositions
Ex. 2–4 Present Continuous
Ex. 5   Simple Present or Present Continuous
Ex. 6   *be* or *do*?

SOMETHING'S HAPPENING (SB p. 77)

something/nothing . . .

> ⚠ **POSSIBLE PROBLEMS**
>
> Students will have learned words like *something*, *nothing*, *everybody*, etc. as lexical items in individual sentences, but are unlikely to know that we can form a set of compounds by joining *some*, *any*, *every*, and *no + thing*, *body*, and *where*. As with …*body*, compounds with …*one* can be used to refer to people. (As in Units 4 and 8, we do not suggest that you explore the use of *any* to mean "it doesn't matter which," as in *Sit anywhere you like*.)
>
> Students shouldn't have problems with meaning as the compounds are presented in context, but there may be confusion in the following areas:
>
> - The difference between *something/somebody*, etc. and *anything/anybody*, etc., is the same as the difference between *some* and *any*, so you may need to review the general rules, especially with weaker students: *something/somebody*, etc., mainly in affirmative sentences, and *anything/anybody*, etc., mainly in negative sentences and questions.
> - *Something/somebody*, etc., (not *any…*) is used in questions that are requests or offers, e.g., *Could I have something to drink? Would you like somebody to help you?*
> - These compounds are singular, e.g., *Everywhere was closed. Something is wrong*, etc.
> - Compounds with *no…* are used with an affirmative verb, e.g., *She said nothing* (NOT *She didn't say nothing.*) *Nobody answered my letter* (NOT *Nobody didn't answer my letter.*) Check for these double negatives and be prepared to correct them carefully.

1 Focus students' attention on the first photo and elicit the first answer as an example. Give students a few moments to complete the rest of the sentences. Students check their answers in pairs before checking the answers with the class.

Answers
1 something
2 anything
3 everything
4 Nothing

Focus students' attention on the chart and elicit the missing compound with *some* (*somewhere*). Put students in pairs to complete the chart. Monitor and help as necessary. Check the answers, asking students to spell each word. Make sure students stress the words correctly (*on the first syllable*). Also check the change in vowel sound in the compounds with *no…*:

nothing /ˈnʌθɪŋ/ *nobody* /ˈnoʊbədi/ *nowhere* /ˈnoʊwɛr/

Answers

some	any	every	no
something	**anything**	**everything**	**nothing**
somebody	anybody	**everybody**	nobody
somewhere	anywhere	everywhere	**nowhere**

▶▶ Read Grammar Reference 10.3 on p. 137 together in class, and/or ask students to read it at home. Encourage them to ask you questions about it.

2 This exercise highlights common mistakes. Focus students' attention on the example and ask *Why "something" and not "anything?"* (it's an affirmative sentence). Students choose the correct word in the other sentences, working individually.

Give students time to check their answers in pairs before checking the answers with the whole class. If students have problems, highlight the meaning of the prefix *every* and *no*, and review the difference in use between *some* and *any* (see *Possible problems*).

Answers

1 something	3 Everybody's	5 Nobody's
2 anywhere	4 anybody	6 everything

PRACTICE (SB p. 77)

Everything was too expensive!

1 **CD3 20** This exercise practices each set of compounds according to the endings *…thing*, *…body*, and *…where*. Give students time to read the incomplete conversations. Elicit what each one is about (*1 shopping, 2 a party, 3 going out on Saturday night*).

Focus students' attention on the example. Then give students time to complete the task, working individually.

Students check their answers in pairs. Then play the recording as a final check.

Answers and audio script
1 **A** Did you buy anything for yourself at the mall?
   B No. Nothing.
   A Why not?
   B **Everything** was too expensive.
   A Oh, that's too bad.
   B But I bought **something** for you. Happy Birthday!
2 **C** Did you talk to **anybody** at the party?
   D No. **Nobody**.
   C Why not?
   D **Everybody** was dancing and the music was really loud!

   C Oh!
   D But I danced with **somebody** nice – a woman named Kate.
3 **E** Did you go **anywhere** on Saturday night?
   F No. **Nowhere**.
   E Why not?
   F **Everywhere** was closed. There wasn't one place open.
   E That's incredible!
   F So next weekend I'm going **somewhere** more interesting.

2 Let the pairs of students choose two of the three conversations. Give them time to practice the conversations a few times to memorize them. Monitor and help as necessary. If students have problems with pronunciation, play selected lines of the recording again and drill chorally and individually. If students sound flat, encourage a wide voice range, drilling again as necessary.

Students act out their conversations in front of the class. Encourage them to prompt each other if they have problems remembering their lines. In larger classes, you may have to divide the class into groups for the acting stage or return to it in a later lesson.

Check it

3 This exercise covers the compounds from the previous section and also two examples of the Present Continuous. Focus students' attention on the first pair of sentences and elicit the answer (*Somebody is on the phone for you.*). Ask *Why "somebody" and not "anybody"?* (it's an affirmative sentence). Students choose the correct sentences, working individually.

Give students time to check their answers in pairs before checking the answers with the whole class.

Answers
1 Somebody is on the phone for you.
2 I don't have anything for your birthday.
3 I want to go somewhere hot for vacation.
4 I'm learning English.
5 She isn't working hard.

Photocopiable Activity
UNIT 10 Something's happening TB p. 153
Materials: One copy of the worksheet with sentences 1–12 cut up and the key words chart left uncut for each pair/team of students. If you are short on time or with weaker students, the worksheet can also be used uncut so that the sentence halves appear in the correct order.

Procedure: Explain that students are going to do a language race to practice *something/nothing*, etc. Pre-teach/check students' understanding of *to pick up the phone, garbage* (n), *designer shop*, and *in the corner*.

• Divide the students into pairs or teams of three students. Hand out copies of sentences 1–12 cut up and give a key words chart to each pair/team. Explain that students need to match the sentence halves and choose the correct word from the chart to complete the sentences. They should cross off the missing key words in the chart as they go, using pencil in case of mistakes! The first pair/team to complete the sentences accurately wins. (Alternatively, students can

do an uncut version of the worksheet and just work as quickly as possibly to complete sentences 1–12, crossing off the key words as they go.)

- Students complete the task in their pairs/teams. Check the answers as students finish. If students have made a mistake, have them go back and try to correct their mistake. Establish which pair/team is the winner.

Answers
1 I spent an hour looking for my car keys, but I couldn't find them **anywhere**.
2 I called the police because **somebody** tried to steal my car.
3 I invited all of my friends for Sunday lunch but **everybody** was busy that weekend.
4 My old apartment wasn't in a very nice area because there was garbage **everywhere**.
5 The weather in my city was awful last year so I decided to go **somewhere** warm this summer.
6 I had to stand on the train to work because there was **nowhere** to sit.
7 I didn't enjoy my French course very much because I didn't know **anybody** in the class.
8 I watched an old DVD because there was **nothing** interesting on TV.
9 I wanted to buy some new clothes, but **everything** in the designer shop was too expensive.
10 I woke up suddenly because I heard **something** strange in the corner of the bedroom.
11 I picked up the phone and said "hello," but there was **nobody** there.
12 I was very hungry when I got home, but there wasn't **anything** in the fridge.

- As an extension, put students in new pairs/groups and ask them to use one of the complete sentences as the first line of a mini-story/anecdote.

READING AND LISTENING (SB p. 78)

The International Space Station

NOTE
At the end of this section, there is a project activity about the astronauts on the International Space Station. You will need to build in time for students to do some research on their chosen astronaut and make notes in order to give a short presentation. Students can also bring in pictures/visuals, if available.

ABOUT THE TEXT
This skills section picks up on the theme of space exploration first introduced in Unit 7, with a focus on the International Space Station (ISS). 15 countries participate in the ISS project, including the United States, Russia, European countries, Canada, and Japan.

The reading text gives a general description of the station and its goals, along with an insight into the everyday lives of the crew on board. The language has been simplified to make the text accessible to students

and has also been chosen to reinforce the difference between Simple Present and Present Continuous. The use of a range of numbers in the texts provides for a number referencing task. The listening task is in the form of an interview with a Japanese astronaut. Although the language has been simplified, students may need help with the following references:

Mars – the fourth planet from the sun and the closest planet to Earth. Due to its relative proximity to Earth, a manned mission to Mars has often been the subject of science fiction, and more recently has become a realistic aim for the 21st century.

Zero gravity – the condition in which the apparent effect of gravity is zero, as when a body is in orbit.

There is an example of the Present Perfect in the section headed *The station*. This is for recognition only, as there is a full presentation and practice of this tense in Unit 12.

Encourage students to use the context to help them with new vocabulary and to pool knowledge with other students, or use a dictionary. With weaker classes or if you are short on time, ask students to look up some of the following vocabulary before the lesson:

Homework prior to the lesson
laboratory, to orbit, to develop, on board, supply ship, zero gravity, to do experiments, effect (n), *oxygen, the origin of the universe, weightlessness, muscle, bone, can, envelope, to float away, spicy, sense of taste, compartment, attached, manned.*

1 Focus students' attention on the photos and ask them what they can see. Use this as an opportunity to provide/review some of the key language (see *About the text* above) e.g., *the station orbiting the Earth, astronauts on board the station, astronauts in zero gravity/floating, a compartment of the station.*

2 Explain that students need to read just the introduction and the sections headed *The station* and *Goals*. Set a time limit of about two minutes to encourage students to read the first part of the text quickly. Have students ask others in their group for help with vocabulary if you didn't pre-teach the items listed in *About the text* or assign them for homework. Monitor and help with any queries.

Focus students' attention on the examples and then put students in pairs to answer the other true/false questions.

Check the answers with the class, having students correct the false sentences. Ask students if they found any of the answers surprising.

Answers
1 true
2 false. It's flying at a distance of 240 miles from Earth.
3 true
4 false. New supplies arrive about eight times a year.
5 false. The space agencies from the different countries are working together.
6 true
7 false. They are studying the Earth's weather and geography.
8 false. They are looking at planets and stars to understand the origin of the universe.

3 Ask students to think about everyday life for the astronauts on the ISS. Focus students' attention on the prompts. Put students in pairs to form the questions. Then check the answers with the class.

Give students time to think of four or five additional questions of their own. Make sure that they use the Simple Present, as the text focuses on the astronauts' routine.

Elicit a range of possible questions from the class.

> **Answers**
> Do you work every day?
> What time do you wake up?
> What do you do in your free time?
> What do you eat?
> Where do you sleep?
> How do you wash?
> What exercise do you do?
>
> **Possible additional questions**
> How can you eat in zero gravity?
> Do you prepare your own food?
> Do you work long hours?
> What do you wear on board the station?

4 Give students time to read the second part of the article – *An astronaut's day*, *Food*, *Personal lives*, and *Future of the ISS*. Again, set a time limit of about two–three minutes to encourage students to read quickly. Have students ask others in their group for help with vocabulary if you didn't pre-teach the items listed in *About the text* or assign them for homework. Monitor and help with any questions students may have.

Students read and find the answers to their questions in exercise 4, both those in the Student Book and the ones they wrote themselves.

Check the answers with the class. Ask students if they found any of the answers surprising and if any of their questions weren't answered.

> **Answers**
> Do you work every day? **I work Monday to Saturday, but not Sunday.**
> What time do you wake up? **We wake up at 6:00.**
> What do you do in your free time? **I send emails home, read, and play games. What I like to do most is look out of the windows at Earth below.**
> What do you eat? **All our food is in cans or envelopes. We have fresh fruit only when a supply ship comes. I like spicy food because in space the sense of taste isn't very strong.**
> Where do you sleep on the station? **We have our own sleeping compartment. We sleep in bags attached to the wall and we sleep "standing up."**
> How do you wash? **No information provided.**
> What exercise do you do? **We do two hours' exercise every day.**
>
> **Possible additional questions**
> How can you eat in zero gravity? **We eat with a spoon. It is a good idea to have food with a sauce so that it stays on the spoon and doesn't float away!**
> Do you prepare your own food? **No, we don't. There isn't a real kitchen. All our food is in cans or envelopes.**
> Do you work long hours? **We work very long hours during the week – 10 hours a day – and five hours on Saturday.**
> What do you wear on board the station? **It's warm on board so we usually wear shorts and T-shirts.**

5 Refer students back to the final section of the article and check the answer to the question.

> **Answer**
> There will be a manned trip to Mars.

6 Elicit the reference for the first two numbers, *100 billion* and *1998* (see *Answers*.) Then give students time to complete the task, working in pairs. Monitor and help as necessary.

Check the answers with the class, making sure students can read aloud the numbers accurately as well as understand what they refer to.

> **Answer**
> 100 billion – the cost of the station in dollars
> 1998 – the year the first part of the station went into space
> six – the number of months the astronauts stay at a time
> 200 – the number of visitors there have been
> 15 – the number of different countries that visitors have come from
> eight – the number of times each year supply ships arrive
> zero – the number used in the expression zero gravity

Listening

7 **CD3 21** Focus students' attention on the photo of Soichi /ˈsoʊitʃi/ and ask where students think he is from. Pre-teach/check students' understanding of the following vocabulary from the recording: *aeronautical engineer*, *to do a space walk* (a period of physical activity by an astronaut outside a spacecraft), *to check the instruments*, *to make sure something is working properly*, *crew*, *commander*.

Two space agencies are mentioned in the recording: *JAXA* (the Japan Aerospace Exploration Agency) and *Roscosmos* (the Russian Federal Space Agency) and two parts of Tokyo (*Yokohama* and *Kanagawa*). Write these proper nouns on the board and explain what they are to help students follow the recording.

Read the questions as a class. Have students predict the types of words Soichi might use in the answers. Play the recording once without stopping. Have students work in pairs and pool their information to answer the questions. With weaker students, you can play the recording in sections, pausing after each section of information.

Play the recording again to allow students to check/complete their answers.

Check the answers with the class. You can decide if you want students to give long answers, as shown in parentheses below, or just the key information.

> **Answers and audio script**
> 1 He works for JAXA (the Japanese Aerospace Exploration Agency).
> 2 He studied aeronautical engineering at the University of Tokyo.
> 3 He's from Yokohama, Kanagawa, which is part of Tokyo. Yes, he's married, and he has three children.
> 4 He likes jogging, basketball, skiing, and camping with his kids.
> 5 He's part of the Russian crew. He's studying weather conditions in space, and doing experiments with plants (to see how they grow in zero gravity). (He's) doing space walks, (going out into space), and checking the instruments on the outside of the space station, (to make sure they're working properly).
> 6 He spends a lot of time looking down at the Earth.

7 He thinks how lucky he is to be there, and he thinks that maybe people would stop fighting if they could see how beautiful our planet is.

CD3 21

I = Interviewer   S = Soichi

I Soichi, what exactly is your job?

S I'm an aeronautical engineer, and I'm a JAXA astronaut.

I What is JAXA?

S JAXA is the Japan Aerospace Exploration Agency.

I What did you study in college?

S Well, I studied engineering, of course! Aeronautical engineering.

I Where did you study? What college?

S I studied at the University of Tokyo, and I graduated in 1991.

I What part of Japan are you from?

S I'm from Yokohama, Kanagawa, which is part of Tokyo.

I Are you married?

S Yes. I have three children.

I What do you like doing when you're on Earth?

S Well, I guess my hobbies are jogging and basketball. And I like skiing and camping with my kids.

I What are you doing on the space station right now?

S I'm doing quite a few space walks. I'm going out into space, and I'm checking the instruments on the outside of the space station to make sure they're working properly.

I You're part of the Russian crew. What does that mean?

S It means that my commander is Oleg Kotov, from Roscosmos, and I'm working on his team. We're studying weather conditions in space, and we're doing experiments with plants to see how they grow in zero gravity.

I What do you do when you aren't working?

S Well, I spend a lot of time just looking down at you on Earth! And I think how lucky I am to be here. And I wish that everyone could see Earth from space. Maybe people would stop fighting if they could see how beautiful our planet is.

Project

See *Note* at the start of this section. Ask students to use the questions in exercise 7 to help them do the research and organize their notes. If appropriate, encourage them to bring in pictures/photos to support their presentations. If you have access to computers, students can give their talk with the support of a presentation program.

When students give their presentation, ask them to come to the front of the class (or stand up in front of their group in larger classes) and make sure the rest of the class is quiet and pays attention. Allow students to refer to their notes, but don't let them read the information from a script. Encourage the class/groups to ask questions to the presenter. Be generous with praise after students have presented their talk, as it can be rather nerve-wracking, especially for weaker students.

EXTRA ACTIVITY

Students use the information they have researched in the *Project* section to roleplay an interview. Students work in pairs. Student A plays the interviewer and prepares a set of questions for the interview and Student B plays the astronaut. Students roleplay their interview and then change roles. If appropriate, have some pairs act out their interview for the class.

ADDITIONAL MATERIAL

Workbook Unit 10
Ex. 9   *something/nothing*

VOCABULARY AND LISTENING (SB p. 80)

Describing people

This section reviews structures students have already learned in the context of describing people – *be* + adjective, *have* + color/style of hair/color of eyes, and Present Continuous: *be wearing* + clothes.

1 **CD3 22** Focus students' attention on the photos. Briefly review the key vocabulary for the clothes and colors shown in the photos. Use the photos to teach *striped* and *checked*. Make sure that students can pronounce the vowel sounds in the following words correctly:

skirt / shirt	/skərt/ /ʃərt/
boots	/buts/
suit	/sut/
tie	/taɪ/

Play the whole recording and let students choose the correct person. Allow students to check their answers in pairs before checking the answers with the class.

Answers and audio script

1 Tanya   2 John   3 Stephanie   4 Ben

CD3 22

1 She has dark brown hair and she's very pretty. She's wearing boots, and a hat, and a red scarf, and she's jumping in the air. She looks really happy!

2 He has short dark hair. He's wearing sneakers, and a purple T shirt, and he's carrying a ball. He isn't very tall.

3 She's wearing a scarf. She's pretty, and she has long, blond hair, and blue eyes. She isn't smiling. She doesn't look very friendly.

4 He doesn't look very happy. Maybe he's a businessman. He's wearing a white shirt and a striped tie. He's also wearing glasses.

2 Pre-teach/check students' understanding of *pretty* and make sure that students understand the difference between *good-looking* (general), *handsome* (for men), and *pretty* (for girls/women).

Focus students' attention on the photo of Mark and elicit a description. (*He's tall and good-looking. He's wearing jeans, a T-shirt, and sneakers, and he's wearing a scarf.*) Elicit one or two other descriptions from the whole class, drilling the sentences as necessary. Students continue in pairs.

Possible answers

Amy is a little short. She has short, dark hair and she's very pretty. She's wearing boots and a checked coat. She's also wearing a scarf. She's smiling and she looks friendly.

Cheryl has long red hair and brown eyes. She's very pretty. She's wearing a black coat, a red scarf, and a hat.

Grace isn't very tall. She's about seven or eight years old. She's wearing a black and grey dress with a pink bow. She's wearing pink shoes and a big hat. She looks very happy.

Matt is very tall and he has short dark hair. He's wearing a purple T-shirt, white shorts, and sneakers. He's carrying a ball and he is smiling just a little.

3   Choose a photo on p. 80 and give a description of the person. Have the class guess who you are describing. Put students into groups of three or four to continue the guessing game. Monitor and check for accurate use of *have* and the Present Continuous. Highlight and correct any common mistakes after the game.

4   Students now personalize the game by describing their classmates. Focus their attention on the examples. Ask a confident student to choose a classmate without saying who it is. Ask *yes/no* questions, e.g.,

   Is it a girl?

   Yes, it is.

   Is she sitting near the door?

   No, she isn't.

   Elicit other questions, drilling the pronunciation chorally and individually if necessary, until students guess the correct person.

   Continue the game with the whole class. Remind them to use only *yes/no* questions and not to ask questions that are too personal! Monitor and check for accurate formation of *yes/no* questions and short answers. Highlight and correct any common mistakes after the game.

The famous person game!

5   Focus students' attention on the examples in the Student Book. Choose someone in the news and describe them in the same way. Have students guess who it is. Students then continue in pairs/small groups. Monitor and check for correct use of *be* + adjective, *have*, and the tenses. Highlight and correct any common mistakes after the activity.

ADDITIONAL MATERIAL

Workbook Unit 10
Ex. 7   Reading
Ex. 8   Listening
Ex. 10   Clothes

WRITING (SB p. 111)

Comparing and contrasting

Linking words *but, however, although*

The writing syllabus continues with a focus on three linkers of contrast – *but*, *however*, and *although* – and how they can be used to join sentences. This builds on the practice of linkers students studied in Units 4 and 6. Students do a sentence joining task and complete a description of two people before going on to write a short comparison of two people in their family.

1   Read the notes with the class. Ask what the linking words express (*contrast*). Make sure students understand that the sentences show three ways of saying the same thing. Highlight the position of each linker in the examples. Point out that we cannot use *but* in the same way as *although*, i.e., we can't say **But I love travel, I don't like flying – I prefer the train.*

• Elicit which sentences are the most formal.

> **Answers**
> I love travel. **However**, I don't like flying – I prefer the train.
> **Although** I love travel, I don't like flying – I prefer the train.

2   This exercise makes sure that students know how to use each of the linkers to join sentences. Elicit the answers to number 1 as an example. Students then join the sentences in 2 and 3 in three ways.

   Allow students to check their answers in pairs before checking the answers with the whole class. Ask students to give the punctuation in each sentence.

> **Answers**
> 1 I like Peter, **but** I don't love him.
>   I like Peter. **However**, I don't love him.
>   **Although** I like Peter, I don't love him.
> 2 My apartment has a balcony, **but** it doesn't have a yard.
>   My apartment has a balcony. **However**, it doesn't have a yard.
>   **Although** my apartment has a balcony, it doesn't have a yard.
> 3 My brother's older than me, **but** he's smaller than me.
>   My brother's older than me. **However**, he's smaller than me.
>   **Although** my brother's older than me, he's smaller than me.

3   This task covers the linkers from this section and also reviews those from earlier units. Focus students' attention on the photo and elicit a brief description of the two brothers. Pre-teach/check students' understanding of *twins*. Have students read the text through quickly to get an idea of the content. Encourage students to use the context to help them understand new vocabulary, or let them use a dictionary. With weaker students, or if you are short on time, pre-teach/check students' understanding of *to look alike, to dress alike, individual* (n), *to have something in common, IT (information technology), personality.*

   Elicit the answer to number 1 as an example and then have students continue the task, working individually. Remind them to read all the text around each blank and to use the punctuation to help them choose the correct linker. Students check their answers in pairs before checking the answers with the class.

> **Answers**
> 1 although   7 so
> 2 However   8 but
> 3 because   9 Although
> 4 when   10 but
> 5 when   11 However
> 6 However

> **SUGGESTION**
>
> It can be helpful to have students talk about the content of a writing task as part of the planning stage. In this case, give students a few moments to choose the two people for their description. Then divide the class into pairs to talk about the people and their appearance, personality, and likes and dislikes. Students can make brief notes at this stage if it helps them.

4 Give a brief example by describing the similarities and differences between two people you know. Briefly review key structures, e.g., *My (brother and sister) both (have blue eyes); My (mom) likes (classical music), but my (dad) prefers (jazz); Although my (sister) is sometimes (annoying), I love (her) very much.*

Before having students write their own comparison, focus their attention on the highlighted expressions in the model text. Check students' understanding of their use by asking the following questions: Which expression:

– introduces the first comparison? (*First of all …*)

– introduces another comparison? (*Something else …, Another thing is that …*)

– gives an example? (*For example, …*).

– introduces the last point/paragraph? (*Finally, …*)

Focus students' attention on the writing plan and elicit possible sentences for each bullet point. Have students write brief notes for each section, if they didn't do so earlier (see *Suggestion* above). Remind students to write paragraphs of roughly equal length.

Give students time to write their description in class or assign it for homework. If possible, display the descriptions on the classroom wall or noticeboard to allow students to read each other's work. If appropriate, have them vote for the most interesting description. When you check the students' work, point out errors, but allow students to correct them themselves. Try to limit correction to major problems to avoid demoralizing students.

EVERYDAY ENGLISH (SB p. 81)

Social expressions (2)

This is the second focus on social expressions, building on the language students practiced in Unit 3.

> **NOTE**
>
> This exercise introduces the use of the Present Continuous to refer to arrangements in the near future. At this stage, this is intended for recognition, rather than active production. Students are introduced to the *going to* future in Unit 11 and the use of Present Continuous with future meaning is also covered there. The conversations also include examples of *will* for spontaneous decisions. These are also for recognition, so there's no need to go into a full presentation of this use of *will* at this stage. The area of future forms and the concepts that they express in English is very complex, and we do not suggest that you explore it in detail at this level.

1 Focus students' attention on the photos and elicit who and where the people are in each one (*1 friends in a restaurant, 2 customer and shop assistant at a store. 3 customer and mechanic at a garage, 4 friends in town, 5 a little boy and a man next to a vending machine, 6 a secretary in an office, 7 friends in a park, 8 friends in a car saying goodbye.*)

Focus students' attention on the example. Elicit a possible reply for number 2. Then have students continue the activity, working in pairs. Monitor and help as necessary. Elicit several possible replies from the class.

2 **CD3 23** Focus students' attention on photo 1 again and ask two students to read the sentences that go with it. Then elicit the correct sentence from the box for photo 2. Students continue matching the sentences from the box to complete the task, working in pairs.

Play the recording and have students check their answers. Remind students that *I'm afraid* in number 6 means *I'm sorry*.

Play the recording again and have students focus on the extra sentences. Elicit some of the wording in a short feedback session.

> **Answers and audio script**
> 1 A Patrick and I are getting married.
> B Wow! That's fantastic! Congratulations!
> A Thanks. We're both very excited. And a little nervous.
> 2 C Can I help you?
> **D No, I'm just looking, thanks.**
> C Just tell me if you need anything.
> D OK, thanks very much.
> 3 E I'm afraid you need a new cylinder.
> **F Sorry, what does that mean?**
> E Well, it means you should probably get a new car. This is a very expensive problem to fix.
> 4 G We're going to the movies tonight.
> **H Oh, nice. Well, I hope you like the movie!**
> G Thanks. I'll tell you all about it.
> H Great!
> 5 I Excuse me! This machine isn't working.
> **J I'm sorry. Let me have a look. Oh! It isn't turned on. That's why!**
> I Oh, great! Thank you very much.
> J No problem.
> 6 K Hi. Can I speak to Dave, please?
> **L I'm afraid he isn't here right now. Can I take a message?**
> K Yes. Could you ask him to call Kevin?
> L Sure. I'll do that.
> 7 M Thanks for the invitation to your party, but I'm afraid I can't come.
> **N Oh, that's too bad. We'll miss you.**
> M I'm going away that weekend.
> N That's OK. Another time.
> 8 O/P Bye! Have a safe trip!
> **Q/R Thanks. We'll see you in a couple of days!**
> O/P I hope you have a good time.
> Q/R We'll try.

3 Put students in pairs to practice the conversations. Weaker students can refer to **CD3 23** on SB p. 126, though encourage students to work from memory as much as they can. Monitor and help as necessary. If students have pronunciation problems, play sections of the recording again. Students listen and repeat, paying special attention to stress patterns and intonation, following the model as closely as possible.

If you have time, students can memorize one or two of the conversations and act it out for the rest of the class.

ADDITIONAL MATERIAL

Workbook Unit 10
Ex. 11 Social expressions (2)

Don't forget!

Workbook Unit 10
Ex. 12 Verb forms
Ex. 13 *-ing* form as noun
Ex. 14 *have* + noun

Grammar Reference (SB p. 137)

Word list Unit 10 (SB p. 144)
Students can translate the words, learn them at home, or transfer some of them to their vocabulary notebook.

Tests (Online)
Unit 10 Test

Video (iTools and Online)

Additional photocopiables and PPT™presentations (iTools)

11 Going far

going to future • **Infinitive of purpose** • **What's the weather like?**
• **Making suggestions**

VIDEO◄ New Year's Resolutions

The theme of this unit is planning the future, including travel plans. We focus on the *going to* future for plans and intentions, and for predictions from what you can see now. We do not at the same time introduce and contrast the Simple Future with *will* (this rather complex distinction is for a later stage of learning), but in the *Everyday English* section *will* for spontaneous decisions is included for recognition. The second presentation in the unit is the infinitive of purpose, which is relatively simple to operate in English, but is often realized differently in other languages. The skills work includes an article about a young woman who can run all day, every day! This continues the theme of travel and adventure, and provides opportunities to review the grammar not only of this unit, but also of previous units (Simple Present and Simple Past).

LANGUAGE INPUT

GRAMMAR

going to (SB p. 82)
* Understanding and practicing *going to* for future plans and predictions.

Infinitive of purpose (SB p. 85)
* Understanding and practicing the infinitive to answer the question *Why ...?*

VOCABULARY

What's the weather like? (SB p. 88)
* Understanding and practicing language to talk about the weather.

EVERYDAY ENGLISH

Making suggestions (SB p. 89)
* Understanding and practicing expressions to make and respond to suggestions.

SKILLS DEVELOPMENT

READING

Meet Zoë (SB p. 86)
* An article about a young woman with an unusual hobby.

LISTENING

Two people talk about travel plans (SB p. 85)
* Listening to hear the order of countries on a trip **CD3 29** (SB p. 127).

A weather forecast (SB p. 88)
* Listening for key information in a weather forecast **CD3 31** (SB p. 127).

SPEAKING

Talking about you (SB p. 83)
* Asking and answering questions about plans.

When ...? Why ...? (SB p. 85)
* Asking and answering questions about where you went and why.

Role play (SB p. 86)
* Roleplaying an interview between a journalist and Zoë Romano.

WRITING

Describing a vacation – Writing a postcard (SB p. 112)
* Understanding adjectives to describe a vacation, then writing a vacation postcard.

MORE MATERIALS

Photocopiables – Making suggestions (TB p. 154)   **Tests** (Online)   **Video** (iTools and Online)

STARTER (SB p. 82)

1 Read aloud *I'm going to India* and *I went to India*. Establish what time they refer to by asking *Past, present, or future?* about each one. Students should recognize *went* as the past of *go*, but make sure that they realize *going to* refers to the future. (Do not go into a full presentation of the tense at this stage.)

Pre-teach/check students' understanding of the meaning of *retire*. Students work in pairs and make sentences using the time references in the second column. Check the answers with the whole class.

Answers
I'm going to India soon/next month/a year from now/when I retire.
I went to India when I was a student/two years ago.

PLANNING MY FUTURE (SB p. 82)

going to

⚠ POSSIBLE PROBLEMS

The *going to* future is made easier by the fact that students already know the present forms of the verb *to be*, both on its own and as part of the Present Continuous, which they learned in Unit 10. These are, of course, intrinsic parts of this structure. Also, this is the first main future form students have encountered, apart from the Present Continuous with future meaning, which was included in Unit 10 for recognition and is revisited in this unit. The problem of when to use *going to* in relation to other future forms (always an area of difficulty for students) is deferred to later levels of the course, so that students can simply concentrate on *going to*. The two uses of *going to* are introduced in the unit: plans and intentions, such as *I'm going to be a photographer*; and making predictions based on present evidence, such as *It's going to rain./He's going to fall.*

Students may need help with the following aspects of the presentation:

- With the verbs *go* and *come* we often avoid using the full *going to* future form, and just use the Present Continuous.

  She's going to go to Rome next week. → *She's going to Rome next week.*

- The Present Continuous can be used for future arrangements and is often interchangeable with the *going to* future. This is not such a leap for students, even though in their own language this concept may be expressed by the equivalent of the Simple Present.

  I'm going to see the doctor tomorrow./I'm seeing the doctor tomorrow.

- To express an arrangement in the near future, the Present Continuous usually needs a future time reference, e.g.,

  I'm doing my homework. (= now)
  I'm doing my homework tonight.

- The *when* clauses in exercises 1 and 2 use the Simple Present. Sometimes students find it strange that the Simple Present is used to talk about future events; they might want to say *When I will get home …*, etc. You can correct individual mistakes if necessary, but don't try to give a detailed explanation of this point at this stage.

The context for the presentation of *going to* is the plans of a range of people in different situations. These show the use of *going to* for short-term plans, e.g., *When I get home …*, and longer-term plans, e.g., *When I retire …*.

There is a reference to Koh Samui Island in one of the examples. This is an island on the south-east coast of Thailand, popular with tourists for its beaches and scenery.

1 Focus students' attention on the photos of the people and check pronunciation of *Leila* /ˈleɪlə/ and *Ayesha* /ˈaɪʃə/. Pre-teach/check students' understanding of *get a raise* and *grow up*. Focus their attention on the thought bubbles and explain that each person is thinking about his/her future. This can be something happening soon, e.g., this evening, or farther in the future, e.g., their career.

Ask *What is Alex doing? What is he thinking about?* as an example (He's going home. He's thinking about his evening after work.) Then put students in pairs to talk about the other people. Monitor and help as necessary.

Check the answers with the class.

Answers
Alex is going home. He's thinking about his evening after work.
Brendan is sitting at his desk at work. He's thinking about money.
Jason is playing in his bedroom. He's thinking about his future job.
George is teaching a class. He's thinking about his retirement.
Leila is sitting on a plane. She's thinking about her vacation.
Yvonne is looking after her children. She's thinking about her evening after the children's bedtime.
Ayesha is sitting at her desk at school. She's thinking about her plans for after class/school.

2 **CD3 24** This is the first time that students see *going to*. Allow them to focus on the context to help convey the meaning, but if students ask about *going to*, just explain that we use it to talk about future plans.

Pre-teach/check students' understanding of *race-car driver* and *ring* (n). Give students time to read the sentences quickly. Answer any other questions about vocabulary. Focus students' attention on sentences 1–3 and on the example. Then ask students to continue matching just the names, working in pairs. Check the answers.

Focus students' attention on the prompt for sentence 4 and elicit the complete sentence (*I'm going to buy my girlfriend a ring.*) Give students time to complete the plans in sentences 5–7, working in pairs. Monitor and check for correct use of *going to*. If students have a lot of problems, correct common errors carefully and drill one or two example sentences before letting students continue the pairwork.

Play the recording and have students check their answers.

3 **CD3 25** Draw a large question mark on the board to signal that you are going to introduce the question form. The formation and pronunciation of the question should not cause students too much difficulty because they are already familiar with the Present Continuous. With weaker students, you can highlight the change from first person to third person (*I'm going to* – *Alex is going to*) before focusing on the question forms.

Give students time to read the examples. Then play the recording. Focus on the weak pronunciation of *to* in *going to*: /ˈɡoʊɪŋtə/. Practice it in isolation first, and then as part of a full sentence, drilling the examples in the book. If students have problems, have them focus on the main stresses and then repeat the questions and answers in open pairs.

What's Alex going to do?   He's going to relax.

You can also drill a few questions and answers about different people in exercise 1 to provide additional support.

Put students in pairs to practice the questions and answers. Monitor and check for correct question forms and pronunciation. If students have a lot of problems, correct common errors carefully and drill one or two more examples before having students continue the pairwork.

4 **CD3 26** Explain that this exercise practices the negative. Tell students the recordings are in the same order as the speakers in exercise 2. Focus students' attention on the examples about Alex and Jason and play numbers 1 and 2 on the recording. With weaker students, you can highlight the negative form at this stage.

Pre-teach/check students' understanding of *do the laundry*. Play the rest of the recording and have students focus on the negative forms in each set of sentences. With weaker students, you can write the key verbs for what

each speaker isn't going to do in random order on the board as additional support.

Give students time to talk about each of the speakers. Monitor and check for correct use of *going to*, both affirmative and negative forms. If students have a lot of problems, correct common errors carefully and drill one or two example sentences before having students continue the pairwork.

Talking about you

5 Now we move away from the people in the Student Book and get students to talk about themselves in an exercise practicing *yes/no* questions.

Drill the example in the Student Book individually and chorally. Have one or two students demonstrate the second question in open pairs. Then have students work in closed pairs, asking and answering the rest of the questions. Monitor and check as they do this, checking for correct use of the *yes/no* questions. Pay attention to all aspects of pronunciation – sounds, stress, and intonation.

6 Focus students' attention on the examples. Highlight the use of *both* for plans that students have in common. Ask students to tell the class about themselves and their partner. This provides practice in the third person singular and first person singular and plural.

GRAMMAR SPOT

Demonstrate that the form of *going to* builds on what students already know by having the whole class say together first the affirmative and then the negative forms of the verb *to be*. (Conjugating verbs may be deemed old-fashioned in these communicative days, but it is an effective way of reinforcing grammatical forms!)

1 Read the notes with the whole class and then have students complete the chart, using contracted forms. Check the answers with the whole class.

Answers

I	'm	
He/She	's	going to cook tonight.
You/We/They	're	

2 Have students figure out the question and negative forms in pairs, and then write the answers on the board, or refer students to the Grammar Reference on p. 138.

Answers
Questions

Am	I	
Is	he/she	going to cook tonight?
Are	you/we/they	

Answers
Negatives

I	'm not	
He/She	isn't	going to cook tonight.
You/We/They	aren't	

3 Focus students' attention on the uses of the Present Continuous for the future and *going to*. Establish that there is little difference between the two sentences.

▶▶ Read Grammar Reference 11.1 and 11.2 on p. 138 together in class, and/or ask students to read it at home. Encourage them to ask you questions about it.

PRACTICE (SB p. 84)

Careful! You're going to drop it!

Here we introduce the second use of *going to*, when we can see now that something is sure to happen in the future. Students should understand this concept from the pictures and contexts, but with weaker students be prepared to refer to the note on this use at the start of the section and explain it, in L1 if possible.

1 **CD3 27** Focus students' attention on picture 1 and the example. Students then write a sentence for each picture, using *going to* and the correct verb in the box. If students have access to dictionaries, have them look up new words, or they can ask you. Students can work in pairs so that they can help each other with vocabulary. With weaker students, you can match the verbs to each picture before students write the sentences.

Read the note aloud about the use of *going to* as a class if you didn't do so at the start of the section.

Play the recording and have students check their answers.

Answers and audio script
1 It's going to rain. He can't play tennis. That's too bad.
2 Look at the time! He's going to be late for his meeting.
3 Come on! Come on! She's going to win. Great!
4 Oh no! Jack's on top of the wall! He's going to fall.
5 Careful! She's going to drop the vase. Too late!
6 He's going to sneeze. "Aaattishooo!" "Bless you!"

2 **CD3 27** There are some useful expressions included in the sentences: *That's too bad. Look at the time. Bless you!* Illustrate the meaning of these when you go over the exercise and have the class repeat them. It can also be interesting and fun to discuss what is said in the students' own language(s) when someone sneezes.

Students listen to the recording again and then practice saying the sentences with a partner and have fun practicing the stress and intonation in the expressions.

Check it

3 Elicit the answer to number 1 as an example. Students work in pairs and complete the exercise.

Answers
1 He's going to watch the soccer game.
2 We're going to the movies tonight.
3 She isn't going to cook.
4 Is it going to rain?
5 When are they going to get married?
6 I'm going to the library.

ADDITIONAL MATERIAL

Workbook Unit 11
Ex. 1–3   *going to* – future intentions
Ex. 4   *going to* – predictions

WE'RE OFF TO SEE THE WORLD! (SB p. 85)

Infinitive of purpose

⚠ **POSSIBLE PROBLEMS**

The infinitive of purpose answers the question *why*, replacing *because I wanted to*, e.g., *Why did you go to the store? Because I wanted to buy a newspaper./To buy a newspaper.*

There is often a problem for learners when they attempt to translate this item from their own language and insert *for*, which is wrong in English.

Common mistakes
I went to the store for to buy a newspaper.
I went to the store for buy a newspaper.
I went to the store for buying a newspaper.

ABOUT THE TEXT

If students ask about some of the places in exercise 1, the following notes may be helpful.

- **Mount Kilimanjaro** /kɪləmənˈdʒɑroʊ/, at 5,895m is the highest mountain in Africa. There are six official routes up the mountain, and although not an easy climb, it has become an increasingly popular activity with tourists.
- **Ayers** /ɛrz/ **Rock** is a very large red rock in the Northern Territory, Australia. Known in the Aboriginal language as *Uluru*, it is a very popular tourist site because it changes color in different lights.

- **Machu Picchu** /mɑtʃu ˈpitʃu/ is an ancient ruined city high in the Andes mountains in Peru. It was built by the Incas, a native people of South America in about 1500 AD. The site with its terraces and buildings is a must-see for tourists for all over the world.
- **Yellowstone Park** is a large national park in Wyoming, in the northwest US. It is known for its hot springs and geysers (natural springs of hot water that rise suddenly into the air). They are fueled by heat from a large reservoir of partially molten rock from one of the world's largest volcanic systems.
- **Lake Tonlé Sap** is a lake and river system of major importance to Cambodia. Approximately 1.2 million people make their living by fishing in the lake, and they live in floating villages on and around the lake. The majority of Cambodia's freshwater comes from Tonlé Sap. These fisheries account for 16 percent of national GDP, making the fish industry not only essential to the diet of local populations, but to the Cambodian national economy.

1 The goal of this activity is to set the scene and learn/review the vocabulary needed for the presentation dialogue in exercise 2.

First, have students look at the photos and ask them which places they recognize. The photos will also help with understanding some of the vocabulary needed for the matching exercise. Briefly check the pronunciation of the names of the places, focusing on *Tanzania* /ˌtænzəˈniə/, *Peru* /pəˈru/, *Antarctica* /ænˈtɑrktɪkə/, *Egypt* /ˈidʒɪpt/, and *Cambodia* /kæmˈboʊdiə/ in particular.

Elicit the activity for Australia as an example (*take photos of Ayers Rock at sunset*). Ask students to point to the correct photo. Students work in pairs to match the places with the activities and also the photos.

Check the answers with the class, correcting pronunciation as you go. If necessary, point out the silent letter in *climb* /klaɪm/ and the vowel sound in *cruise* /kruz/.

Ask students if they have visited any of the places on the list, and which place and activity they would like to try.

Answers
Australia – take photos of Ayers Rock at sunset
Tanzania – climb Mount Kilimanjaro
Peru – visit Machu Picchu
Antarctica – fly over the coldest place on Earth
Egypt – take a cruise down the Nile River
Cambodia – visit the floating villages in Lake Tonlé Sap
The US – see the supervolcano at Yellowstone Park
India – go on a tiger safari

SUGGESTION

Rob and Becky's conversation with their friend incorporates review of *going to* and also highlights the fact that with the verb *go* we do not usually say *going to go*, but simply use the Present Continuous. The notes in the *Grammar Spot* spell this out in more detail. You can read this with your students either after they first read the conversation, or after they have listened to check the answers.

2 **CD3 28** Focus students' attention on the photo and ask students to point to Rob and Becky. Explain that they are talking to a friend about their world trip. Go over the conversation with the whole class, asking three students to take the roles of the characters, read the sentences, and complete the missing words.

Play the recording for your students, not only to check the wordings, but also to familiarize them with the stress and intonation patterns in the conversation. Students then practice the conversation in pairs.

Answers and audio script
R = Rob   F = Friend   B = Becky
R First we're going to Egypt.
F Why? To see the pyramids?
B Well, yes, but also we want to **take a cruise down the Nile**.
F Great! Where are you going after that?
R Well, then we're going to Tanzania to …

GRAMMAR SPOT

1 Read the notes with the class (if you have not done so earlier) and point out the use of *going/coming* rather than *going to go/going to come*.

2 Focus students' attention on the sentences and have students decide if they mean the same.

Answer
Yes, the sentences do mean the same.

Explain, in L1 if possible, that the infinitive can be used in answer to a *Why … ?* question.

▶▶ Read Grammar Reference 11.3 on p. 138 together in class, and/or ask students to read it at home. Encourage them to ask you questions about it.

Why did you come to NYC?

PRACTICE (SB p. 85)

Listening and speaking

1 **CD3 29** Tell students they are going to hear Rob and Becky continuing their description of their trip.

Ask students *What is one of the main tourist attractions in Egypt?* (the pyramids). *And in India?* (the Taj Mahal). Pre-teach/check students' understanding of *a day trip* and *grizzly bear*.

Focus students' attention on the examples and play the recording as far as *… climb Kilimanjaro*. Tell students that one of the countries needs to appear twice. Play the rest of the recording without stopping and have students write the rest of the countries on the itinerary.

Check the answers and then have students pool any additional information they understood.

Answers and audio script
Egypt, Tanzania, India, Cambodia, Australia, Antarctica, Peru, the US

CD3 29

R = Rob   F = Friend   B = Becky

R First we're going to Egypt.
F Why? To see the pyramids?
B Well, yes, but also we want to take a cruise down the Nile River.
F Great! Where are you going after that?
R Well, then we're going to Tanzania to …
F Wow! You're going to climb Kilimanjaro.
R Yes, and then we're flying to India.
F Are you going to visit the Taj Mahal?
B Of course, but we're also going on a tiger safari.
F You're going to see tigers!
R Well, we hope so. Then we're going to Cambodia to visit the floating villages in Lake Tonlé Sap and …
B … then to Australia to see Ayers Rock. We want to take photos of it at sunset. Did you know it turns from pink to purple at sunset?
F Really! And are you going to Sydney?
R Oh, yes we're taking a flight from Sydney to Antarctica.
B Yeah, it's a day trip to fly over the coldest place on Earth.
F I can't believe this. How many more places?
R Two. We're flying from Sydney to Peru to …
F … to visit Machu Picchu of course.
R Yes, and then from Peru back to the US to Yellowstone Park to see the supervolcano and maybe some grizzly bears.
B Then home!
F Amazing! What a trip! How long is it going to take?
R Nine months to a year – we think.

2   Focus students' attention on the example and have a student read the first sentence aloud. Elicit the continuation (*Then, they're going to Tanzania to climb Kilimanjaro.*)

Put students into groups of four so that the activity can be completed quickly. Ask them to take turns telling part of Rob and Becky's planned journey. Remind them to use the adverbs *first, then, next, after that,* and *finally.*

Sample answer
Student 1: First they're going to Egypt to see the pyramids and to take a cruise down the Nile River. Then, they're going to Tanzania to climb Kilimanjaro.
Student 2: Next they're going to India to visit the Taj Mahal and to go on a tiger safari. Then they're going to Cambodia to visit the floating villages in Lake Tonlé Sap.
Student 3: After that they're going to Australia to take photos of Ayers Rock at sunset. Then they're going to Antarctica to see the coldest place on earth.
Student 4: Next they're going to Peru to see Machu Picchu. Finally, they're going to the US to Yellowstone Park to see the supervolcano and maybe some grizzly bears.

EXTRA ACTIVITY

Students work in groups of four to plan their own round-the-world trip. Write the following headings on the board and elicit possible examples:

Place	Reason
China	*walk along the great wall*
Japan	*visit Mount Fuji*

Ask students to plan seven or eight countries and activities for their trip, and decide on the order of travel. Students then change groups to talk about their trip, using language from exercise 2. With smaller classes, students can present their plans to the whole class. If appropriate, ask students to vote for the most exciting trip.

When …? Why …?

3   This activity personalizes the infinitive of purpose. It also moves away from practicing the structure with *going to,* and reviews the Simple Past.

You can introduce the activity by just going over the examples in the Student Book, but it is much more interesting if you say some names of places you visited in the past and then have students ask you why you went there and when, for example:

Teacher   I went to Milan.
Student(s) When did you go to Milan?
Teacher   Eighteen months ago.
Student(s) Why did you go?
Teacher   To visit a friend and to practice my Italian.

Model the highlighted stress patterns in the examples, drilling as necessary.

Ask students to write down the names of some places they visited in the past – countries, cities, villages, or any places of interest. Then put them into pairs to ask each other questions about the places. Let this go on for as long as students are interested if you have time.

Finish the activity by asking students to share their partner's answer with the class.

SUGGESTION

If you think your students need more practice with the infinitive of purpose, you can follow the same procedure as exercise 3, but focus on the future. Remind students of the expressions of future time that they can use, e.g., *soon, next week/month/year, in a few weeks' time,* etc. Give an example about a place you are going to visit, e.g.,

Teacher   I'm going to New York.
Student(s) When are you going to New York?
Teacher   Next Christmas.
Student(s) Why are you going?
Teacher   To do some sightseeing and to go shopping.

Students work in pairs and ask each other questions about the places. Ask one or two individuals to share their partner's answers with the class.

Workbook Unit 11
Ex. 5   Infinitive of purpose

WRITING (SB p. 112)

Describing a vacation

Writing a postcard

This unit of the writing syllabus gives students the opportunity to write a vacation postcard. It gives further practice in a range of tenses.

1   Read the instructions as a class. Pre-teach/check students' understanding of *rental car* and then give students time to read the information in the chart.

2   **CD3 30** Focus students' attention on the example. With weaker classes, you can focus on the *Grammar Spot* before students complete the questions.

Give students time to write the questions, using the prompts in the *Questions* column of the chart. Monitor and help as necessary.

Then put students in pairs to ask and answer about Luke and Tina's vacation. Monitor and check for accurate question formation and use of Present Continuous and *going to*.

Play the recording and have students check their answers. Ask *Why "going to" and not Present Continuous in number 6?* (Present continuous would mean '*now*'.)

Answers and audio script
1 Where are they going?
   To Brazil.
2 When are they going?
   On October 15th.
3 How are they traveling?
   By plane and rental car.
4 How long are they staying?
   For ten days.
5 Where are they staying?
   In a house in a village.
6 What are they going to do?
   They're going to swim, go shopping in the markets, read and relax, and eat in good restaurants.

GRAMMAR SPOT

Read the notes and examples as a class. Check students' understanding of *arrangement* (a plan or preparation for a future event). Elicit examples of what students are doing after class, e.g., *We're going for a coffee. I'm meeting my friend for dinner*, etc.

▶▶ Read Grammar Reference 11.2 on p. 138 together in class, and/or ask students to read it at home. Encourage them to ask you questions about it.

---

3   As an introduction to the writing section, ask what information people typically include in a postcard (*weather, accommodation, food, activities, places to visit*).

Have students read the postcard quickly and ask *Who is on vacation?* (Luke and Tina), *Where are they?* (in Brazil), *Who is the postcard to?* (their friends, Toby and Mel).

Pre-teach/check students' understanding of *loud* and *peaceful*. With weaker students, go over the adjectives in the box first and elicit a possible context for each one. Point out that *warmer* is in the comparative form.

Students then read the postcard again and fill in the blanks with the missing adjectives. Remind them to use each adjective only once. It's a good idea if they use pencil so that they can change any answers they get wrong earlier in the task.

Check the answers with the class.

Answers
1 wonderful   9 sunny
2 old   10 colorful
3 beautiful   11 expensive
4 hot   12 delicious
5 warmer   13 peaceful
6 huge   14 relaxed
7 loud   15 busy
8 scared

---

4   Divide the class into pairs and have them discuss the questions, giving examples where possible. Elicit any interesting examples from the class. You can ask students to share their partner's examples with the class.

5   Focus students' attention on the writing plan and elicit possible ideas for each point. Make sure that students use the correct tense for things they do often/most of the time (Simple Present), things they did yesterday (Simple Past), and things they are going to do tomorrow (*going to*/Present Continuous).

If possible, bring in real postcards for students to write on to add authenticity and encourage them to base their ideas on a real vacation if appropriate. Remind them to use adjectives like those in exercise 3 to make their writing interesting.

Give students time to write their postcard in class or assign it for homework. Students then take turns reading their postcard aloud to a partner.

If possible, display the postcards on the classroom wall or noticeboard to allow students to read one another's work. If appropriate, you can have students vote for the best/worst vacation described in the postcards. When you check the students' work, point out errors, but allow students to correct them themselves. Try to limit correction to major problems to avoid demoralizing the students.

READING AND SPEAKING (SB p. 86)

Meet Zoë

> **NOTE**
>
> At the end of this section, there is a project activity about someone who raises money for an organization and how they do it. You will need to build in time for students to do some research and make notes on their person of choice, probably for homework. Students then give a short presentation about their chosen person to the class. In larger groups, you may need to stage the presentations across a series of lessons or have students give their presentations in groups.

> **ABOUT THE TEXT**
>
> The reading section continues the theme of travel and adventure with an article about a young woman who has an unusual hobby – she runs very, very long distances to raise money for a charitable organization.
>
> The text describes how long she runs, how often she runs, and some of her more amazing achievements. It also tells why she runs and what her life is like today. It has been chosen to review a range of structures from this and recent units. It also consolidates present and past tenses.
>
> The places mentioned in the text are:
>
> **Coast to coast/cross-America** These two phrases describe an east to west (or vice versa) direction, generally from somewhere on the mid-Atlantic coastline of the US to somewhere in the mid-California Pacific coastline.
>
> **Tour de France course** The Tour de France is the most prestigious cycling race in the world. Traditionally, the race is held in the month of July. The route changes every year, but the general format of the race stays the same. Part of the race always goes through the Pyrenees and the Alps and it finishes on the Champs Elysses in Paris. There are 21 day-long segments over 23 days and it covers about 2200 miles. The 2014 edition consisted of 9 flat stages, 5 hilly stages, 6 mountain stages with 5 high-altitude finishes, and 1 individual time-trial stage. The race alternates between clockwise and counter clockwise circuits of France.
>
> Encourage students to use the context to help them with new vocabulary and to pool knowledge with other students, or use a dictionary. With weaker classes or if you are short on time, ask students to look up some of following vocabulary before the lesson:
>
> **Homework prior to the lesson**
>
> *typical, marathon, half marathon, challenge, competition, without a break, adventure, pediatric, donate, dream big*

1 Focus students' attention on the photos. Explain that her name is Zoë /ˈzoʊi/

Put students in pairs to answer the questions. Then check the answers with the class. Ask students what they think the young woman is doing and why. Elicit several possible ideas, but don't confirm or reject answers at this stage.

> **Answers**
> She is on top of a hill and on a country road. She's running.

2 This exercise focuses on the first part of the article as far as *... invited her to stay in their homes.* Have students read this part of the text quickly, asking others for help with vocabulary if you didn't pre-teach the items listed in *About the text* or assign them for homework. Monitor and help with any questions.

Elicit the correction to sentence 1. Then let students continue the task, working in pairs.

Check the answers with the class.

> **Answers**
> 1 Zoë doesn't run without shoes. She always runs with shoes.
> 2 Zoë didn't run from Canada to Mexico. She ran across the United States from coast to coast.
> 3 Zoë didn't run a marathon when she was 19. She ran a half marathon.
> 4 Zoë doesn't always run alone. Sometimes other people run with her for a few miles.
> 5 Zoë didn't cycle across the US. She ran across the US.

3 Explain that students are going to read the second part of the text from *Soon after that amazing challenge ...* to the end. Set a time limit of about two–three minutes to encourage students to read quickly.

Students read and find the answers to the questions in exercise 3, working in pairs. Encourage them to ask other students for help with vocabulary if you didn't pre-teach the items listed in *About the text* or assign them for homework. Monitor and help with any questions.

Check the answers with the class. Ask students if the predictions they made about Zoë before reading the text were correct.

> **Answers**
> 1 She wanted to do something even more difficult.
> 2 France
> 3 She ran the same course as the Tour de France cyclists ride.
> 4 She loves adventure.
> 5 An organization called the World Pediatric Project.
> 6 They help to take care of sick children around the world.
> 7 $200,000
> 8 She writes magazine articles and she is writing a book.
> 9 She is teaching people that they can dream big and do great things.
> 10 She is not sure, but it will be exciting!

What do you think?

Put students into groups of three or four to discuss their answers. Monitor and help as necessary, but don't interrupt or over-correct as this is primarily a fluency task.

Allow the discussion to continue for as long as students' interest is held, and exchanges are taking place mainly in English! Elicit a range of opinions from the class.

> **Possible answers**
> She likes a big challenge. She likes meeting new people and seeing different places. She wants to tell as many people as possible about the World Pediatric Project Answers will vary for questions 2 and 3.

Role play

4 This gives students the opportunity to transfer the information in the text to a speaking activity. Put students into A/B pairs and assign the role of journalist to the A students and the role of Zoë to the B students.

Give students time to prepare their roles. The A students can use the questions in exercise 3 as a starting point, but encourage them to think of their own questions, too. The B students can look back at the text and take notes on the key information. Encourage them to use their imagination to add details about Zoë's way of life and philosophy.

Demonstrate the activity by having two students ask and answer the questions from the prompts in the Student Book. Students continue the roleplay in their pairs. (If you want to do the *Extra Activity* below, have the journalist in each pair write down any interesting information to use in their report.) Monitor and help as necessary. Write down any common errors, but don't correct these until after the roleplay.

SUGGESTION

You can ask pairs of students to act out their interview for the whole class. If you have access to recording equipment, it is a great idea to record some of the role plays and play them back to the whole class for them to comment on and correct. Students often find this very productive and satisfying.

EXTRA ACTIVITY

Students follow up their role play with a written task. The A students (journalists) write up the notes from the interview into a report for their newspaper. The B students (Zoë) write the text for a podcast, telling the story of one of their walks.

Project

See *Note* at the start of this section. Ask students to use some of the following headings to help them do the research and organize their notes:

Short biography of the person: name, age, country, interests

Name of organization

Organizations' goals

How person raises money

If appropriate, encourage students to bring some visuals to support their presentation, e.g., a picture of the person, poster about the organization, etc. If you have access to computers, students can give their talk with the support of a presentation program.

When students give their presentation, ask students to come to the front of the class (or stand up in front of their group in larger classes) and make sure the rest of the class is quiet and pays attention. Allow students to refer to their notes, but don't let them read the information from a script. Encourage the class/groups to ask questions to the presenter. Be generous with praise after students have presented their talk, as it can be rather nerve-wracking, especially for weaker students.

ADDITIONAL MATERIAL

Workbook Unit 11
Ex. 6 Reading
Ex. 7 Listening

VOCABULARY AND LISTENING (SB p. 88)

What's the weather like?

NOTES

The last task in this section asks students to write a short weather forecast for the coming weekend. If possible, have students research the weather for the country they are studying in ahead of the lesson.
Americans are well known for their interest in the weather and students may well have their own ideas about weather conditions in the US. A few points to note:

- Weather is often the initial topic in any conversation in the US. Students can be encouraged to talk about the weather as a "safe" opening topic, particularly with people they don't know.
- The US is a very large country with many different kinds of weather in its different parts. The places with the most pleasant weather are the south and central parts of California and Honolulu, Oahu in the Hawaiian Islands. The Pacific Northwest is known for having very rainy weather. Not surprisingly, northern Alaska has the coldest temperatures.
- Go over the place names that the weather forecaster uses: the Midwest States are: in the northern-central part of the continental US (Illinois, Indiana, Iowa, Kansas, Michigan Minnesota, Missouri, Nebraska, North Dakota, Ohio, South Dakota and Wisconsin).

  New England is in the northeast corner of the country: Maine, Massachusetts, New Hampshire, Vermont, Rhode Island, and Connecticut.

⚠ POSSIBLE PROBLEMS

What … like? for descriptions always creates some difficulty because of the different use of *like*. Be prepared to make these two points clear to your students:

1 It has nothing to do with the verb *like*. The note on *What … like?* will help you do this.

2 The answer does not contain the word *like*. *What's the weather like? It's sunny.* NOT **It's like sunny.*

1 **CD3** **31** Focus students' attention on the photo and ask *What's her job?* (She's a weather forecaster.) Then focus their attention on the map. Point to the following cities and elicit the names, checking pronunciation as you go: Boston, New York, Chicago, Minneapolis, St. Louis, Denver, Dallas, Seattle, Atlanta, Miami, Mexico City, Guadalajara, Cancun.

Explain that students are going to hear a weather forecast for the US and Mexico. They don't need to understand every word, but just listen for the temperatures to add to the map and for the correct season.

Play the recording as far as ... *Minneapolis, 60 degrees* and elicit the temperature for the cities of Boston and New York. Point out that for some temperatures students will hear the name of a region, not a city. Play the rest of the recording without stopping. Have students check their answers in pairs. Play the recording again if necessary and have students check/complete their answers.

Check the answers with the class.

Answers and audio script
Sunny: southern California, Mexico
Raining: the Midwest states, New England, Northwest and Seattle
Atlanta 82° F
Miami 90° F
Chicago 65° F
Minneapolis 60° F
Boston 68° F
New York City 68° F
Denver 59° F
Seattle 70° F
St. Louis 70° F
Mexico City 87° F
Guadalajara 87° F
Cancun 93° F
Dallas 75° F

The season is late summer.

CD3 31

News anchor: Here's Kristin with the weather for the United States and Mexico for the next 24 hours.

Kristin: Hello there. Here's the forecast for Mexico and the United States today. Right now there's some wet and windy weather over the Midwest states, and this is going to move east over the New England states. Temperatures in Boston and New York are now about 68°, but it's cooler in Chicago, 65°, and even cooler in Minneapolis, 60°. To the south it's a little warmer, in St. Louis, 70°, but to the west cool and cloudy in Denver, where it's a welcome 59° after all that extreme summer heat. Moving south it's getting warmer, 75° in Dallas. It's going to be cloudy and showery across much of the northwest, with heavy rain in Seattle and a temperature of 70°. Southern California is going to be warm and dry. In the southeast, it will be hot and stormy, 82° in Atlanta and even warmer in Miami, with temperatures up to 90°. It's going to be sunny all over Mexico, with a high of 75° in Mexico City, 87° in Guadalajara, and 93° in Cancun. And that's your weather for today. I'll be back at lunchtime with an update.

News anchor: Thank you, Kristin, and now...

2 Ask students to look at the weather symbols on the map. Elicit words for symbols students already know and then have them continue working in pairs to match the remaining symbols and words. If students have access to dictionaries, have them look up words they don't know.

Go over the answers with the class.

Answers
sunny =
rainy =
windy =
cloudy =
stormy =
snowy and foggy are not in the forecast

3 This exercise is to practice which pairs of adjectives commonly go together to describe weather. This will vary in different countries according to the climate, for example it can be warm and windy in many climates but is only rarely so in most parts of the US.

Introduce the topic by asking students for their ideas about US weather.

Focus students' attention on the examples. Then have students continue making sentences, working in pairs. Monitor and help as necessary.

Sample answers

cool and cloudy	cold and windy
cool and rainy	warm and sunny
cool and windy	hot and sunny
cold and cloudy	cold and foggy
dry and cloudy	cold and rainy
wet and windy	cold and snowy

Also you often hear the pairs *warm and dry*, *cold and wet* together.

SUGGESTION

If you have time, you can have a mini-discussion comparing which pairs of words go together to describe the climate in different parts of the US and which for the climate of their own country.

CD3 32 Draw a large question mark on the board to signal that you are going to introduce a question form.

Play the recording and have students repeat chorally and individually. Read the note on *What ... like?* with students (See *Possible problem* above).

4 Practice the question and elicit possible answers about where you are and about other places that students know. Encourage students to use some of the sentences from exercise 3. Drill the pronunciation as necessary.

5 **CD3 33** Give students a few moments to read the incomplete conversation. Play the recording and have students write in the weather for today, yesterday, and tomorrow. Check the answers.

Students practice the questions and answers about the weather where you are in open and then closed pairs. Monitor and check for correct tense use.

6 This is an information-gap activity. Divide the class into A/B pairs. If possible, have students sit facing each other so they can't see each other's books. Tell Student A to look at the world weather information on p. 147 of the Student' Book and Student B at the information on p. 150.

Demonstrate the activity by doing the first question and answer about Seoul with the class. This is a good time to encourage the use of the modifiers *very* and *really*, if you feel your students can cope with it. Make sure they realize that this is tomorrow's weather and therefore they need to use *going to* in the questions and answers.

Have students continue the activity in closed pairs. Monitor and check as they do it.

Check the answers with the whole class. Have students read aloud their answers as complete sentences, e.g., *It's going to be rainy and (really) cold in Moscow tomorrow.*

Answers
World weather: tomorrow

		°F	It's going to be:
Beijing	C	43	cloudy and cold
Boston	Fg	42	foggy and cold
Cairo	S	64	sunny and warm
Hong Kong	S	75	sunny and warm
Istanbul	Fg	50	cloudy and cold
Lima	S	74	sunny and hot
London	R	50	wet/rainy and cool
Luxor	S	82	sunny and very hot
Mexico City	C	76	cloudy and cold
Moscow	Sn	30	snowy and very cold
Mumbai	C	84	cloudy and hot
Rio de Janeiro	R	75	wet/rainy and hot
Seoul	S	45	sunny and cold
Sydney	C	72	cloudy and warm

S = sunny   C = cloudy   Fg = foggy   R = rainy   Sn = snowy

7 Elicit/pre-teach the points of the compass (*north, south, east, west*). Also pre-teach/check students' understanding of other useful vocabulary when referring to regions of a country, e.g., *in/over the mountains, on the coast,* etc. Have students think about different areas of the country where they are studying and make notes about the weather for the coming weekend. Students can use the information they researched before the lesson (See *Notes* above) or base their forecast on recent weather conditions.

Give students time to write their forecast. Monitor and help as necessary. Students read their forecast to a partner and compare the details for each area.

ADDITIONAL MATERIAL

Workbook Unit 11
Ex. 8 The weather

EVERYDAY ENGLISH (SB p. 89)

Making suggestions

NOTE

In order not to overload students, we have restricted the functional content to two of the most common expressions for asking for and making suggestions:

- *should* to ask for suggestions and make suggestions, e.g., *What should we do?/Should we go out for dinner?*
- *Let's* to make a suggestion for everyone, e.g., *Let's go to the movies.*

Will for spontaneous decisions is also included, but just for recognition.

1 Focus students' attention on the headings in the chart and the two examples. Then elicit a few more activities for good weather (*go for a walk, play tennis, do some gardening,* etc.) and some for bad weather (*read a book, do a jigsaw puzzle, play chess,* etc.) Students continue the two lists, working individually and then compare their lists with a partner.

Elicit examples from the whole class and build more lists on the board. Tell students that they will need their lists later in the lesson.

2 **CD3 34** Tell students that they are going to hear two conversations, one for good weather and one for bad. Ask them to read the incomplete conversations quickly. With weaker students, have them predict possible words for each blank.

Play the recording and have students complete the conversations.

Check the answers. Then have students listen and repeat chorally. First focus on the question, and then practice the answer. Encourage good stress and intonation.

What should we do?   /wʌt ʃʊd wi du/
Let's go for a walk.   /lɛts goʊ fərə wɔk/

Ask students to practice the conversations in pairs.

Read the notes on *Should we* and *Let's* with the whole class. In a monolingual class, you can ask students to translate the sentences.

3 **CD3 35** Ask your students to work in pairs. Ask them first to find the "good weather" lines and then the "bad weather" lines. Then ask them to put each set in order to complete the conversations from exercise 2.

Play the recording and have students listen and check their answers.

Students work in their pairs to practice the conversation. Monitor and check. If students have problems with pronunciation, play key lines of the recording again, drilling chorally and individually. Then have students continue practicing the conversation in closed pairs.

4 Students continue to work in pairs, changing partners if appropriate. Ask them to look at the lists they made in exercise 1. Demonstrate the activity by asking for examples of a good weather and a bad weather activity and building the conversations with the whole class. Have students continue in pairs, using the activities in their lists. Monitor and check. Write down any common errors, but don't discuss these until after the activity.

SUGGESTION

To finish the activity in exercise 4, you can either ask a couple of pairs to act out their conversations for the whole class, or record a few conversations and play them for the class to correct any mistakes in the language and the pronunciation.

Photocopiable Activity

UNIT 11 Making suggestions TB p. 154

Note: This activity should be used in a later lesson as reinforcement and not straight after finishing SB p. 89.

Materials: One copy of the worksheet for each student.

Procedure: Explain that students are going to do a worksheet to practice making suggestions. Introduce the topic by asking *What's the weather like today? What activities could we do?* Elicit a range of possible answers.

- Hand out a copy of the worksheet to each student. Elicit an example of a good and a bad weather activity for exercise 1. Students complete the task, working in pairs. Check the answers.

- Focus students' attention on the flow diagram in exercise 2. Elicit possible lines in an example conversation with the whole class. If students have problems with pronunciation, drill key lines as necessary. Encourage a lively delivery with a good voice range. With weaker classes, write the conversation on the board to provide added support.

- Put students in pairs and give them time to build their conversation, using the prompts in parentheses. Monitor and help as necessary.

- Students work with a new partner and make another conversation. Encourage them to choose a different type of weather and different activities. Students act out their conversation(s) for the rest of the class.

- As an extension, divide the class into groups of three and have them plan an evening out for the class. They need to make suggestions on when/where to meet and what activities to do. Students present their ideas to the class and then vote for the idea they like best.

ADDITIONAL MATERIAL

Workbook Unit 11

Ex. 9   What should we do?

Don't forget!

Workbook Unit 11

Ex. 10   *I/my/mine*

Ex. 11   Prepositions

Grammar Reference (SB p. 138)

Word list Unit 4 (SB p. 144)

Students can translate the words, learn them at home, or transfer some of them to their vocabulary notebook.

Tests (Online)

Unit 11 Test

Video (iTools and Online)

Additional photocopiables and PPT™presentations (iTools)

12 Never ever!

Present Perfect • *ever, never, yet,* and *just* • *take* and *get*
• **Transportation and travel**
VIDEO Experiences

This unit introduces one of the most difficult tenses for students of English. The Present Perfect is one of the most commonly used tenses in English, especially spoken English, but its presentation has been left until Unit 12. This is because until students understand the concept that the Simple Past refers to the definite past, they will not be able to grasp the idea that the Present Perfect refers to the indefinite past. The second grammar section brings together all the key tenses students have covered in *American Headway Level 1*.

The theme of this unit is "in my life," and various people's experiences in life and travel are explored. The skills section focuses on experiences at the Glastonbury Music Festival. The *Everyday English* section further develops the travel theme with a focus on transportation by bus, train, and plane.

LANGUAGE INPUT

GRAMMAR

Present Perfect + *ever* and *never* (SB p. 90)
Present Perfect + *yet* and *just* (SB p. 92)

- Understanding and practicing the Present Perfect to talk about experiences.
- Understanding and practicing the Present Perfect with the adverbs *yet* and *just*.

VOCABULARY

take and *get* (SB p. 96)

- Understanding and practicing words and expressions that go with *take* and *get*.

EVERYDAY ENGLISH

Transportation and travel (SB p. 97)

- Understanding and practicing useful words and expressions in travel situations.

SKILLS DEVELOPMENT

READING

The Glastonbury festival (SB p. 94)

- An article about the Glastonbury Music Festival.

LISTENING

Two people talk about experiences at a music festival (SB p. 95)

- Listening for key information in two anecdotes about a music festival **CD3 43** (SB p. 128).

SPEAKING

Talking about you (SB p. 92)
What do you think? (SB p. 95)
Talking about you (SB p. 96)

- Asking and answering questions about experiences.
- Discussing the Glastonbury Music Festival.
- Asking and answering questions to practice words and expressions that go with *take* and *get*.

WRITING

A poem – Choosing the right word (SB p. 113)

- Choosing words to complete a poem, then writing additional verses.

MORE MATERIALS

Photocopiables – Have you ever …? (TB p. 155), **Tests** (Online) **Video** (iTools and Online)

STARTER (SB p. 90)

This section is a fun way of getting students into the topic of places people have visited.

1 Focus students' attention on the first two flags and elicit the names of the corresponding countries and their capitals. Students continue the task, working in pairs/small groups.

Check the answers with the whole class. If students have problems with the pronunciation of the countries, drill them chorally and individually.

Answers

a Italy – Rome	b Switzerland – Bern
c Argentina – Buenos Aires	d Egypt – Cairo
e Mexico – Mexico City	f Chile – Santiago
g Australia – Canberra	h Brazil – Brasília
i China – Beijing	j Japan – Tokyo
k The US – Washington DC	l Korea – Seoul

2 Tell students the countries you have been to. Students then choose the countries they have visited. Elicit a range of examples from the class.

BEEN THERE! DONE THAT! (SB p. 90)

Present Perfect + *ever* and *never*

> ⚠ **POSSIBLE PROBLEMS**
>
> In this unit, the coverage of the Present Perfect is staged across the two presentations. In this first section, we introduce one of the main uses of the Present Perfect – to refer to an experience at some time in your life. On p. 92, we focus on another use – to refer to the present result of a past action – with the adverbs *yet* and *just*. We do not introduce at all the third main use of the Present Perfect, which is to refer to unfinished past (*I have been a teacher for ten years*), nor do we teach the Present Perfect Continuous.
>
> The goal of this unit is to provide an introduction to the Present Perfect, but do not expect your students to master it quickly! It takes a long time (and a lot of mistakes, correction, and re-teaching) before students feel confident with this tense.
>
> The following aspects of the tense often present problems:
>
> • A similar form of auxiliary verb *have* + past participle exists in many European languages, but it is used in a very different way. In English, the Present Perfect expresses the concept of an action happening at an indefinite time before now, and so it cannot be used when a definite time is given.
>
> **Common mistakes**
>
> *I have seen him last week.
>
> *When have you been to the States?
>
> *Did you ever try Chinese food?
>
> *In my life I went to most countries in Europe.

1 **CD3 36** Focus students' attention on the photo and read the instructions. Ask students to identify Kyle and Lara. Ask *What nationality are they?* (Australian) and *Where are they?* (In a camping/travel store).

Read the questions as a class. Then play the conversation and elicit the answers.

Answers and audio script
They are talking about Lara and Mel's trip to Europe.
Mel is Lara's friend.
Lara wants to end the conversation because Mel is waiting for her and they have a lot to do.

CD3 36

K = Kyle   L = Lara
K Hi Lara! Are you and Mel ready for your trip?
L Yeah, almost. We leave next Monday for Hong Kong.
K Ah, Hong Kong, I've been to Hong Kong many times.
L Well, I've never been there. It's my first time in Asia.
K Really? What about your friend Mel?
L She's been to Tokyo and Taipei, but she hasn't been to Hong Kong.
K Ah, Tokyo and Taipei. I've been there too. I studied in Tokyo for a year before I went to work in Toronto. Have you ever been to Canada?
L No, I haven't, I haven't traveled much at all so I'm really excited.
K Oh, I've been to Asia, North *and* South America so many times and I've …
L I'm sure you have, Kyle. Oh no, look at the time! Mel's waiting for me. We have so much to do. Bye, Kyle, we'll send you a postcard.

2 **CD3 37** Ask students to do this task from memory. With weaker students, you can ask *Who has traveled a lot?* (Kyle) *Who hasn't visited many countries?* (Lara), but don't give an explanation of the Present Perfect at this stage.

Focus students' attention on the example. Give students time to complete the task and check their answers in pairs before checking answers with the class.

Play the recording of the sentences and have students repeat chorally and individually. Make sure that students can reproduce the contracted forms in each sentence. Correct any mistakes carefully.

Remember that students will probably never have seen the Present Perfect tense before, and *been* will be unfamiliar. If students ask about the tense, explain, using L1 if possible, that *have been* is an example of the Present Perfect tense. Don't try to do a full presentation at this stage, but just explain that the sentences refer to the idea of "at some time in your life." Focus students' attention on the highlighted contracted forms. Also elicit the full form of *hasn't* (*has not*) and *haven't* (*have not*).

Answers and audio script
1 I've been to Hong Kong many times. **(Kyle)**
2 I've never been there. **(Lara)**
3 She's been to Tokyo and Taipei. **(Mel)**
4 She hasn't been to Hong Kong. **(Mel)**
5 I haven't traveled much at all. **(Lara)**
6 I've been to Asia, North and South America. **(Kyle)**

3 Demonstrate the activity yourself with information about the countries you have and haven't visited. Ask students to read the examples in the Student Book aloud. Then ask students to make similar sentences, saying which countries they have/haven't been to. Elicit examples from several students, so you can check students' accuracy in the use and pronunciation of the structure.

Students then continue the activity in groups. Monitor and check. Correct any mistakes carefully with the class after the groupwork.

4 **CD3 38** This activity introduces the question form and covers the "experience" use of the Present Perfect in contrast to the Simple Past.

Give students a few moments to read the incomplete conversation. Then play the recording and have students complete the replies.

Have students read the conversation in open pairs. If necessary, highlight the main stresses in the Present Perfect questions and short answers:

Have you ever been to Chile?

No, I haven't.

Play the recording again or model the sentences yourself and have students repeat.

Focus students' attention on the question form of the Present Perfect and name the tense. Then focus on *When did you go? Where did you go?* and *Did you have a good time?* Ask *What tense this is?* (Simple Past). Just name the tenses at this stage and do not try to explain the different uses. (These are given in the *Grammar Spot* below.)

Have students ask you questions about countries you have been to, following the model in exercise 4. Encourage them to ask *When did you go? Where did you go?* and *Did you have a good time?* and give appropriate answers.

Students continue in open pairs asking and answering about countries they have been to, when and where, and if they had a good time. This might sound repetitive, but remember you are introducing students to a very new concept with the Present Perfect tense and they need practice with forming questions, answers, and negatives.

Answers and audio script
A Have you ever been to Chile?
B No, I **haven't**.
A Have you ever been to Brazil?
B Yes, I **have**.
A When did you go?
B Two years **ago**.
A Where did you go?
B Rio, Salvador, and Recife.
A Wow! Did you have a good time?
B Yes, I **did**. It was great!

5 Students write down the names of two countries or cities and make similar conversations, working in pairs. Monitor and check for accuracy in the use and pronunciation of the two tenses. Highlight and correct any mistakes carefully.

6 This practices the third person singular in a personalized way. Students will need to make the change from *have/*

haven't to *has/hasn't*. Focus students' attention on the examples and elicit the full form of *Maria's* (*Maria has*). Drill the examples chorally and individually. Then elicit examples from several students about their partner.

GRAMMAR SPOT

1 Read the notes with the whole class. Point out the use of *ever* with the Present Perfect in the question form to mean "at any time in your life." Stress that we do not use *ever* in the answer.

2 Read the notes with the whole class. Focus students' attention on the use of the Simple Past to say exactly when something happened. Elicit other past time references that can be used with the Simple Past, e.g, *last month*, *a long time ago*, *yesterday*, etc.

3 Read the notes with the whole class and have students complete the charts. Check the answers with the class.

Answers			
	Affirmative	**Negative**	
I/You/We/They	**have**	**haven't**	been to
He/She	**has**	**hasn't**	Mexico City.

4 Students complete the sentences with *ever* or *never*. Check the answers with the class.

Answers
Has he **ever** been to Rio de Janeiro?
He's **never** been to Seoul.

▶▶ Read Grammar Reference 12.1 and 12.2 on p. 138 together in class, and/or ask students to read it at home. Encourage them to ask you questions about it.

SUGGESTION

If your students have a similar tense form in their language, and if you can use L1, you might want to make a brief comparison between the way L1 and English use the auxiliary verb *have* + past participle. Be careful, however! Keep it short, and as simple as possible, because it would be very easy to overload students with too much information at this early stage of their exposure to the Present Perfect.

7 This exercise presents the past participle of a range of high-frequency verbs. Many of them are used in exercises that come later in this unit and they are very common verbs when talking about experiences.

Remind students of the terms *past participle* and *base form* and elicit examples for *been* (be/go) and *lived* (live). Tell students that they will often be able to guess which base form a past participle comes from.

Students write the base forms for the rest of the verbs. Have students check their answers in pairs before checking the answers with the whole class. Elicit which two verbs are regular.

8 Elicit the Simple Past forms of *be (was/were)* and *live (lived)* and have students continue the list in pairs.

▶▶ Refer students to the list of irregular verbs on SB p. 152 and have them check their answers.

9 Focus students' attention on the examples. Say a few more verbs in the infinitive and elicit the Simple Past and past participle. Students continue the task in pairs, taking turns testing each other. Encourage students to get faster and faster as they do the task.

PRACTICE (SB p. 92)

Talking about you

This section reinforces the use of Present Perfect to ask about experiences and the Simple Past to talk about exactly when/how something happened.

1 Focus students' attention on the bulleted list and pre-teach/check students' understanding of the following vocabulary: *foreign* /ˈfɔrən/, *sunrise*, *tent*, and *marathon*.

First ask students to go over the list and choose the things they have done. Focus students' attention on the example exchanges in the Student Book. Elicit complete examples of follow-up questions in the Simple Past, e.g., *Why did you go there? Who did you go with?/Who did you meet? How did you travel? Where did you stay?/Where did you visit?*

Have students ask and answer the questions, giving true answers. If necessary, highlight the contrastive stress in the third speech bubble in exercise 2:

Well, I have.

2 Put students into groups of three or four to ask and answer the questions in the list. With weaker students, you can go over other possible follow-up questions for some of the prompts, e.g., *Have you ever worked all night? Why did you do that? How did you feel? What time did you go to bed?*

Give students time to work through the list, encouraging a reasonably fast pace so that students don't stay on the same question for too long. Monitor and check for correct formation of the questions and short answers, both Present Perfect and Simple Past, and for accurate

pronunciation. If students have problems, drill key forms chorally and individually and then have students repeat the groupwork.

3 Focus students' attention on the example. Students tell the class about people in their group. Make sure they give follow-up information in the Simple Past where appropriate, e.g., *Kati has flown in an airplane. She flew from London to New York five years ago.*

ADDITIONAL MATERIAL

Workbook Unit 12
Ex. 1–4   Present Perfect and Simple Past

Present Perfect + *yet* and *just*

> ⚠️ **POSSIBLE PROBLEMS**
>
> The concepts expressed by *yet* and *just* are very subtle and they are expressed by different structures in different languages. We do not ask any questions in the Grammar Spot that test concept (only form), because the language required would be more complex than the target items themselves. Students should be able to understand the meaning through context and use, but you need to make sure, probably via translation into L1 if possible, that students understand them. Explain that *(not) yet* means "(not) before now" whereas *just* means "a short time before now." Use examples from the text and/or write additional examples on the board.
>
> Note that American English usually uses the Simple Past with *just,* and sometimes with *yet.*
>
> *Did you do your homework yet? I just did it.*

SUGGESTIONS

- Be prepared to prompt and help with the questions in the *Grammar Spot,* as students may find them hard.

1 **CD3 39** Focus students' attention on the photo of Lara. Elicit information about her (*She's Australian. She's planning a trip to Hong Kong.*) Ask *Who is the other girl?* (Mel, Lara's friend.) *Is she going to Hong Kong with Lara?* (Yes, she is.)

Focus students' attention on the "Things to do" list and ask students to locate it in the photo. Read the list as a class, referring to the photo to add support, and check students' understanding of *packing, print tickets,* and *check in online.* With weaker students, elicit the past participle for each verb in the "Things to do list" (*bought, finished, gotten, emailed, checked, printed, checked*).

Read the instructions for exercise 1 as a class. Play the recording as far as *we did that a while ago* and focus students' attention on the example. Students listen to the rest of the recording and choose the things Lara and Mel have done. Only play the recording a second time if students had problems doing the task.

Check the answers with the class.

> **Answers and audio script**
> **Things to do …**
> 1 buy new backpacks ✓
> 2 finish packing ✗
> 3 get Hong Kong dollars from bank ✓
> 4 email Mel's aunt in Tokyo ✓
> 5 find out weather forecast for Hong Kong ✓
> 6 print tickets ✓
> 7 check in online ✗

> **CD3 39**
> **L = Lara   M = Mel**
> L   Where's the list?
> M   I have it. OK, let's check it. Umm we've bought new backpacks, we did that a while ago.
> L   They look pretty big. I hope we can carry them.
> M   Oh, don't worry. We're strong! I haven't finished packing mine yet. Have you?
> L   Not yet, just one or two more things to go in. Oh, have you gotten the Hong Kong dollars from the bank?
> M   Yup. I got five thousand for you and five thousand for me.
> L   All our savings. I hope it's enough!
> M   No worries. We can stay with my aunt in Tokyo.
> L   Have you emailed her yet?
> M   Yeah, she's just emailed back. She's going to meet us at the airport when we fly in to Tokyo from Hong Kong.
> L   Great. Hey, look, I've just checked the weather in Hong Kong for next week. Hot and sunny!
> M   Yeah, it's going to be so good. We're going to leave winter here and arrive in the middle of summer in Hong Kong.
> L   What about the tickets?
> M   I think we only need passports, but I printed our tickets just in case, but I haven't checked in online yet. You can only do that 24 hours before the flight.
> L   Oh, Mel! I am so excited. I can't wait.

2 **CD3 39** Refer students back to the "Things to do" list. If you didn't do so in exercise 1, elicit the past participle of each of the verbs in the list (*bought, finished, gotten, emailed, checked, printed, checked*). Drill the examples in the Student Book and elicit one or two more examples. If students ask about the use of *yet,* just explain it means "before now."

Students continue working in pairs, saying what Lara and Mel have and haven't done. Monitor and check for the correct form of the Present Perfect and the correct position of *yet.*

Play the recording again so that students can check their answers. Then check the answers with the whole class.

Refer students to **CD3 39** (SB p. 128). Have them practice the conversation in pairs. If students have problems with pronunciation, drill key lines chorally and individually and then have students repeat the pairwork.

> **Answers**
> 1 They've bought new backpacks.
> 2 They haven't finished packing yet.
> 3 They've gotten Hong Kong dollars from the bank.
> 4 They've emailed Mel's aunt in Tokyo.
> 5 They've checked the weather forecast for Hong Kong.
> 6 They've printed their tickets.
> 7 They haven't checked in online yet.
> See exercise 1 for **CD3 39**.

GRAMMAR SPOT

Look at the questions in the Grammar Spot as a class.

1 Have students think about which form of *have* they need to complete the sentences. Allow students to check their answers in pairs before checking the answers with the class. Focus on the use of *yet* and

just in the sentences, and check comprehension (see *Possible problems*).

2 Elicit the answers to the questions about the position of *yet*.

3 Allow students time to figure out the rules for the use of *yet*. Check the answer with the class.

▶▶ Read Grammar Reference 12.3 on p. 138 together in class, and/or ask students to read it at home. Encourage them to ask you questions about it.

PRACTICE (SB p. 93)

Tense review

Exercises 1 and 2 help to review and reinforce the tenses students have covered in this level – Simple Present and Present Continuous, Simple Past and Present Perfect, and *going to*. Exercise 1 covers affirmative and negative forms, and exercise 2 *wh*-question forms in a range of tenses.

> **NOTES**
> The places mentioned in Lara's description are:
>
> **Perth** The largest city in south-west Australia, located on the Swan River 20 km inland from the Indian Ocean.
>
> **Cairns** A city and port on the north-east coast of Australia, in the state of Queensland.
>
> **Great Barrier Reef** The largest coral reef in the world (about 2000 km long), located off the north-east coast of Australia.
>
> A **747** refers to the Boeing passenger plane, often used for long-distance flights.

1 **CD3 40** Tell students they are going to hear Lara talking about traveling and her trip to Asia. Pre-teach/check students' understanding of *to scuba dive*. Read the first sentence with the class and elicit the answer to number 1 (*haven't traveled*).

Put students in pairs to continue the task. With weaker students, you can write the range of tenses covered in the text on the board (see the note at the start of this section). Ask students to underline any answers that they are unsure about or can't agree on.

Elicit the numbers of the answers that students had problems with and write them on the board. Play the recording and have students check their answers. Go back

to the "problem" sentences on the board and confirm the correct answers. Ask students to explain the answers as best they can. If necessary, refer them back to the Grammar Reference at the end of the Student' Book.

2 Have two students ask and answer question 1 as an example. Students then answer the questions, working individually. Monitor and help as necessary.

Put students in pairs to ask and answer the questions. Encourage students to give full answers so that they practice statement forms, too. Monitor and check for correct question formation and verb forms in the answers.

Students ask and answer the questions in open pairs to check their answers with the whole class. Highlight and correct mistakes carefully.

No, not yet!

3 **CD3 41** Focus students' attention on the examples. Drill the question and possible answers, encouraging students to imitate the intonation and main stress. Students give one or two more examples in open pairs. Remind them that they will need to use different pronouns in their answers (*it/him/her*) and that they should try to use *not yet* or *just* where possible.

Students continue working in closed pairs. Monitor and check for correct question formation and use of *yet* and *just*.

Play the recording and have students compare their answers. If you think students need further practice, put them in new pairs and have them practice the questions and answers from **CD3 41** in closed pairs.

Audio script

1 **A** Have you checked your emails yet?
  B Yes, I just checked them, but there wasn't one from you.
2 **A** Have you done the shopping?
  B No, I haven't. I'm too tired to go out.
3 **A** Have you washed your hair?
  B Yes, I just washed it.
4 **A** Have you cleaned the car yet?
  B Yes, I just cleaned your car and mine!
5 **A** Mom, have you made dinner yet?
  B Yes, dinner's ready. Go and wash your hands.
6 **A** Have you done the dishes yet?
  B No. I did them last night. It's your turn!
7 **A** Have you met the new student yet?
  B Yes, I have. I met her on the way to school this morning.
8 **A** Have you finished this exercise?
  B Yes, I just finished it. Thank goodness!

Check it

4 This exercise reviews the grammar just covered in the unit and also reinforces the main tenses covered in the course.

Students work in pairs to choose the correct sentence. Then check the answers with the whole class.

Answers
1 I saw Kyle yesterday.
2 Have you ever met my cousin?
3 When did she go to New Zealand?
4 What are you going to do in Hong Kong?
5 He doesn't like flying.
6 Has Lara finished packing yet?
7 Have you ever been to a rock concert?

ADDITIONAL MATERIAL

Workbook Unit 12
Ex. 5–7   *yet* and *just*
Ex. 8   *Reading*

READING AND LISTENING (SB p. 94)

The Glastonbury festival

This skills section continues the theme of experiences with a focus on the Glastonbury Music Festival – considered a must-do experience by fans of contemporary music from all over the world.

NOTE

The following artists and bands are mentioned in the article on Glastonbury: Paul McCartney, Bruce Springsteen, Robbie Williams, rapper Jay Z, and soul singer Amy Winehouse, REM, Radiohead, Coldplay, Arctic Monkeys, and Sigur Ros (an experimental rock band from Iceland). Students are likely to be familiar with many of the artists, but if you would like your students to hear examples of their music, you can bring in short extracts or ask your students to provide some of them.

ABOUT THE TEXT

Glastonbury /ˈglæstʌnbɛri/, known as *Glasto* for short, is one of the largest open-air music and performing arts festivals in the world. It is best known for its contemporary music, but also features dance, comedy, theater, circus, and cabaret. Since the first festival in 1970, the event has grown in scope and popularity, with a number of different stages/performance areas dedicated to different styles of music and acts. Since 1981, the festival has been organized by local farmer and site owner Michael Eavis. Much of the profit from the festival is donated to local and international charities. Note that the 2012 festival was canceled because all the portable toilets were being used at the London Olympics.

Exercise 2 has an extract from a song by Turin Brakes, a folk-rock duo from London. They performed the song *They Can't Buy the Sunshine* at Glastonbury. See the above *Note* about other performers/bands mentioned in the article.

Sonar is an annual three-day music festival held in Barcelona, Spain.

Encourage students to use the context to help them with new vocabulary and to pool knowledge with other students, or use a dictionary. With weaker classes or if you are short on time, ask students to look up some of following vocabulary before the lesson:

Homework prior to the lesson

acre /ˈeɪkər/, *farmland, act* (n), *to attend, slogan, mud, knee, to be great fun, highlight, complaint, atmosphere, toddler, crowd.*

1 Introduce the topic by asking students *What's your favorite type of music?* and list different styles on the board. Ask *Do you prefer to listen to music on CD/iPod or hear music live?*

Then ask and answer the questions in exercise 1 with the class, eliciting a range of experiences and opinions. Elicit what students know about the Glastonbury Music Festival. If they haven't heard of it, focus their attention on the photos and elicit impressions of the event and the people who attend it.

2 **CD3 42** Tell students they are going to hear an extract from a song that was played at Glastonbury (see *About the text* above). Play the recording and elicit students' opinion of the song.

3 Have students read the facts about Glastonbury quickly, asking others for help with vocabulary if you didn't pre-teach the items listed in *About the text* or assign them for homework.

Students read and find the answers to the questions, working in pairs. Monitor and help with any questions.

Check the answers with the class. If appropriate, play extracts of music by the performers listed in the article (see *Note* above) and ask students for their opinions.

Elicit students' reactions to the facts about the Glastonbury.

Answers

1 It takes place in 1,000 acres of farmland in southwest England, in June. It lasts four days.
2 There are 21 hours of music every day.
3 In 1970, 1,500 people attended the first festival. They paid £1 a ticket. Last year, 190,000 people attended. They paid £205 for a ticket.
4 Students' own answers.
5 In 2009, Michael Jackson died during the festival and T-shirts with the slogan "I was at Glastonbury when Michael Jackson died" went on sale.
6 In 2005, it rained every day and people danced in the mud. It is a good song because the festival is famous for its rain.

4 This exercise focuses on the second part of the article and the experiences of people who have been to Glastonbury. The goal of the task is to have students scan the paragraphs for the information they need to match the names to the questions. Stress that students don't need to understand every word to be able to do the task and that they may need more than one name for each question.

Focus students' attention on the photos of the four people and say each of their names. Set a time limit of about two minutes to ensure that students don't spend too long on the details in the article. If appropriate, you can set the task up as a race, with students working in pairs.

Students read quickly to find the correct names to match the questions. Check the names, eliciting the lines from the article that gave students the answers.

Answers

1 Marina (I've now been six times!)
2 Dave (my first time …), Izzi (This was my first year at Glastonbury.)
3 Marina (I loved it!), Len (We loved everything.), Izzi (It was amazing. Long live Glastonbury!)
4 Dave – mobile phones (Only one complaint – there were so many mobile phones.)
5 Len (I've taken my kids to Glastonbury twice. We watched Radiohead with my 11-year-old son.)
6 Izzi (I traveled 10,000 miles to be there.)

5 This exercise allows students to read the second part of the article again, this time more slowly so that they can process the information to answer the true/false questions.

Elicit the answer to number 1 as an example. Then put students in pairs to answer the other true/false questions. Have students ask others in their group for help with vocabulary if you didn't pre-teach the items listed in *About the text* or assign them for homework. Monitor and help with any questions.

Check the answers with the class, having students correct the false sentences.

Answers

1 False. She took off her shoes and danced in the mud up to her knees.
2 True.
3 True.
4 False. He thought there were too many cell phones.
5 True.
6 False. The crowds all moved back so his son could see better.

Listening

6 **CD3 43** Read the instructions to exercise 6 as a class. Pre-teach/check students' understanding of *highlights*, *sausages*, *House music* (a type of modern electronic music that developed in the 1980s), *hang out*. With weaker students, you can play the recording through once and elicit who had the best experience (*Daniel*) and then play it again and ask students to focus on the detail.

Write the headings *food*, *drink*, *music*, and *people* on the board. Tell students to listen for the information for each category. Point out that Daniel doesn't say anything about food or drink.

Play the recording of both Elsa and Daniel and have students make notes for each person. Students check their answers in pairs. Play the recording again to allow students to check/complete their answers.

Go over the key information with the class and elicit who had the best experience.

Answers and audio script
Elsa
Food: the best sausages and fries ever
Weather: sunny and beautiful every day
Music: disappointed with the music on Saturday night. DJs played House music all night, but it was awful.
People: went back to her tent to hang out with friends.
Daniel
Music: really great
People: 100,000 friendly people – can have good conversations with people at Glastonbury.
Daniel had the best experience.

CD3 43
1 Elsa from New York
OK, I've been to Glastonbury twice now. My highlights this year were: the weather - it was sunny and beautiful every day, and the food van with the best sausages and fries ever. However, I was very disappointed with the music on Saturday night. DJs played house music all night. I love House, but this was awful. I got really bored, so I went back to my tent to hang out with friends!
2 Daniel Evans from Wales
Last Wednesday at 2:30 in the afternoon, I decided that I wanted to go to Glastonbury. I was lucky! I found a ticket online. I'm so glad I went. The music was really great. Sometimes it took a long time to get to the stages. The lines were long, but people were always friendly. In the busy "real world" it's difficult to have good conversations with people. At Glastonbury you can do this. It's a great festival, with a great crowd of people. What more could you want? 100,000 friendly people. I wish the rest of life was the same! Four days out of 365 is a good start!

What do you think?

Discuss the questions as a class. Encourage students to give reasons for their answers. Vote on how many students would/wouldn't like to go to Glastonbury and why.

EXTRA ACTIVITY

Students work in small groups to plan their own one-day music festival for an international audience of different ages. Tell them they need to plan who will perform on stage, the order of acts, and what facilities they want to offer to the public, e.g., food, things to buy, other entertainment, parking, etc. Also ask them to decide the schedule, pricing of tickets, and also the name of a charity which will benefit from some of the profits.

Give students time to discuss their plans, making notes on their final choices. Students present their ideas to the rest of the class, who in turn ask questions/give opinions on each of the planned festivals. Students then vote for the one they like best.

ADDITIONAL MATERIAL

Workbook Unit 12
Ex. 9 Listening

VOCABULARY AND SPEAKING (SB p. 96)

take and *get*

The last vocabulary section in this level highlights an important feature of English – the use of high-frequency verbs like *take* and *get* that change their meaning according to the noun or expression that follows, e.g., *take photos/a break/a long time/it easy*, etc.

1   Introduce this section by writing on the board: *photos, married, a seat,* and *up in the morning*. Elicit which two examples go with *take* (*photos/a seat*) and which two with *get* (*married/up in the morning*).

Read the instructions to exercise 1 as a class. Then give students time to look at the sentences. Elicit the base form of the expressions with *take* (*take place/take off/take a long time*) and *get* (*get along well/get bored*).

2   **CD3 44** Elicit the answer to number 1 as an example. With weaker students, you can elicit the expressions students need to use in each conversation in the base form and have students put them into the correct tense.

Play the recording and have students check their answers. Then put students into pairs to practice the conversations. Monitor and check. If students have problems with pronunciation, drill key lines chorally and individually and then have students repeat the pairwork.

> **Answers and audio script**
> 1 **A** It's really hot in here.
>   **B** Why don't you **take off** your sweater?
> 2 **A** Is your office near where you live?
>   **B** No, it **takes a long** time to **get to** work
> 3 **A** What are your co-workers like?
>   **B** Great! We all **get along** really **well**.
> 4 **A** How often are there exhibitions in the museum?
>   **B** They **take place** regularly, every two months.
> 5 **A** Do you like learning English?
>   **B** It's OK but sometimes I **get** really **bored**!

3   Focus students' attention on the example. Then ask students to work in their pairs to categorize the words and expressions according to the verb.

Check the answers with the class. If appropriate, point out that *get* is often followed by an adjective to express the idea of "become," e.g., *get ready/wet*.

> **Answers**
>
> | take | | get | |
> |---|---|---|---|
> | a test | photos | home late | on/off the bus |
> | a long time | it easy | married | ready |
> | a break | | a lot of emails | better soon |
> | | | very wet | |

4   **CD3 45** Elicit the answer to number 1 as an example. With weaker students, you can elicit the tenses students need to use in each sentence as a class and then have students write the correct forms.

Give students time to complete the sentences, working individually. Students then take turns reading the sentences aloud. Ask them to write down any differences in their answers.

Play the recording as a final check. Be prepared to explain the tense use if students had problems.

> **Answers and audio script**
> 1 I usually **take** a coffee break at around 10:00 in the morning.
> 2 How long **does** it **take** if you go by train?
> 3 Could you please **take** a picture of us?
> 4 Sue **has taken** her driving test three times and she's failed every time.
> 5 Are you still **getting** ready?! We're going to be so late!
> 6 The doctor told me to **take** it easy if I want to **get** better soon.
> 7 It rained on the day we **got** married. We **got** very wet, but still had a great day.
> 8 You can't **get** on the bus with that big dog. Please, **get** off!

Talking about you

5   Tell students that they need to use a range of tenses in this exercise, as in exercise 4. Elicit the answer to number 1, then have students complete the sentences, using the correct form of *take* or *get*. Monitor and help as necessary. With weaker classes, check that students have completed the sentences correctly before they do the pairwork.

Put students in pairs to ask and answer the questions in closed pairs. If necessary, have students ask and answer in open pairs as a final check.

> **Answers**
> 1 How long does it **take** you to **get** to school?
> 2 What time do you **get** back home after school/work?
> 3 What time do you usually **get** up in the morning?
> 4 Have you **taken** any exams this year?
> 5 Does it **take** you a long time to **get** ready before you go out?
> 6 Are you **getting** tired of this exercise?

ADDITIONAL MATERIAL

Workbook Unit 12
Ex. 10 *get*
Ex. 11 *take*

EVERYDAY ENGLISH (SB p. 97)

Transportation and travel

This final *Everyday English* section continues the travel theme with a focus on the situational language used when traveling by bus, train, and plane.

1   Introduce this section by asking students *When was the last time you traveled by bus, train, or plane? Were there any problems?* Elicit a range of examples, writing any relevant vocabulary on the board.

Focus students' attention on the chart and elicit an example for the *bus* column. Students work in pairs to complete the task.

Check the answers with the class, dealing with any pronunciation difficulties as you go. If necessary, remind students that the first part of compound nouns have greater stress, e.g., airport, round-trip ticket, bus stop.

Answers

bus	train	plane
round-trip ticket	round-trip ticket	airport
ticket office	arrivals	round-trip ticket
bus stop	train station	arrivals
	platform	boarding pass
	ticket office	customs
	departures	security check
		carry-on bags
		flight
		departures

2   **CD3 46** Tell students they are going to hear three travel announcements. They need to listen for the key words to match them to *bus*, *train*, or *plane*.

Play the recording and have students compare answers in pairs before checking answers with the class.

Answers and audio script

1   train   2 bus   3 plane
1   The 1:35 for San Diego stopping at San Luis Obispo, Santa Barbara, and Los Angeles is now ready to board on Track 2. There is a dining car on this train. Please make sure that you have all your luggage with you.
2   This is the number 22 for Springfield. Next stop Greenfield. Stand back from the doors, please.
3   Flight BA1536 to New York is now ready for boarding at Gate 58. Will passengers in rows 12 to 20 please board first. Passengers are reminded to keep their carry-on bags with them at all times.

3   **CD3 46** Pre-teach/check students' understanding of *gate* (the place in an airport where you get on/off a plane) and *row* /roʊ/ (a line of seats in a plane). Play announcement 1 again and elicit the numbers and what they refer to (1:35 – the train time, 2 – the track number).

Play the rest of the recording and have students write down the numbers in announcements 2 and 3. Allow students to check their answers in pairs before checking answers with the class.

Elicit any places in the announcements that students can remember. Play sections of the recording again as necessary.

Answers

See exercise 2 for **CD3 46**
1   Numbers: 1:35 – the train time, 2 – the track number
Places: San Diego, San Luis Obispo, Santa Barbara, Los Angeles
2   Numbers: 22 – the bus number
Places: Springfield, Greenfield
3   Numbers: BA 1536 – the flight number, 58 – the gate number, 12 to 20 – the number of the rows
Places: New York

4   This exercise helps to prepare students for exercises 5 and 6, as the lines are taken from the conversations in those tasks.

Elicit the answer for sentence 1. Have students complete the task in pairs. Then check the answers with the class.

Answers

1   bus   2 train   3 bus   4 plane   5 plane   6 train

5   **CD3 47** Explain that Exercise 5 contains the lines from conversations 1 and 2 in scrambled order. The lines for speaker A and speaker B appear in separate columns of the charts.

Focus students' attention on the example for conversation 1 and then elicit the next sentence (*A round trip to Washington, DC, please.*) Put students in pairs to continue figuring out the correct order for each conversation. With weaker students, you can put all of the lines in conversation 1 in order as a class activity and then let students do conversation 2 in pairs. Monitor and help as necessary.

Play the recording and have students check that they have ordered the lines correctly. Ask them to practice the conversations in their pairs.

6 **CD3 48** Focus students' attention on the photo of Mel and Lara. Ask students what they can remember about them. (*They are friends from Australia. They are planning a trip to Europe.*)

Check that students understand that A in the conversation stands for *Assistant*. Pre-teach/check students' understanding of *scales*. With weaker classes, give students time to read the conversation through before playing the recording.

Play the recording and have students complete the conversation. Elicit where Lara and Mel are and check the missing words in the conversation.

7 Give students time to practice the conversations in their pairs. Monitor and check. If students have problems with pronunciation, drill key lines chorally and individually and then have students repeat the pairwork.

Students choose one or two conversations and rehearse them a few times to help them memorize the lines. Monitor and help. Students act out their conversation(s) to the class.

EXTRA ACTIVITY

Students review the language of traveling by plane by putting in order the key steps of getting a flight. Dictate the following sentences *in random order* and then have students number them in the correct order. (This is based on a passenger with just a carry-on bag.)

1 You check in online.
2 You print your boarding pass.
3 You arrive at the airport.
4 You show the ticket agent your boarding pass and carry-on bags.
5 You go through passport control and the security check.
6 You wait in the departure lounge.
7 You hear the announcement for the gate number for your flight.
8 You go to the gate and board the plane.

Students can then personalize the language by telling a true anecdote or imagining a story about an experience they had when waiting to board a flight.

ADDITIONAL MATERIAL

Workbook Unit 12
Ex. 12 Transportation and travel

WRITING (SB p. 113)

A poem

Choosing the right word

The final unit in the writing syllabus appeals to students' creative side with a guided task on writing verses of a poem. The model poem *Why did you leave?* goes well with the unit theme of travel and moving on, but is also open to interpretation, allowing students to use their imagination in discussing the poem and writing their own verses.

1 This task reviews question words and prepares students for the question and answer format of the poem.

Elicit the matching answer to *What ...? (A suitcase)*. Check that students understand that *Whose ...?* asks about possession, e.g., *Whose cell phone is that? It's Mike's*. Then put students in pairs to continue the task. Check the answers with the class.

Elicit a possible complete answer for the *What ...?* question, e.g., *What are you taking on vacation?* Students then continue the task, working in their pairs.

Elicit a range of possible answers from the class. Different tenses are possible in some of the questions but make sure students use the Simple Past in questions for *Last September* and *Because I needed a vacation*.

Answers
What ...? A suitcase.
Where ...? Mexico.
When ...? Last September.
Why ...? Because I needed a vacation.
Who ...? Nobody.
How ...? By boat.
Which ...? The small brown one.
Whose ...? It's mine.

Possible complete questions
What are you taking on vacation? A suitcase.
Where are you going on vacation? Mexico.
When did you go to the US? Last September.
Why did you go to Italy? Because I needed a vacation.
Who are you traveling with? Nobody.
How are you going to travel? By boat.
Which backpack is yours? The small brown one.
Whose suitcase is this? It's mine.

2 Focus students' attention on the title and give students time to read the poem. Tell them not to worry about the missing words for now. Explain that there are no "right" answers to the questions in exercise 2. Give students a few moments to think about their answers and then put them in pairs/small groups to compare their ideas.

Elicit several ideas from the class, encouraging students to give reasons for their answers.

3 Focus students' attention on the pairs of words for each incomplete line of the poem and answer any questions about vocabulary. Students work in their pairs/small groups to discuss the words they think fit best. With weaker classes, you can give students time to choose the words independently first and then move on to the discussion stage. Again, explain that there are no "right" answers to the choice of words, but encourage students to justify their ideas as best they can.

Ask a student from each pair/group to read aloud a verse of their version of the poem. Establish if most of the class have made similar or very different choices.

4 **CD3 49** Tell students they are going to hear a version of the poem. Play the recording and have students circle the word chosen each time.

Students then compare their version with the recording. Ask which they think is better and why.

5 Focus students' attention on the framework for the next verses in the poem. Point out the repetition in the questions and that students need to write a different answer each time. With weaker students, elicit the type of language that can complete each answer and write examples on the board, e.g.,

I met — *a wise old man/a young child/a happy traveler*
someone sitting on the beach/someone walking in the hills/someone traveling the world
You — *can listen to my story/give me food and water/offer me a place to sleep*
I've learned — *to be patient/not to judge people*

Give students time to write their verses in class or assign the task for homework.

Students take turns reading their verses aloud, either later in the same lesson or in a subsequent class. Let students compare the different versions and choose which they find most interesting.

If possible, display the poems on the classroom wall or noticeboard. When you check the students' work, point out errors, but allow students to correct them themselves. Try to limit correction to major problems to avoid demoralizing the students.

SUGGESTION

If your students enjoyed the poem-writing task, you can have them bring along an illustration that they feel fits with the words. This can be a photo of their own, an image taken from a magazine, or for the artistic ones, a drawing/painting they have done themselves. These can be displayed on the wall/noticeboard with the students' poems.

Don't forget!

Workbook Unit 12
Ex. 13 *The* or no article with places
Ex. 14 Phrasal verbs
Grammar Reference (SB p. 138)
Word list Unit 12 (SB p. 144)
Students can translate the words, learn them at home, or transfer some of them to their vocabulary notebook.

Tests (Online)
Unit 12 Test
Skills Test 1 (Units 9–12)
Stop and Check 1 (Units 9–12)
Video (iTools and Online)
Additional photocopiables and PPT™ presentations (iTools)

AMERICAN Headway¹ THIRD EDITION

Student A

1 Read the conversations with a partner. Find out the missing words.

Conversation 1

A Thank goodness it's Friday! Bye, Harry.
B _____
A Thanks. Same to you.
B _____

Conversation 2

C Hello, Mr. Harrison. How are you?
D _____
C Very well, thanks.

Conversation 3

E Good morning!
F _____
E Yes, of course! Anything else?
F _____

Conversation 4

G _____
H No, thank you. I'm just looking.
G _____

2 Work with a new partner. Practice the conversations.

Student B

1 Read the conversations with a partner. Find out the missing words.

Conversation 1

A _____
B Bye, Tessa. Have a good weekend.
A _____
B See you on Monday.

Conversation 2

C _____
D Fine, thank you. And you?
C _____

Conversation 3

E _____
F Good morning! Can I have a coffee, an espresso, please?
E _____
F No, thank you.

Conversation 4

G Good afternoon! Can I help you?
H _____
G That's OK.

2 Work with a new partner. Practice the conversations.

	About you	Make a question	What's the job?
START	my age ▶	Your teacher = married?	He takes care of people's teeth. ▼
Make a question Where / your favorite actor come from? ▼	**Opposites** the opposite of *cheap*	**Make a question** What / your phone number?	**What's the job?** She works with money. ◀
Make a question Where / your best friend work? ▶	**What's the job?** She designs buildings.	**About you** my job	**What's the job?** He cuts hair. ▼
Make a question Where / your teacher live? ▼	**Make a question** What / your best friend's job?	**What's the job?** She writes news stories.	**Opposites** the opposite of *nice* ◀
Make a question What time / now? ▶	**About you** I like …	**Opposites** the opposite of *old*	**Make a question** Your teacher = speak Italian? ▼
FINISH	**Make a question** What / your best friend like doing?	**About you** I / married.	**Make a question** How / spell your last name? ◀

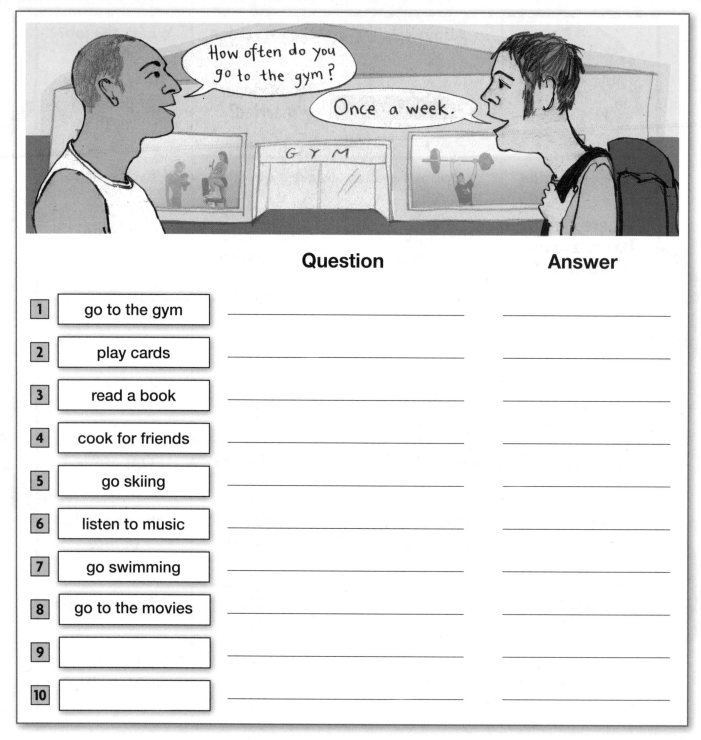

1 Write questions for 1–8. Use your own ideas for 9 and 10.

2 Work in pairs. Ask and answer the questions. Write your partner's answers.

3 Work in groups of four. Talk about your answers and find …

• an activity your group does every day
• an activity your group never does.

1   Do the numbers quiz. Then compare your answers with a partner.

Numbers 84 1500 60 47,000,000 MI 26 $9.99 $3			
1 How many players are there on an ice hockey team?	a 6	b 4	c 5
2 How many letters are there in the English alphabet?	a 24	b 26	c 30
3 How many seconds are there in an hour?	a 3600	b 3000	c 36,000
4 How many keys are there on a piano?	a 66	b 77	c 88
5 At what age can you vote in the US?	a 16	b 18	c 21
6 Which of these are coins in the US?	a 20¢, 25¢, $5	b 5¢, $1, $5	c 10¢, $1, 5¢
7 What's the usual speed limit on a large highway in the US?	a 65mph	b 6.5mph	c 165mph
8 What is the population of the US in 2014?	a about 320, 563,000	b about 380,563,000	c about 220,563,000

2   How much are these things in your country and in the US? If you are not sure, guess.

Prices	Your country	the US
a day train/subway pass in the capital city		
a coffee and a daily newspaper		
a movie ticket for an adult		
a month's food shopping for two adults		
dinner for two in a 3-star restaurant		
a top-20 CD		
a gallon of gas		
a month's rent in a small apartment in the capital city		

3   Compare your answers to Exercise 2 in small groups. What things are expensive in your country? And in the US?

me a hand with the dishes?	Can you ride	a motorcycle?	Do you live
on the third floor?	How often do you take	care of the children?	Can I try
on these jeans?	Do you send	a lot of text messages?	How many languages
can you speak?	Could you tell	me the time, please?	Do you like listening
to music?	Can I have	a black coffee, please?	Do you earn
a lot of money?	Could I speak	to you for a second?	Can I borrow
your pen, please?	Do you watch	television a lot?	Do you wear
a suit and tie for work?	Can you lend	me $20 until next week, please?	Can you play
the guitar?	Could you mail	this letter for me?	Can you give

1 Read the sentences and circle the correct adjectives in *italics* (*-ed* or *-ing*).

2 Change the <u>underlined</u> information in the sentences to make them true for you.

3 Compare your answers in pairs or small groups.

1	The most *tiring/tired* part of my week is <u>commuting to work</u>.
2	As a child, I was *frightening/frightened* of <u>dogs</u>.
3	I'm always *annoying/annoyed* when <u>people use their cell phone in a restaurant</u>.
4	I was really *embarrassing/embarrassed* when <u>I fell down in the street</u>.
5	My best friend's most *irritating/irritated* habit is <u>talking all the time.</u>
6	My most *interesting/interested* teacher at school taught <u>French</u>.
7	I was really *boring/bored* when <u>I saw the movie *Avatar*</u>.
8	I was a bit *worrying/worried* <u>before my driving test</u>.
9	The most *exciting/excited* sport is <u>soccer</u>.
10	I was very *surprised/surprising* when <u>my brother got married</u>.

close the door ...		ride a motorcycle ...	
quietly		carefully	
drive ...		go to sleep ...	
badly		quickly	
play the piano ...		study ...	
well		hard	
skateboard ...		arrive ...	
slowly		late	
breathe ...		do the housework ...	
deeply		happily	
get up ...		drink tea ...	
early		noisily	
eat an ice cream ...		sit down ...	
quickly		carefully	

Student A

1 Answer Student B's questions about your recipe.

Aromatic chicken

Ingredients
- 1 tbsp oil
- 2 onions, chopped
- 3 cloves garlic, chopped
- 1 tsp ginger
- 1 lb chicken, chopped
- 2 c chicken stock
- ½ cup dried apricots
- 3 tbsp almonds, chopped

1 Heat the oil in a medium saucepan. Fry the onion and garlic until soft.

2 Add the chicken and the ginger. Cook for about 5 minutes. Then add the stock.

3 Boil, then cover the pan with a lid and cook on a low heat for about 15 minutes.

4 Take off the lid and add the apricots. Mix well and cook for another 10 minutes until the sauce is thick and the chicken is cooked.

5 Sprinkle the almonds on top of the chicken. Serve with couscous and a green salad.

2 Ask Student B about his/her recipe. Complete the information.

Fresh tuna with tomatoes

Ingredients
- _____ tuna steaks
- _____ tbsp olive oil
- _____ small onion, chopped
- _____ clove garlic, chopped
- _____ c tomatoes, peeled and chopped
- _____ c vegetable stock
- _____ tbsp anchovies, mashed
- _____ c black olives

1 Heat the oil in a frying pan. Fry the tuna for about _____ minute until brown on both sides. Move the fish to a warm plate.

2 Add the onions and _____ and fry until soft. Mix in the _____, tomatoes, and anchovies.

3 _____, then cover the pan and cook on a low heat for about _____ minutes.

4 Put the fish back in the pan and cook for another _____ minutes.

5 Add the _____ and mix gently. Serve with crusty _____ and a green salad.

3 Which recipe would you like to try? What was the last thing you cooked at home?

Student B

1 Ask Student A about his/her recipe. Complete the information.

Aromatic chicken

Ingredients
- _____ tbsp oil
- _____ onions, chopped
- _____ cloves garlic, chopped
- _____ tsp ginger
- _____ lb chicken, chopped
- _____ c chicken stock
- _____ c dried apricots
- _____ tbsp almonds, chopped

1 Heat the oil in a medium saucepan. Fry the _____ and _____ until soft.

2 Add the chicken and the _____. Cook for about _____ minutes. Then add the stock.

3 Boil, then cover the pan with a lid and cook on a low heat for about _____ minutes.

4 Take off the lid and add the _____. Mix well and cook for another _____ minutes until the sauce is thick and the chicken is cooked.

5 Sprinkle the _____ on top of the chicken. Serve with couscous and a green salad.

2 Answer Student A's questions about your recipe.

Fresh tuna with tomatoes

Ingredients
- 4 tuna steaks
- 3 tbsp olive oil
- 1 small onion, chopped
- 1 clove garlic, chopped
- 1 and ½ c tomatoes, peeled and chopped
- ½ c vegetable stock
- 2 tbsp anchovies, mashed
- ¼ c black olives

1 Heat the oil in a frying pan. Fry the tuna for about 1 minute until brown on both sides. Move the fish to a warm plate.

2 Add the onions and garlic and fry until soft. Mix in the stock, tomatoes, and anchovies.

3 Boil, then cover the pan with a lid and cook on a low heat for about 10 minutes.

4 Put the fish back in the pan and cook for another 8 minutes.

5 Add the olives and mix gently. Serve with crusty bread and a green salad.

3 Which recipe would you like to try? What was the last thing you cooked at home?

1 Complete the questions with the superlative form of the adjectives. Then write the answers for your country. Don't always choose your own city / region!

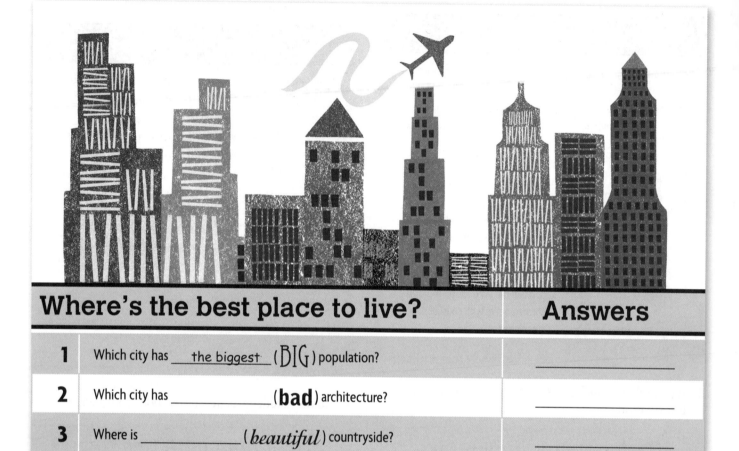

	Where's the best place to live?	Answers
1	Which city has ___the biggest___ (BIG) population?	_____
2	Which city has _____ (**bad**) architecture?	_____
3	Where is _____ (*beautiful*) countryside?	_____
4	Which region has _____ (**good**) reputation for food?	_____
5	Where are _____ (*interesting*) tourist attractions?	_____
6	Which airport is _____ (busy)?	_____
7	Which region is _____ (**expensive**)?	_____
8	Who are _____ (friendly) people?	_____
9	Which city is _____ (**dangerous**)?	_____
10	Which region has _____ (**modern**) public transportation?	_____

2 Work in groups and discuss your answers. Give reasons for your answers.

3 Work as a class. Tell your classmates about the best region / city in your country. Try to persuade them to live there!

1	I spent an hour looking for my car keys, but	I couldn't find them _____.
2	I called the police because	_____ tried to steal my car.
3	I invited all of my friends for Sunday lunch, but	_____ was busy that weekend.
4	My old apartment wasn't in a very nice area because	there was garbage _____.
5	The weather in my city was awful last year so	I decided to go _____ warm this summer.
6	I had to stand on the train to work because	there was _____ to sit.
7	I didn't enjoy my French course very much because	I didn't know _____ in the class.
8	I watched an old DVD because	there was _____ interesting on TV.
9	I wanted to buy some new clothes, but	_____ in the designer shop was too expensive.
10	I woke up suddenly because	I heard _____ strange in the corner of the bedroom.
11	I picked up the phone and said "hello," but	there was _____ there.
12	I was very hungry when I got home, but	there wasn't _____ in the fridge.

Key words

everything	**nobody**	**somewhere**
nothing	**anybody**	**everywhere**
anything	**somebody**	**anywhere**
something	**everybody**	**nowhere**

1 Write the activities in the correct column.

go to the beach   go to a gallery
have a picnic   play cards
go to the movies   go for a walk
go fishing   update our blog
play golf   make a cake
watch a movie   do some gardening

Good weather	Bad weather

2 Work with a partner. Have a conversation. Talk about the weather and make suggestions about what to do.

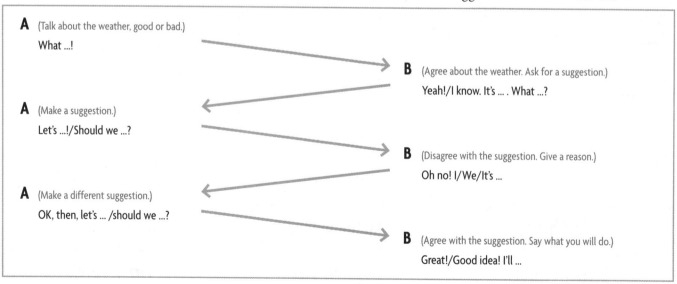

A (Talk about the weather, good or bad.)
What ...!

B (Agree about the weather. Ask for a suggestion.)
Yeah!/I know. It's ... . What ...?

A (Make a suggestion.)
Let's ...!/Should we ...?

B (Disagree with the suggestion. Give a reason.)
Oh no! I/We/It's ...

A (Make a different suggestion.)
OK, then, let's ... /should we ...?

B (Agree with the suggestion. Say what you will do.)
Great!/Good idea! I'll ...

3 Work with a new partner. Make another conversation.

1 Have you ever bought anything on the Internet ?   Yes/No

What did you buy?

_____

(your own question)

_____

2 Have you ever written a blog ? Yes/No

How many people read it?

_____

(your own question)

_____

3 Have you ever won a competition ? Yes/No

What did you win?

_____

(your own question)

_____

4 Have you ever broken a bone ? Yes/No

How did it happen?

_____

(your own question)

_____

5 Have you ever eaten Mexican food ? Yes/No

What was it like?

_____

(your own question)

_____

6 Have you ever been to South America ? Yes/No

Where did you go?

_____

(your own question)

_____

7 Have you ever lost something important ? Yes/No

What was it?

_____

(your own question)

_____

8 Have you ever slept on the beach ? Yes/No

Why did you do that?

_____

(your own question)

_____

9 Have you ever seen an accident ? Yes/No

What did you do?

_____

(your own question)

_____

10 Have you ever done anything for charity? Yes/No

What did you do?

_____

(your own question)

_____

Workbook Answer Key

Unit 1

1 1 your, are, 'm, you, 's

2 's, last name, spell, where, 'm

2 2 English 3 Brazilian 4 Korean
5 Mexican 6 Saudi Arabian
7 Peruvian

3 1 1 What's, she, is, her, What's her,
Is she, isn't

2 What's, he, from, he, his,
What's his, Is he, he isn't

2 2 She isn't 3 I'm 4 I'm not
5 He's 6 He isn't 7 You're
8 You're not

4 1 3 mother's 4 sister's 5 brother's
6 cat's

2 3 is 4 P 5 is 6 is 7 P 8 P

5 2 go 3 live 4 like 5 live
6 go 7 have 8 like

6 Across   **Down**
8 sister   1 mother
9 wife   2 aunt
10 son   4 husband
11 nephew   5 grandmother
15 children   6 niece
16 daughter   7 grandfather
                      12 parents
                      13 father
                      14 uncle

7 1 2 cold 3 old 4 good 5 young
6 easy 7 small 8 nice

2 1 sunny 2 fast 3 friendly
4 beautiful 5 interesting 6 great

8 1 2 houses 3 Ellie 4 76 5 children
6 Marganne 7 go 8 like

2 2 Joe 3 George 4 Catherine
5 Dave 6 Sandra

9 2 f 3 g 4 a 5 b 6 d 7 h 8 e

10 1 A day E tea I Hi O no
U you R car G me J day
Q you Y my Z we

2 2 Melissa
3 Suzi
4 Bishop
5 Kelly
6 Liz Jones
7 pnash@tmail.com
8 jennyblack@bz.com

11 2 my 3 Her 4 Their 5 our
6 His

12 buses, sandwiches, glasses
cities, parties, ladies
days
women, children, people

Unit 2

1 2 He works in an office. He earns a lot of
money.
3 She cooks dinner for her family. She
goes shopping every day.
4 He cooks in an Italian restaurant. He
works in a kitchen.
5 She studies every day. She likes her
teacher.
6 He works outside. He lives in the
country.

2 2 er 3 or 4 er 5 er 6 er 7 or
8 er 9 er

3 1 2 studies 3 works 4 writes
5 earns 6 teaches 7 goes
8 does 9 watches 10 has
11 finishes 12 lives

2 1 plays
2 teaches, writes
3 goes, studies
4 works, finishes
5 does, lives
6 has, watches

4 2

/s/	/z/	/ɪz/
writes	studies earns goes does has lives	watches finishes

5 2 What time 3 Who 4 How
5 How many 6 Why 7 How old
8 What

6 1 2 takes a shower
3 gets dressed
4 has breakfast
5 goes to work
6 starts work
7 has lunch
8 finishes work
9 goes home
10 has dinner
11 watches TV
12 goes to bed

2 2 does she have
3 does she work
4 does she start
5 does she have
6 does she do

3 2 She doesn't work in a store. She
works in an office.
3 She doesn't start work at 10:00. She
starts work at 9:00.
4 She doesn't have lunch with her
sister. She has lunch with her friend.
5 She doesn't watch sports on TV. She
watches dramas.
6 She doesn't go to bed at 10:30. She
goes to bed at 11:00.

7 1 3 F Eurostar trains don't run 365 days
a year. They run 364 days a year.
4 F The first train to Paris doesn't
leave before 5:00 a.m. It leaves at
5:25 a.m.
5 T
6 F He doesn't start work early every
day. Sometimes he starts late.
7 F He doesn't always go home in the
evening. Sometimes he stays in
Paris.
8 T
9 F He does earn a lot of money. He
earns £45,000.
10 T

2 3 starts 4 finishes 5 takes 6 travels
7 earns 8 likes 9 works 10 has

3 **Angela** French, 25,000, walks
Toby 16, store, 30–35, goes to bed
late, listens to loud music

8 1 2 live 3 have 4 watch 5 wear
6 play 7 drive 8 earn 9 read
10 help 11 go 12 want

9 1 2 hairstylist
   3 accountant
   4 lawyer
   5 taxi driver
   6 architect
   7 journalist
   8 pilot
   9 dentist
   10 receptionist

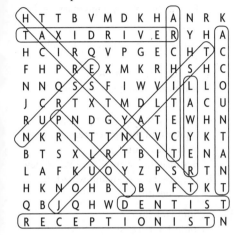

10 1 2 2:15
   3 ten o'clock
   4 quarter after three
   5 eight thirty
   6 twenty to two
   7 six thirty
   8 ten after twelve

  2 1 about 2 just after 3 nearly

  3 2 3:10 3 9:15 4 1:45 5 4:40
   6 7:25

11 1 2 has 3 does 4 's 5 does
   6 does 7 Is 8 's 9 Does
   10 has

12 1 2 a 3 an 4 an 5 a 6 a
   7 a 8 an

Unit 3

1 **Across**   **Down**
  Thursday   Sunday
  Wednesday Saturday
  Friday   Tuesday
  Monday

2 1 2 works 3 flies 4 earns
   5 doesn't have 6 go 7 watch
   8 have 9 don't take 10 collects
   11 has 12 love

  2 2 do, work
   3 do, fly
   4 do, fly
   5 do, earn
   6 do, go
   7 does, do
   8 do, have

3 2 doesn't 3 don't 4 aren't
   5 don't 6 doesn't 7 'm not
   8 doesn't

3 1 2 mean 3 want 4 come
   5 understand 6 live 7 know
   8 love, love 9 prefer 10 like

4 1 2 I sometimes go to the movies.
   3 We often go to Mexico for vacation.
   4 I never drink coffee in the morning.
   5 I usually start work at 9:00.

  2 2 usually goes
   3 He sometimes has / Sometimes he has
   4 He never works
   5 He often goes

5 1 2 a 3 e 4 d 5 b

  2 3 go 4 go 5 play 6 go
   7 play 8 go 9 play 10 go

6 1 **Seasons** summer, fall, winter
    Months February, April, May, July,
                August, November, December

  2 1 summer 2 winter 3 spring

  3 1 She likes summer best because her
    cousins from *Portugal* often come
    to stay. She *doesn't like* sunbathing.
    They all like water sports, such as
    surfing and waterskiing. Marisa loves
    Carnival time too because there's a
    party that lasts *five* days.

   2 She says that in Thailand they have
    three seasons. She likes winter best
    because it's not too hot, it's warm
    in the day and cold at night. She
    loves the Flower Festival in *February*
    because she goes there with her
    sisters, and they all sing and dance.

   3 Canadians *love* their cold winters,
    but Noah says that *spring* is
    his favorite season because he
    goes skiing and snowboarding.
    Sometimes he and his *friends* still
    go skiing in May and June. Summer
    in Canada is warm but not very long.

  4 1 December to February.
   2 They go surfing and waterskiing.
   3 They have a big party and barbecue
    on the beach.
   4 No, she doesn't. She lives in the north
    of Thailand.
   5 November to February.
   6 There are a lot of beautiful tropical
    flowers in February.
   7 December to February.
   8 Spring.
   9 June to late August or September.

7 1 1 Violinist.
   2 Skiing.

  2 1 In Zermatt, Switzerland.
   2 She goes skiing.
   3 In the summer.
   4 Her dog, Max.
   5 A ski resort in France.
   6 Yes, he does.
   7 Max, my dog; boyfriend; grandmother;
    violin.

  3 2 do you go
   3 do you get
   4 do you do
   5 do you have

  4 3 goes
   4 takes
   5 gets
   6 works
   7 doesn't cook
   8 wants

  8 2 d 3 a 4 e 5 g 6 h 7 c 8 i 9 f

  9 2 busy 3 hungry 4 thirsty 5 happy

  10 2 's 3 are 4 'm 5 does 6 's

  11 3 — 4 an 5 a 6 a,— 7 —
     8 a, a 9 — 10 —

  12 2 to, by 3 with, in 4 for, in
     5 of, on, in 6 to 7 for 8 in

Unit 4

1 1 1 bathroom
   2 bedroom
   3 kitchen
   4 living room

  2 2 k 3 o 4 l 5 h 6 g 7 n
   8 q 9 m 10 b 11 c 12 r 13 e
   14 i 15 d 16 f 17 a, j

2 1 3 There's 4 There's 5 There are
   6 There's 7 There isn't

  2 2 Are there, there are
   3 Is there, there's
   4 Are there, there aren't
   5 Is there, there is
   6 Are there, there are
   7 Is there, there isn't

3 2 next to 3 above 4 on 5 outside
   6 near 7 in 8 across from 9 under

4 2 any, some
   3 any, any, some
   4 any, some
   5 any, some
   6 any, a lot of
   7 any, any
   8 any, a lot of

5 2 that 3 This 4 those 5 These
   6 this 7 that 8 those

6 1 2 old   3 some   4 is, is
5 dark   6 near

2 3 **F** They give you a key.
4 **T**
5 **F** The lounge has cell windows.
6 **F** The restaurant isn't too expensive.
7 **T**
8 **T**

7 1 2 Donna
3 Nagendra and Anita
4 Nagendra and Anita
5 Kelly
6 Donna
7 Donna
8 Kelly
9 Nagendra and Anita

2 2 teacher   3 is   4 has   5 bank
6 train   7 don't live   8 isn't
9 living room

8 1 b 70   c 68   d 20   e 260   f 810
g 2,000   h 15,000

2 a eight   b eighteen   c two hundred
eighty-eight   d six hundred
e five thousand   f one million

3 b 51   c 28   d 670   e 1,500
f 2 ½   g 10.3   h 484 555 6721

9 1 b $10   c £6.50   d 80 cents   e €100
f €86   g $45   h $20

2 2 The shoes are thirty-five euros.
3 The book is six pounds ninety-nine.
4 The TV is three hundred dollars.
5 The sunglasses are forty dollars.
6 The newspaper is two dollars
seventy-five cents.

10 2 sofa   3 fruit   4 notebook
5 lipstick   6 lamp   7 key
8 yard   9 cup   10 clothes

11 1

Subject pronoun	Object pronoun
I	me
you	you
he	him
she	her
it	it
we	us
they	them

2 2 her   3 me   4 us   5 you
6 him   7 it

Unit 5

1 2 can't   3 can   4 can't   5 Can't
6 can, can't   7 can't   8 Can't

2 2 can't ride, can't drive
3 can use, can't program

4 can play, can't play
5 can't ride, can't drive
6 can ride a motorbike
7 can use a computer
8 can program a computer

3 1 2 Can, run; he can
3 Can, cook; she can
4 Can, ride; can't, can drive
5 Can, do; can

2 2 She can't cook at all.
3 She can speak English pretty well.
4 He can speak Arabic a little.
5 Her baby's only one, but he can walk
very well.
6 My sister's only five, but she can read
pretty well.
7 My brother can program computers
really well.
8 I can understand Japanese a little,
but I can't speak it at all.

4 3 Was   4 was   5 Were   6 were
7 Was   8 wasn't   9 weren't   10 was
11 was

5 2 could   3 couldn't   4 couldn't
5 couldn't   6 could, Could

6 1 **Kyle** New York, New York, dad – taxi
driver / mom – cleaner,
play soccer, no

Olivia Tanzania, mom – Tanzania /
dad – California, teachers,
play outside, yes

2 1 Next to his house.
2 Because he wasn't very popular.
3 In downtown New York City.
4 He's a journalist.
5 On the same street.

3 2 children does she have; Two,
a daughter
3 were, Africa
4 Is, isn't, English
5 were, teachers
6 Were, parents, were
7 Was, wasn't, was
8 couldn't, play; was hot, were snakes

7 **Across**   **Down**
5 run   1 speak
7 watch   2 sing
9 dance   3 paint
12 fly   4 drive
13 walk   6 ride
14 jump   8 cook
16 eat   10 call
                   11 swim
                   15 play

8 2 gas station   3 sunglasses
4 living room   5 handbag   6 bus stop
7 motorcycle   8 traffic lights
9 bookstore

9 1 2 His father was a famous musician.
3 He was a student at the University of
Pisa. / He was a professor at the
University of Padua.
4 He was the father of three children.
5 His theory was that the earth went
around the sun.
6 He spent his last years at his house in
Florence.
7 He was completely blind when he died.

2 1 Italian.
2 An astronomer and a philosopher.
3 1564.
4 The University of Pisa.
5 Professor of mathematics and
astronomy.
6 Moons going around the planet
Jupiter and the planet Venus going
around the sun.
7 Because they were different and new.
8 Because he was 70 and wasn't in
good health.

10 1 could you, Sure
2 Could I, Of course, Could you
3 Can I, Could you, the problem
4 could I, Can you, Can I have

11

Country	Nationality
Brazil	Brazilian
China	Chinese
the United States	*American*
Peru	*Peruvian*
Saudi Arabia	Saudi Arabian
Japan	*Japanese*
Thailand	Thai
England	*English*
Mexico	*Mexican*
Spain	Spanish

12 2 and   3 because   4 but
5 so   6 because   7 and   8 so

13 2 on   3 at   4 in   5 at   6 on
7 in   8 at   9 in   10 at

14 2 c   3 d   4 a   5 f   6 e   7 h
8 j   9 g   10 l   11 i   12 k

Unit 6

1 1 2 started   3 worked   4 recorded
5 played   6 traveled   7 earned
8 enjoyed   9 received   10 produced
11 stopped   12 joined

2 2 did they start
3 did they record
4 did they play
5 did, produce
6 did they stop
7 did, join

158   Workbook Answer Key

3 2 didn't work
  3 didn't record
  4 didn't play
  5 didn't stop
  6 didn't join

2 1

/t/	/d/	/ɪd/
watched	received	
talked	joined	recorded
stopped	earned	wanted
finished	opened	started
walked	stayed	
liked	enjoyed	
	traveled	
	played	

3 1   **Across**   **Down**
    5 had   1 made
    6 went   2 sent
    8 gave   3 won
  11 took   4 caught
  12 left   6 wrote
  13 came   7 began
             9 lost
          10 met

  2 2 met 3 left 4 saw 5 bought
    6 sent 7 made 8 had

  3 2 wrote 3 took 4 put 5 saw
    6 had 7 began 8 sent

4 2 yesterday afternoon
  3 last year
  4 last week
  5 yesterday evening
  6 last September
  7 last Friday
  8 yesterday morning

5 1 2 he was 17
    3 1960
    4 200 concerts
    5 *Abbey Road*
    6 1970
    7 Central Park

  2 2 did, die
    3 did, go
    4 did, start
    5 did, go
    6 did, stop
    7 did, marry
    8 did, move
    9 did, write, sing
   10 did, shoot

6 1 1 1965, Shea Stadium, New York City.
    2 Yes, he did.
    3 over 55,000
    4 over 2,000.
    5 They went crazy. They climbed over
      each other to get closer.

  6 The screaming was so loud you
    couldn't hear the music.
  7 30 minutes. 12 songs.
  8 $5.75.
  9 "I wanna hold your hand."

  2 2 noisy, excited / excited, noisy
    3 wild / crazy
    4 best
    5 cheap

7 1 2 d 3 a 4 f 5 b 6 g
    7 i 8 e 9 h

  2 3 bored 4 boring
    5 excited 6 exciting
    7 annoying 8 annoyed
    9 worrying 10 worried

8 1 25th twenty-fifth
    10th tenth
    1st first
    19th nineteenth
    30th thirtieth
    3rd third
    9th ninth
    5th fifth
    12th twelfth

  2 2 June 10
    3 August 9
    4 November 12
    5 December 25
    6 March 19

  3 2 the tenth of March
    3 the fifteenth of May
    4 the second of June
    5 July fourteenth
    6 August third
    7 September eighth
    8 November fifth

  4 2 1996 3 1961 4 1865 5 2003
    6 2009 7 2010 8 2015

9 2 was 3 Did 4 didn't 5 Was
  6 had 7 didn't 8 Were 9 Did
  10 had 11 do 12 Does

10 3 the 4 — 5 — 6 the
  7 the, the 8 the 9 — 10 the
  11 — 12 the

Unit 7

1 1 2 spent 3 used 4 began 5 sent
    6 became 7 went 8 took 9 said
    10 landed 11 walked 12 ended
    13 met 14 joined 15 won

  2 2 did, begin
    3 did, send
    4 did, become
    5 did, go
    6 did, take

  7 did, land
  8 did, end

2 1 2 They didn't have much money.
    3 They didn't own any land.
    4 But sometimes he didn't work very
      hard.
    5 He didn't grow very tall.
    6 He didn't land on the moon.
    7 But he didn't go into space again.
    8 Investigators didn't know why his
      plane crashed.

  2 2 We didn't go
    3 I didn't
    4 He didn't
    5 I didn't
    6 They didn't

3 1 2 f 3 c 4 a 5 d 6 e 7 l
    8 i 9 h 10 g 11 k 12 j

  2 2 What time did you get up this
      morning?
    3 What did you have for dinner last
      night?
    4 When did you last travel by train?
    5 What did you do last Sunday?
    6 Where did you go on vacation last
      summer?

  3 1 2 Did you
      3 did you have
      4 Was it

    2 1 was it
      2 How many people
      3 did Alison wear
      4 Did you

4 2 in 3 in 4 at 5 on 6 in 7 on
  8 in 9 on 10 in 11 on 12 in

5 2 5 minutes ago
  3 0.0.2 seconds ago
  4 3 days ago
  5 13 days ago
  6 5 months ago
  7 3 months ago
  8 10 years ago

6 1 2 did, Pittsburgh, 1905
    3 were, 4,000
    4 did, half an hour
    5 was, names

  2 2 Why, the sunshine and scenery
    3 What, Westerns
    4 When, 1914
    5 How many, the world's movies
    6 Who, Charlie Chaplin

  3 2 No, it wasn't. It was made in 1927.
    3 No, it wasn't. The time of "talkies" was
      called "The Golden Age of Hollywood."
    4 No, it didn't. It lasted until the 1940s.

7 1 2 *Pride and Prejudice*, Keira Knightley
3 *High Noon*, Gary Cooper
4 *Gone with the Wind*, Clark Gable
5 *Star Wars VI: Return of the Jedi*,
Carrie Fisher
6 *Breakfast at Tiffany's*, Audrey Hepburn

2 1 Sam 2 Emily 3 Derek 4 Nora
5 Mandy 6 Frank

8 1 3 beautifully 4 beautiful 5 badly
6 bad 7 really 8 real 9 quiet
10 quietly 11 slow 12 slowly

2 2 fast 3 well 4 hard 5 late

9 1 New Year, Happy, Year, Goodbye, new
2 card, party, came, presents, a present,
Here, birthday
3 big day, in, ring, like it, invitation,
congratulations
4 goodness, weekend, You, See you

10 2 She speaks English very well.
3 We played tennis all afternoon.
4 I always make the same mistakes.
5 I wrote some emails this morning.
6 I liked the movie very much.
7 Do you know Tokyo well?
8 I went to the theater last week. / Last
week I went to the theater.
9 I often go out with my friends on
weekends. / On weekends I often go
out with my friends.
10 Do you ever go to concerts?

11 2 for 3 to, in 4 in 5 at 6 of
7 for 8 about 9 on 10 around

Unit 8

1 2 C 3 N 4 C 5 N 6 N 7 C
8 C 9 N 10 N 11 C 12 N 13 C
14 N 15 C 16 N

2 2 an 3 some 4 a, some
5 some, a 6 a
7 some 8 some 9 an, a 10 some, an

3 2 going to the
3 going, cooking dinner
4 relaxing, likes exploring
5 swimming, sunbathing, likes going on
6 reading

4 1 2 d 3 a 4 c 5 f 6 g 7 e 8 h

2 2 would you like to drink
3 would you like to go
4 would you like
5 would you like
6 would you like

5 1 2 A 3 B 4 A 5 B 6 A

2 2 She'd like 3 I'd like
4 Would, like 5 We like
6 She'd like

6 1 2 What would you like to drink
3 Are you ready to order
4 I'd like the steak please
5 How would you like it cooked
6 Do you want tap or bottled water
7 Could we have the check please
8 Is service included

2 1 No, they didn't. 2 Yes, there is.
3 Sodas. 4 Tomato.
5 Vegetable tart. 6 Salmon with a
salad. 7 Medium. 8 French fries.
9 Bottled. 10 No, they don't.
11 No, it isn't. 12 Yes, they did.

7 1 2 any 3 any 4 some 5 any
6 any 7 any 8 some, any
9 some 10 any

2 2 any food 3 some gas
4 any stamps 5 any eggs
6 some French fries 7 some friends
8 some ice

8 2 How much 3 How much
4 How many 5 How much
6 How many

9 1 2 food 3 cookies 4 cookies
5 sick 6 taste what he cooks
7 everything 8 meat

2 2 like 3 'd like to eat 4 'd love

10 1 **Vegetables** onion, pea, broccoli, carrot
Meat beef, turkey, sausage
Fruit banana, orange, tomato,
strawberry, raspberry
Dairy products cheese, ice cream,
butter, yogurt

2 ●● yogurt, orange, sausage

●●● broccoli, strawberry, raspberry

●●● potato, tomato, banana,

11 2 battery 3 envelope 4 magazine
5 toothpaste 6 light bulb
7 Band-Aid 8 aspirin 9 chocolate
10 pencil 11 flowers 12 shampoo

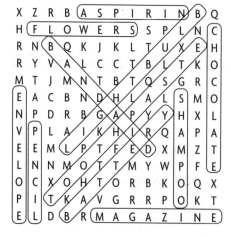

12 1 mean, understand, much
2 small, many, too, enough

13 1 3 — 4 a 5 — 6 a/some
7 — 8 some/an

2 2 is made from milk.
3 is full of vitamins.
4 come from chickens.
5 comes from Japan.

14 2 later 3 especially 4 pretty
5 again 6 together 7 nearly 8 too

Unit 9

1 1 taller
hotter
nicer
more polite
easier
prettier
more exciting
more beautiful
more important

2 more expensive
more dangerous
slower
dirtier
noisier
more boring
easier
older
worse

2 2 Pete's car is cheaper than Ann's car.
3 is newer than Pete's car.
4 Ann's car is more comfortable than
Pete's car.
5 bigger
6 The house is more expensive than the
apartment.
7 is nearer
8 The apartment is more modern than
the house.

3 1 2 smarter 3 friendlier 4 better
5 worse

2 2 more interesting 3 bigger
4 stronger 5 easier

4 2 Lisa is, than Kelly
3 Lisa is, than Kelly
4 Kelly is, Lisa isn't
5 friendly, louder
6 has, has
7 smaller than
8 Kelly, Lisa
9 better, than
10 jobs
11 works, than
12 has, job than
13 skiing
14 worse, than

5 3 younger; the youngest
4 happier; the happiest
5 more beautiful; the most beautiful
6 bigger; the biggest
7 busier; the busiest
8 more intelligent; the most intelligent
9 worse; the worst
10 further; the furthest
11 newer; the newest
12 more dangerous; the most dangerous

6 2 My sister is younger than me.
3 Who is the oldest in the class?
4 The Airbus A380 is the biggest passenger plane in the world.
5 Your/My book is more interesting than my/your book.
6 Peter bought the most expensive TV in the store.
7 Did you buy the cheapest shirt in the store?
8 English/Chinese is much more difficult than Chinese/English.
9 The weather today is much better than yesterday.

7 2 the highest, Everest
3 the biggest, (*student's own answer*)
4 the most popular, (*student's own answer*)
5 the oldest, (*student's own answer*)
6 the youngest, (*student's own answer*)
7 the most intelligent, (*student's own answer*)

8 1 2 When   3 How   4 How many
5 How much   6 How long

2 1 the tallest   2 the fastest
3 the highest

3 1 Six years.
2 A swimming pool.
3 No, it isn't. 1,667 ft
4 The building's structural engineer.
5 The winds.
6 About 5 feet.
7 12,000.
8 The bottom.

9 1 2 exciting
3 a small fishing village
4 friendly, welcome
5 swimming, windsurfing
6 skiing, ski, snow
7 restaurants
8 hotter, rain
9 cheaper, much bigger

2 1 family and friends
2 the seasons
3 walks in the country

10 1 statue   2 train station
4 traffic lights   5 gas station
6 parking lot   7 bridge
8 mall   9 hill
10 apartment building   11 woods
12 farmer's market   13 traffic circle
14 crosswalk

11 The train station

12 1 2 at   3 in   4 at   5 outside
6 at   7 at   8 on   9 At   10 in

2 2 along   3 through   4 up   5 down
6 over   7 past   8 around

Unit 10

1 2 on   3 on   4 at   5 in   6 at
7 in/at   8 in/at   9 on   10 at

2 1 dancing   2 going   3 drinking
4 doing   5 driving   6 reading
7 buying   8 wearing   9 running

3 2 e   3 a   4 f   5 g   6 d   7 b

4 1 2 's driving
3 're watching
4 's reading
5 's washing
6 're drinking.

2 2 What's he driving
3 What are they watching
4 What's he reading
5 What's she washing
6 What are they drinking

3 2 He isn't driving
3 They aren't watching
4 He isn't reading
5 She isn't washing
6 They aren't drinking

5 1 3 is, speaking
4 does, speak
5 'm reading
6 read
7 do, think
8 are, thinking
9 don't eat
10 'm not eating

2 5 She's a teacher.   6 she does
7 she isn't   8 She's playing the guitar.
9 She's a mail carrier.   10 she does
11 she is   12 He's an actor.
13 he does   14 he isn't
15 He's having breakfast.

3 2 I think
3 I'm working
4 I don't understand
5 she's taking

6 2 are, 'm   3 does   4 'm, do
5 doesn't, 's   6 don't   7 are, 're
8 is, 's

7 3 T
4 F Researchers collected four million messages over seven days.
5 F Most tweets are in English.
6 T
7 F The most common sentences are "I'm working" and "I'm sleepy."
8 T
9 F There is not one main reason why people use Twitter.
10 T

8 1 1 Journalist
2 Librarian
3 History teacher
4 Marketing director

2 2 a   3 d   4 c

3 1 The news.
2 Because when a story begins there, it often becomes the most important story of the day.
3 Meat-free Monday.
4 Farmers.
5 A conference for history teachers.
6 He already knew people's problems and could continue discussing them face to face.
7 Both.
8 Different countries and cultures.

9 2 anybody   3 nothing   4 anywhere
5 nobody   6 everything   7 Everybody
8 nowhere   9 anything   10 everywhere

10 2 Tom   3 Jenny   4 Jenny   5 Tom
6 Mike   7 Mike   8 Jenny   9 Mike
10 Tom   11 Jenny   12 Tom

11 2 e   3 g   4 a   5 c   6 h   7 f
8 i   9 d

12 2 ski   3 to ski   4 to listen   5 listen
6 listening   7 learning   8 to learn
9 learn   10 going   11 to go   12 go

13 2 Learning   3 skiing   4 Running
5 living, living   6 saying

14 2 They're having a sale.
3 They're having a lesson.
4 They're having an argument.
5 They're having lunch.
6 They're having a drink.
7 They're having a picnic.
8 They're having a party.

Unit 11

1 2 She's going to be an accountant.
3 She's going to be a nanny.
4 They're going to be athletes.
5 He's going to be a politician.
6 They're going to be explorers.
7 She's going to be a journalist.
8 They're going to be in a band.

2 1 2 What are you going to cook?
3 What are you going to see?
4 When are they going to get married?
5 Are you going to have a party?
6 Are they going to fly?

2 2 I'm not going to cook meat. I'm going to cook fish.
3 I'm not going to see an action movie. I'm going to see a comedy.
4 They're not going to get married this year. They're going to get married next year.
5 I'm not going to have a party. I'm going to go to a restaurant.
6 They're not going to fly. They're going to drive.

3 1 2 Where are they going to stay? They're going to stay at the Star Hotel.
3 How long are they going to stay? They're going to stay for ten days.
4 What are they going to do? They're going to see the architecture, and they're going to visit the Shanghai Museum.

2 2 are you going
3 are you going
4 'm going
5 are you going
6 are you going
7 'm going to
8 'm going to

3 2 aren't going to
3 aren't going to stay
4 isn't going
5 isn't going
6 isn't going to

4 1 2 It's going to rain.
3 She's going to fall.
4 They're going to see a movie.
5 They're going to play tennis.
6 He's going to lose the race.

2 2 are going to win
3 's going to be a difficult week
4 's going to be a nice day
5 're going to miss
6 's going to happen

5 1 2 to buy some T-shirts
3 to get some books
4 to meet a friend
5 to have a talk
6 to confirm her flight
7 to have an early night

2 2 to make an appointment
3 to learn English
4 to ask for a job
5 to open the door
6 to pay my bills

3 2 I need a dictionary to help me with words.
3 I went to town to meet my friends.
4 I go jogging every day to keep fit.
5 I'm saving my money to buy a new car.

6 1 1 Tokyo.
2 American music.
3 New Orleans, Memphis, Nashville, Cleveland, and New York.

2 2 22   3 400,000   4 30   5 600,000
6 24   7 two   8 1951

3 3 **F** They're going to travel from the south to the north of the US.
4 **T**
5 **F** The New Orleans Jazz Fest takes place 30 minutes from the French Quarter.
6 **F** The White House gets more visitors than Elvis Presley's house.
7 **F** The friends aren't going to visit the White House.
8 **T**
9 **T**

7 1 1 No, they're going to stay near Graceland.
2 Heartbreak Hotel
3 In the music room.
4 No, upstairs is private.
5 Yes, he had a lot of cars.
6 Because they're going to see Elvis's grave.
7 Watch a video of one of his concerts.
8 In the Rockabilly's Diner.
9 A cheeseburger and fries and a peanut butter and banana sandwich.

2 Order: 2, 1, 6, 4, 5, 3, 7

8 1 2 rainy   3 windy   4 sunny
5 cloudy   6 snowy   7 foggy

2 2 cold   3 warm   4 dry   5 wet
6 cool

3 2 's cold and wet
3 was cloudy and cool
4 hot and sunny

9 1 go shopping, have lunch in the old town, go to the beach, go swimming

2 2 don't we go   3 'd like   4 Let's do
5 could go   6 don't we catch
7 'd like to look   8 we can go
9 Let's go

10 1

Subject	Possessive adjective	Possessive pronoun
I	my	mine
you	your	yours
he	his	his
she	her	hers
we	our	ours
they	their	theirs

2 2 yours   3 his   4 hers   5 ours
6 theirs

11 2 than   3 from   4 in   5 for
6 at, of   7 like   8 of   9 with
10 about

Unit 12

1

Base form	Simple Past	Past Participle
be	was/were	been
travel	traveled	traveled
have	had	had
live	lived	lived
see	saw	seen
make	made	made
meet	met	met
take	took	taken
buy	bought	bought
do	did	done

2 1 2 started   3 came   4 have traveled
5 went   6 played   7 didn't win
8 hasn't played

2 2 he was   3 No, he didn't.
4 Have they   5 Yes, they have.
6 did they go   7 No, he didn't
8 Has he, played; No, he hasn't

3 2 went
3 didn't like
4 Have, seen
5 went
6 saw
7 didn't enjoy
8 Have, seen
9 went
10 climbed

3 1 3 Have you ever been/gone to New York?
4 Have you ever met the president?
5 Have you ever seen a play on Broadway?
6 Have you ever had a New York pizza?
7 Have you ever lived in the US?

2 3 She's been/gone
4 She's, met
5 She's seen a play
6 She's, had
7 She's lived

4 1 2 met, two years ago
  3 read, last year
  4 lived, when I was 16
  5 had, at 7:30
  6 bought, last Monday
  7 went, in 2010
  8 did, before I got home

  2 last year, when I was 16, at 7:30,
  last Monday, in 2010,
  before I got home

5 2 Have you gotten dressed yet?
  3 Have you brushed your teeth yet?
  4 Have you made your bed yet?
  5 Have you had breakfast yet?
  6 Have you taken a shower yet?
  7 Have you packed your school bag yet?

6 2 He hasn't brushed his teeth yet.
  3 He hasn't had breakfast yet.
  4 He hasn't taken a shower yet.
  5 He hasn't packed his school bag yet.

7 2 e 3 g 4 h 5 d 6 f 7 c 8 a

8 1 1 Three. Author, businessman, and
    adventurer.
  2 Because he suffered a broken heart.
  3 25.
  4 In Hong Kong.
  5 She was the first woman to fly a
    helicopter solo around the world.
  6 He became the oldest man to walk to
    the South Pole.
  7 His marriage.
  8 Stop their parents from having more
    adventures.

  2 2 don't live 3 's had 4 wrote
    5 began 6 have been 7 are trying
    8 don't want

9 2 c 3 c 4 c 5 b 6 b 7 a 8 b

10 1 2 dressed 3 married 4 bored
    5 wet 6 ready

  2 2 get 3 gets 4 get 5 get

  3 2 receive 3 find 4 fetch 5 catch

11 2 break 3 off 4 test 5 photo
  6 time 7 easy

12 2 h 3 g 4 a 5 d 6 c 7 f 8 e

13 3 — 4 the 5 — 6 the 7 the
  8 the 9 the 10 — 11 the
  12 the

14 2 take care of 3 turn on
  4 Take, off 5 Come on
  6 try on 7 look for 8 turn off

OXFORD
UNIVERSITY PRESS

198 Madison Avenue
New York, NY 10016 USA

Great Clarendon Street, Oxford, OX2 6DP, United Kingdom

Oxford University Press is a department of the University of Oxford.
It furthers the University's objective of excellence in research, scholarship,
and education by publishing worldwide. Oxford is a registered trade
mark of Oxford University Press in the UK and in certain other countries

ISBN: 978 0 19 472576 7 TEACHER'S BOOK

Printed in China

This book is printed on paper from certified and well-managed sources

ACKNOWLEDGEMENTS

Illustrations by: Gill Button p.146, p.149, p.154; Debbie Powell p.147, p.152;
Harry Venning p.150.

*We would also like to thank the following for permission to reproduce the following
photographs:* Cover: Paul Harizan/Getty Images, Ralf Hiemisch/fstop/Corbis;
global - antonyspencer/istockphoto.